POETRY OF OPPOSITION AND REVOLUTION

QUÆRIT PATRIA CÆSAREM.

Frontispiece. James III, *de jure* King of Great Britain, 1701–66, with inset medallions of Prince Charles Edward (left) and Prince Henry Benedict (right). In the centre an inset scene of the oppressions of the House of Brunswick. Engraving by George Bickham, 1747.

Poetry of Opposition and Revolution

Dryden to Wordsworth

HOWARD ERSKINE-HILL

CLARENDON PRESS · OXFORD
1996

Oxford University Press, Walton Street, Oxford OX2 6DP

Oxford New York
Athens Auckland Bangkok Bombay
Calcutta Cape Town Dar es Salaam Delhi
Florence Hong Kong Istanbul Karachi
Kuala Lumpur Madras Madrid Melbourne
Mexico City Nairobi Paris Singapore
Taipei Tokyo Toronto
and associated companies in
Berlin Ibadan

Oxford is a trade mark of Oxford University Press

Published in the United States
by Oxford University Press Inc. New York

British Library Cataloguing in Publication Data
Data available

Library of Congress Cataloging in Publication Data
Data available
ISBN 0 19 812177 6

1 3 5 7 9 10 8 6 4 2

Typeset by Pure Tech India Ltd, Pondicherry
Printed in Great Britain
on acid-free paper by
Bookcraft Ltd
Midsomer Norton, Bath

TO

*JESUS COLLEGE, CAMBRIDGE,
COLLEGE OF COLERIDGE
AND WILLIAM FREND*

Acknowledgement

MANY debts have been incurred in the planning and writing of this book. Professor Earl Miner kindly advised me on the late Dryden; Dr Valerie Rumbold and Dr Julian Ferraro kindly read and commented on my chapters on Pope, as did the late Dr David Fleeman, and Dr Graham Nicholls (Curator of the Johnson Museum at Lichfield) my chapters on Johnson. Professor George Dekker and Dr Tim Fulford advised me on my chapters on Wordsworth, and I am exceptionally grateful to Dr Fulford for his generous, detailed, and shrewd guidance. Mr Richard Sharp, of Worcester College, Oxford, has generously assisted me from his expert knowledge of eighteenth-century English print-culture.

Several other colleagues and friends have assisted me with their advice. They are Professor John Beer, FBA, Dr David Brunton, Dr Jonathan Clark, Dr Edward Corp, Dr Eveline Cruickshanks, Dr Mark Goldie, Dr Paul Hopkins, Professor Joseph Loenstein, Mr Bryan Milnes, Dr Peter Swaab and Professor Michael White. My colleagues in Pembroke College, Cambridge, have advised me on a variety of matters: I am grateful to Professor Ian Jack, FBA, Dr Peter McDonald, Professor Michael Reeve, FBA, Mr Colin Wilcockson, and Dr Mark Wormald who have been more than generous in helping me. Nobody acknowledged here necessarily agrees with any of my arguments, and I am of course responsible for errors which may remain in the book.

I thank the National Humanities Center, North Carolina, USA, for electing me an Olin Fellow for the year 1988–9, which enabled me to complete the greater part of the work which became *Poetry and the Realm of Politics* and *Poetry of Opposition and Revolution*. I especially appreciate the regular kindness and helpfulness of all the staff at the Center, extending to personal as well as academic concerns, which made my year in North Carolina so rewarding and happy. At the same time I want to thank the University of Cambridge and Pembroke College, Cambridge, for granting me leave of absence on several occasions, without which I could never have forged ahead with this project.

I am grateful to the staff of the University Library, Cambridge, of Pembroke College Library, of the British Library, and of the National Library of Scotland. I am grateful too to Helen Saunders, in the Cambridge English Faculty Office, for her patience and skill in word-processing most of my manuscript. Mr L. R. Goodey, of The Cambridge University Library Department of Photography, has been particularly helpful in producing good images of eighteenth-century prints and medals.

My interest in Pope and Wordsworth—powerful presences in this book—goes back many years to my schooldays. *The Prelude* has been a kind of poetic companion of my life. I therefore want to thank the two teachers who originally planted and fostered these interests, thus giving me something of quite incalculable value, which I have attempted to pass on: they are Mr G. G. Daniels and Mr Patrick Radley. Later, as an undergraduate, I owed a particular debt to Professor J. T. Boulton, FBA, for helping me extend and deepen these same eighteenth-century and Romantic interests.

H.H.E.-H.

27 September 1994

Contents

List of Illustrations

James III, *de jure* King of Great Britain, 1701–66, with inset medallions of Prince Charles Edward (left) and Prince Henry Benedict (right). In the centre an inset scene of the oppressions of the House of Brunswick. Engraving by George Bickham, 1747 *(Frontispiece)*.

Abbreviations and Short Titles

The Commons, 1715–54	Romney Sedgwick (ed.), *The History of Parliament: The House of Commons, 1715–1754*, 2 vols. (1970)
Corr.	Alexander Pope, *Correspondence*, ed. George Sherburn, 5 vols. (Oxford, 1956)
Dryden, *Poems*	*The Poems of John Dryden*, ed. James Kinsley, 4 vols. (Oxford, 1958)
EY	William and Dorothy Wordsworth, *Letters, The Early Years, 1787–1805*, ed. Ernest de Selincourt; rev. Chester L. Shaver (Oxford, 1967)
JEGP	*Journal of English and Germanic Philology*
Johnson, *Poems*	Samuel Johnson, *The Poems*, ed. David Nichol Smith and Edward L. McAdam; rev. David Fleeman (Oxford, 1974)
Johnson, *Lives of the Poets*	Samuel Johnson, *Lives of the Poets*, ed. G. Birbeck Hill, 3 vols. (Oxford, 1905)
Johnson, *Works*	Samuel Johnson, *Works* (New Haven, 1958–)
MLN	*Modern Language Notes*
MLR	*Modern Language Review*
Norton	William Wordsworth, *The Prelude, 1799, 1805, 1850*, ed. Jonathan Wordsworth, M. H. Abrams, and Stephen Gill (1979)
POAS	*Poems on Affairs of State; Augustan Satirical Verse, 1660–1714*, ed. George de Forest Lord *et al.*, 7 vols. (New Haven, 1963–75)
Poetical Works	William Wordsworth, *Poetical Works*, ed. Ernest de Selincourt and Helen Darbishire, 5 vols. (Oxford, 1940–49)
Prose Works	William Wordsworth, *Prose Works*, ed. W. J. B. Owen and J. W. Smyser, 3 vols. (Oxford, 1974)
RES	*Review of English Studies*
TE	*The Twickenham Edition of the Poems of Alexander Pope*, ed. John Butt *et al.*, 11 vols. (1939–69)

TLS	*Times Literary Supplement*
Works of John Dryden	*The Works of John Dryden*, ed. Sir Walter Scott, revised and corrected by George Saintsbury, 18 vols. (Edinburgh, 1882–93)
Works	John Dryden, *Works*, ed. E. N. Hooker, H. T. Swedenberg, jr., *et al.*, 20 vols. (Berkeley and Los Angeles, 1961–)
Young, *Works*	Edward Young, *The Works of the Author of the Night Thoughts*, 6 vols. (1762)

Introduction

IN a famous moment of literary history Dryden, in his 'Secular Masque' for *The Pilgrim* (1700) gave to Momus the resounding refrain:

> *'Tis well an Old Age is out,*
> *And time to begin a New.* (ll. 96–7)[1]

It is moving that a poet who knows himself not far from death can write in this buoyant way of a new age, but Momus, the laughing sceptical god, does not speak wholly for Dryden, and the turn of the century produced small political and poetical change. Doubtless it is the residual magic of number, persisting even into the late twentieth century, which suggests that a new order of numerals will bring a new order of experience.

The 1688 Revolution, on the other hand, had been a shattering alteration. Then, in a crisis of Protestantism against Roman Catholicism, the Prince of Orange at the head of an invading army expelled the reigning king and precipitated civil war in two British kingdoms. What was done then was revealed even more starkly after the death of Mary II in 1694, since that left her husband the Prince of Orange, now William III, with only a parliamentary title to the crown, and with the Continental war in which he had involved Britain still in full spate. The Peace of Ryswick, in 1697, strengthened William's position and weakened that of the Jacobites supporting James II and the exiled Stuart dynasty. In 1700 the death of the young Duke of Gloucester, son of the Princess Anne, removed any midway solution (if such were conceivable) of the problem of the succession. Either the exiled Stuarts would have to be restored, on the death of the childless William or the now childless Anne, or a Protestant prince still further from the hereditary line would have to be found, in which case the wounds opened in 1688 would hardly be soon healed. The second alternative, however, was always likely to be William's solution, and, by the Act of Settlement (1701), the crown was directed to the House of Brunswick, on the death of Anne. Also

---

[1] John Dryden, *Poems*, James Kinsley (Oxford, 1956) iv. 1765.

in 1700 Louis XIV of France again seized a series of low country fortresses, at the same time recognizing the claim of his grandson Philip to the throne of Spain, and of the young James III to the British kingdoms. He thus violated a whole series of recent treaty obligations; the new situation was so familiar in fact that it might appropriately have occasioned another of the sceptical lines of Dryden's Momus:

Thy Wars brought nothing about

(l. 94)

and it is no surprise that the greater European powers now engaged in a yet further, and wider, continental war: the War of the Spanish Succession. Nothing could more strongly attest to the fact that this continued to be a dynastic era. Dynasticism was the means by which wealth, power, and advancement could be gained, at the national, local, and personal levels. Further, dynasticism, with its focus on a series of specific families, was the human face of politics, in recognition of which public and personal allegiance joined. When, in 1702, William III unexpectedly died from a fall from his horse, the new monarch, Queen Anne, inherited the same realm which William had himself very largely shaped.

All this means that the poetry which Dryden produced in the 1690s—the last decade of his life—was not relegated on the turn of the century. On the contrary, his plays and poems from this period were relevant to the realm of the 1710s. What is more, his literary production at this time was of extraordinary salience, restlessly inventive in form and mode, in translation, collaboration, and original work, looking to both past and future, using earlier literary kinds in new ways. Sometimes, and sometimes at the height of his powers, Dryden is conscious of uttering latest or last words. *Love Triumphant*, a neglected *tour de force*, was his deliberated farewell to the stage, and his last dramatic word on dynastic rivalry, love, and war. In *Alexander's Feast* (1697) he took the musical, masque-like ode in honour of St Cecilia to an astonishing pitch of narrative irony, to mark the return of William III to England in the year of the Treaty of Ryswick. If Milton's *Samson Agonistes* were Milton's menacing last work of poetry, this (Dryden may have thought) was his own. But he lived longer, long enough to put together his *Fables, Ancient and Modern* (1700), which not only incorporated and made pointed comment on *Alexander's Feast*, but also included his pseudo-Chaucerian 'Character of a Good Parson', which really was his last word on the realm of politics he knew in the 1690s, one which would extend until the coming of the Hanovers in 1714. The text for which Dryden's 'Secular Masque' was intended, Fletcher's *The Pilgrim* as reshaped by Vanbrugh, is a fair indication of the newness of the new age celebrated by Momus. It is an intelligent and subtle synthesis of the old and new; or, one may sometimes suspect, no more than old minds under new wigs.

I hope this goes some way to explain why the present book, a study of poetry and the realm of politics in the eighteenth century and early Romantic period, should open with a discussion of Dryden's comparatively neglected last poetry and plays. From Dryden, Pope (a political as well as poetic heir) and Addison (a poetic heir but not a political one) derived at the outset of their careers their major artistic orientations. Not only that, but the eighteenth-century poetry of political opposition has its roots in the post-revolutionary poetry of Dryden. Dryden's cultivation of obliquity, ambiguity, and paradox in political allusion would be an indispensable resource for Hanoverian poetry. Dryden showed the way to mingle topical consciousness with epic narrative and medieval story. Further, eighteenth-century poetry of opposition can sometimes seem self-indulgently partisan

> 'What are you thinking?' 'Faith, the thought's no sin,
> I think your friends are out, and would be in.'

unless the ideological roots of such opposition are exposed. An exploration of Dryden's 1690s work is probably the best way of achieving this, for the relation of his writings to the high politics of the time is, at least at first sight, more obvious than is the case with Pope and Johnson.

A word must be said here about my choice of poets for discussion in this book. Pope must be thought to nominate himself: at the very least he is the most interesting and subtle of the eighteenth-century poets of political opposition, and opposition poetry is the great, new, remarkable feature of the 1720s, 1730s, and 1740s, even remembering the Restoration Marvell, the State Poems, and the Dryden of the 1690s. Samuel Johnson may then seem entirely predictable according to the orthodox literary canon. Johnson's special significance, however, is here a religious one. The opposition of Dryden and Pope to the powers-that-be might plausibly be attributed to religion and religious background alone, Dryden a Roman Catholic convert after 1686, Pope emerging from a Roman Catholic home and never repudiating his early religion. Johnson, however, a devoted Anglican and one who came to have reservations about the two earlier poets, nevertheless developed the opposition poetry of Pope. The opposition poetry of the 1730s and 1740s was not therefore reliant on a set of residual Roman Catholic attitudes. Johnson's decision to follow Pope in the late 1730s, when he might so easily and so much more prudently have found different models in the pro-Hanoverian tradition of Addison and Young, is one of the remarkable moments in the revolution of eighteenth-century political consciousness.

Mention of Addison and Young (the latter to be discussed briefly in relation to Johnson) prompts the point that a different eighteenth century than the one shown here could have been presented. To Addison and Young might have been added Thomson, a considerable poet with a different political vision and a different notion of liberty from Pope and Johnson. But Thomson does not begin to have the political imagination they have. Again, of poets in whom affairs of state assume dramatic salience, William Blake vies with Wordsworth among the earlier Romantics. My decision to conclude this book with Wordsworth—Wordsworth at his most famous—stems from two considerations. First (surprising as it may seem) there are definite points of contact between Wordsworth and the tradition of Dryden, Pope, and Johnson. Wordsworth, like Johnson, imitates Juvenal to convey something of his political vision. Like Pope he resorts to the seventeenth-and eighteenth-century convention of the political card-game. He reworks Renaissance political metaphors such as the ruler as a shepherd, or the high point of hope and happiness as the golden time in the cycles of history: indeed his very concept of revolution partakes as much of the cyclical as of more modern meanings of the word. Like Dryden, Wordsworth can use drama to explore political blindness and uncertainty, as his important play *The Borderers* reveals. But, secondly, Wordsworth commands attention for something scarcely precedented in English poetry: his capacity to combine personal and political consciousness. Scarcely precedented, because the growing habit of poetic self-presentation from Spenser to Pope's *Imitations of Horace* is still qualitatively different from Wordsworth's poetic autobiography and the subtleties with which that received political experience. *The*

Prelude displays, among other things, the cost of high politics in terms of personal suffering. The poem is poised between eighteenth-century political poetry—and eighteenth-century nature poetry—and the nineteenth-century novel. This in turn is the reason why this book concludes with Wordsworth. Neither Byron nor Shelley seems to me to show Wordsworth's combination of high politics with deep personal inwardness, though arguably Byron approaches it in the later cantos of *Don Juan*. The inheritors of the wide and deep vision of *The Prelude* are less obviously Wordsworth's successors in poetry than a new and great generation of novelists in which Stendhal, the Tolstoy of *War and Peace*, and Thomas Mann must be dominant presences, but to which Thackeray and Dickens, George Eliot and Conrad, in different works also belong.

Poetry of Opposition and Revolution is a sequel to an earlier book, *Poetry and the Realm of Politics*. Parts of one enterprise, the two books have a number of common features. They share a concern, less with systematic political parallels in literary texts, than with the more frequent, subtle, glancing, or multiple allusion. Further, their concept of politics is of what seemed most obviously politics at the time: what Camden, or Dryden, or Johnson, or Wordsworth considered politics to be. Not, that is, relationships of power as seen more widely, for example in the family, or in the place of work, but high politics: the decisions and deeds of rulers, debate about their title or right to rule, changes in forms of government, war, and revolution at home and abroad. As in the earlier book, the chief focus is on the governance of the body politic, here the way in which major poetry was aware of, and intervened in, this governance between the first years of William III and the later years of George III. Finally, as will now be clear, the two books are of an historicist rather than a New Historicist trend. They seek proximate historical evidence for the better understanding of literary texts which make political allusion, while at the same time remembering that in history everything is on the move, and, at times of political crisis, rapidly and bewilderingly so. Then the same principles may seem to point in different directions as circumstances change.

New Historicism has been interestingly different in the Renaissance and the Romantic periods. In the former the frontiers of historical evidence have been forced outward, but a somewhat arbitrary selection of material has been produced from the enlarged field. Interpretations of Shakespeare verging on the licentious were the result, since so wide a variety of contexts could now be adduced that the dramatist could be made to appear more or less according to late twentieth-century order. In the latter field, critical practice proved quite different. Here a single body of historical evidence, centred on the earlier phase of the French Revolution, was always insisted on. To a surprising degree recent critical commentary identified itself with the early Jacobin phase of the earlier Romantics. Difficulties at once began to appear.

If it were right that Wordsworth and Coleridge abandoned French Revolutionary commitment for deeper, a-political verities, it would follow, as Jerome McGann has argued, that their new, a-political stance was no more than a concealed political ideology. But how plausible is that? May it not be nearer the mark to say that the earlier Romantics remained faithful to their values, while recognizing that these values had in fact been betrayed by the destructive political programme of Revolutionary and Napoleonic France? New Historicist commentary on Wordsworth, however, remaining ingenuously pro-Jacobin, divided only over whether Wordsworth's Jacobin phase could be made to last into the period of his most famous poems, or whether these same poems had been insufficiently berated for not being Jacobin enough. A critical concept came readily to hand. The notion of significant absence, or displacement, seemed to enable the first group of New Historicists to import Jacobin content into non-Jacobin texts, while it helped the second and more numerous group to convict the poet of a disingenuous occlusion of real politics from his mature poems.[2]

An unsatisfactory approach to the earlier Romantics thus seemed to prevail. What looked to many like traces of covert displacement, or erasure, of revolutionary concern, may in fact have been marks of a continuing political preoccupation, which naturally found new forms after the collapse of an enlightenment programme into the Jacobin Terror. If so this should mean that implausible efforts to

---

[2] For varieties of New Historicism see (on the Renaissance): Stephen Greenblatt, *Renaissance Self-Fashioning* (1980), *Shakespearian Negotiations* (1988), *Learning to Curse* (1990), and Stephen Greenblatt (ed.), *Representing the Renaissance (1988); (on the Romantics)*: Jerome McGann, *The Romantic Ideology: A Critical Investigation* (1983), Marjorie Levinson, *Wordsworth's Great Period Poems* (Cambridge, 1986), Alan Lui, *Wordsworth: The Sense of History* (Stanford, Calif., 1989), Nicholas Roe, *The Politics of Nature: Wordsworth and Some Contemporaries* (1992).

prolong a 'Jacobin Wordsworth' into the period of his most famous poems can be abandoned with relief. Wordsworth's poetry, it seems likely, continues responsibly and feelingly political in subtle, human, and challenging ways long after his Jacobin period comes to an end. It may be suggested that *The Prelude* was designed (at the point of its most ambitious extension) to be a pre-Jacobin and a post-Jacobin work of art, operating as a historical and poetic fiction even while it would preserve much autobiographical content. It would certainly seem doubtful, on this reading, whether (for example) an account of crossing the Alps in the pre-Napoleonic period should be seen as 'displacing' Napoleon's crossing. If Napoleon is meant to be recalled at this point at all, it is more likely as the object of proleptic warning. Much also turns on whether the notion of significant absence is an aesthetic or a biographical concept. If it is the former, some features of the text must plausibly point the absence, as I shall argue is often the case in Dryden, Pope, and Johnson. If the latter, the modern critic is rejecting the original act of choice which created the poem. This in turn means that the poem is being judged by alien, perhaps irrelevant standards which, in the earlier stages of critical discussion at least, can never be helpful for an understanding of the poem under discussion.

If conflicts of methodology have recently dominated attention in literary studies, historians, for their part more deeply imbued in the discipline of their subject, are more preoccupied with the conflicting claims of particular historical hypotheses, and thus of different visions of different periods. Modern literary studies are historically old-fashioned in this regard, old Macaulayan myths of English political progress making their last stand in neo-Marxist dress. Modern, revisionist history, on the other hand, seems more likely to offer reliable accounts of earlier times as those times saw themselves, and thus a better if dauntingly detailed ground for the present project. On the later seventeenth and the earlier eighteenth centuries, therefore, I have followed the more recent historiography which has challenged the long-lingering Whig triumphalist vision of those precarious and uncertain years, and of their unpredictable alternative futures.[3] The first half of the eighteenth century has long

---

[3] J. P. Kenyon, *Revolution Principles: The Politics of Party, 1689–1720* (Cambridge, 1977) is perhaps the book which has most altered our view of the later 17th and earlier 18th cents., though J. G. A. Pocock, *The Ancient Constitution and the*

been portrayed by historians whose vision and methods were oriented chiefly to the second half—so much so that historiographical revisionism on the period of Pope and the young Samuel Johnson remains fiercely controversial.[4] Did the earlier eighteenth century more or less contentedly see a consolidation of the political nation under a Whig oligarchy with all the various forces of religious, dynastic, and economic resistance divided and enfeebled? Or was it dubious ground, claimed by rival ideologies or rival dynasties competing for the same ideology: a conflict which seen in its international dimension may seem more equal than when, as in the old historical way, we looked at England and England's surviving evidence alone? In my view the revisionists of the eighteenth century make better sense of the major writers of that era, whether Whig or Tory, 'court' or 'country', than the expounders of Whig stability.[5] The exceptionally adversarial character of much Augustan satire accords ill with notions of a stable political consensus. 'The recovery of Jacobitism' (J. G. A. Pocock's phrase)[6] seems to me the major achievement of the historians of the last twenty years for an understanding of earlier eighteenth-century political consciousness. This will be a theme in the first half of the present book.

It is no surprise that literary discussion of the earlier Romantics should have so regularly stressed the idealism of those who saw a

Feudal Law (Cambridge, 1957) was a very significant early pointer. New work by Mark Goldie, for example 'The Revolution of 1689 and the Structures of Political Argument: An Essay and an Annotated Bibliography of Pamphlets on the Allegiance Controversy', *Bulletin of Research in the Humanities* (Winter 1980), Edward Gregg, *Queen Anne* (1980) and *The Protestant Succession in International Politics, 1710–16* (New York, 1987), and much new work on Jacobitism by, and edited by, Eveline Cruickshanks, have modified our view on these times.

[4] The work which has been exceptionally challenging, stirring 18th-cent. historiography into a new debate, is J. C. D. Clark, *English Society, 1688–1832: Ideology, Social Structure and Political Practice During the Ancient Regime* (Cambridge, 1985); see also his *Samuel Johnson: Literature, Religion and English Cultural Politics from the Restoration to Romanticism* (Cambridge, 1994).

[5] See e.g. Sir John Plumb, *The Growth of Political Stability in England, 1675–1725* (1967), the most distinguished study in what was a major and influential hypothesis about the 18th cent. What began to open a new view of the earlier 18th cent. is the work on the Tories in *The History of Parliament: The House of Commons, 1715–1754*, ed. Romney Sedgwick, 2 vols. (1970). Eveline Cruickshanks, *Political Untouchables: The Tories and the '45* (1979) carried the political argument forward, while Paul Kleber Monod, *Jacobitism and the English People, 1688–1788* (Cambridge, 1989) has surveyed English Jacobitism as a social phenomenon.

[6] See '1660 And All That . . .', his review of Jonathan Clark's *English Society* in the *Cambridge Review* (Oct. 1987), 127.

dawn, or a beacon, in the early constitutionalist phase of the French Revolution, and have so routinely sounded the note of disappointment and disapproval when the Jacobin Terror forced the poets and men of letters, belatedly enough, to recant their specific political positions. It was time that this easy idealisation of French revolutionary sympathy was challenged—as it has now been by works so different in kind as Simon Schama's *French Revolution* (1989) and John Ehrman's meticulous biographies of Pitt the Younger[7]—and as it was by Burke in the 1790s. This was a new model revolution, the first in the category of 'attempted Utopias culminating in Terror'.[8] This was the first, but in the events of the next two hundred years by no means the last, chastisement of the hubris of intellectuals. The rectification of this imbalance in the presentation of the earlier Romantics, yields, I think, a clearer sense of where their merits and their talents really lie. The Jacobin Wordsworth found expression in the then unpublished version of Juvenal VIII (1795–7). But most of his powerful political poetry arises out of the conflict between his first and his converted idealism. Again, a more balanced political view than has tended to prevail will do justice to the courage and integrity of the first Romantics in moving away from their pro-Jacobin stance when events prompted them to rethink their position. Very recent historical study has laid a much needed emphasis on a loyal nationalism that, partly as a result of the later foreign wars of the eighteenth century (wars not involving the British Succession) grew in the French Revolutionary and Napoleonic periods into an ideal more deserving of loyalty, perhaps, than the Utopian aspirations of Paine and Godwin.[9] The revolutions which Wordsworth came wholeheartedly to support were the nationalist revolutions of Spain and Portugal against the Napoleonic invader, as the poet's tract, *The Convention of Cintra* (1809) makes clear.

Some of the chief proposals of this book have already been touched on in the above explanations. Dryden, master of the oblique, coded, partial, or multiple allusion, seems at first in his poetic fictions of the 1690s to be searching for ways of laying the Jacobite

---

[7] Simon Schama, *Citizens: A Chronicle of the French Revolution* (1989); John Ehrman, *The Younger Pitt: The Years of Acclaim* (1969) and *The Younger Pitt: The Reluctant Transition* (1983).

[8] Conor Cruise O'Brien, *The Great Melody: A Thematic Biography and Commented Anthology of Edmund Burke* (1992), 609; see also 595–604.

[9] Linda Colley, *Britons: Forging the Nation, 1707–1837* (1992).

faith to rest with reverence and honour, though also with criticism. Then, some five years after the Revolution, he found an equilibrium from which he continued to highlight loyal values and Jacobite views while also seeing beyond them to opposing or simply different positions. As a man Dryden seems to have stood by his creed; as a poet he sometimes expresses this creed quite plainly, but his muse is never restricted to it.

Pope, not Dryden, however, must seem the great poet of political opposition in English literature. At first sight Pope's debt to Dryden might suggest that the small Roman Catholic minority in Britain (however dashed after its brief bid for power under James II) had hijacked English poetry for half a century. Comparison of Pope and the young Johnson, however, shows that this was not the case. Rather each drew on what was, after the 1720s, an increasingly widespread opposition culture, a culture stirred by, though not wholly committed to, the primarily Protestant Jacobite movement— Protestant in its leadership and main support, however much it retained the hopes of persecuted Roman Catholics. This opposition culture enabled Pope to become a quite open opposition poet in the 1730s, but the common view that before that decade he was primarily apolitical, social rather than national in his poetic perspectives, is quite wrong. The politics of Pope's earlier poetry are simply more exploratory and subtle than the poetry of the 1730s, less open and defiant. And in the later development of the 1728 and 1729 *Dunciads* Pope may be seen to return to his subtler poetic language at the end of his career. Pope is therefore a complex political case, and the term 'emotional Jacobitism'[10] has recently come into use to refer to his work and to some features of the culture which sustained him in his later writings. This term needs to be treated with great care, particularly in the light of the misleading subtitle of Isaac Kramnick's *Bolingbroke and His Circle: The Politics of Nostalgia in the*

---

[10] The term was coined, I believe, by Douglas Brooks-Davies, in his fascinating study, *Pope's Dunciad and the Queen of the Night* (Manchester, 1985), 7–8. The term is required in order to designate a frame of mind and a structure of feeling not necessarily identical with a readiness to take up arms in support of the *de jure* king at a given moment, but which saw the world in sympathy with the *de jure* claim and did not rule it out as serious politics. My misgiving about the term may be illustrated by Paul Monod's *Jacobitism and the English People*: cultural history with the politics left out. In the earlier 18th cent. at least, 'emotional Jacobitism' was sustained by the seeming possibility of a restoration. Only later did it wane into principled sentimentalism.

Age of Walpole (1968). 'Emotional' may be equated with 'nostalgia' and be understood to refer to residual feeling when action or desired change are assumed to be hopeless. That would be a self-evidently retrospective judgement. Whatever one thinks of Bolingbroke today his politics were not especially backward-looking at the time; whatever one thinks of Walpole it was not clear that Britain was bound to go his way, and that the *de jure* dynasty would not be restored. 'Emotional Jacobitism' should mean that frame of mind which existed when, according to the standards of the time, a Stuart restoration continued to seem possible and (to some) desirable. So far as Johnson is concerned—though not of course other poets or thinkers—the terminus of 'emotional Jacobitism' seems to have been the Treaty of Aix-la-Chapelle (1748) and its immediate aftermath.

Specific biographical background (so often cited in the case of Pope) is likely to be just as significant in Wordsworth's case. Members of a young family who lost both parents at an early age, only to grow up into the realization that their father's employer, the great aristocrat of their native region, refused to discharge the substantial debt he owed to their dead parents, were likely to develop into social radicals. In these circumstances a concern with Milton was unlikely to have been purely poetic. The minority eighteenth-century tradition which favoured the pro-regicide Milton (despite Addison's efforts to sanitize him from such association) continued as a cult that remembered Argyle, Algernon Sidney, and other republican martyrs of the century before. Not only did Wordsworth pick up, inhabit, and thus modify this tradition, but he seems to have responded with peculiar vividness to those parts of Milton's work in which the earlier poet expresses the power of a special providence upon certain individuals—chosen Samsons, perhaps—to fight, suffer, and rise again, in a world of fallen hope.

Like Dryden as well as Milton, Wordsworth uses the pattern of Virgilian epic as a means, if more remote yet still with some sustaining structures and powers, of understanding fall, loss, and revival within the experiential realm of politics. A part of this experience is the process which drew so many purely social radicals of the 1790s back to the historical and social—and physical and regional—loyalty to their native land in its struggles with revolutionary France and, more tellingly, with the structural and statist imperialism of the Emperor Napoleon.

That Wordsworth's *Prelude* is not just a poetic autobiography with two or three books about political experience and ideas included, but a poem whose major political theme is fully integrated into the work as a whole, is the last major proposal of the present book. That *The Prelude* is less a reliable base for biography than a quasi-fictionalized apologia, reading a great deal of the later 1790s back into youth and childhood, I am inclined to suspect—but that is a matter which must be left for future Wordsworthians to investigate. The main aesthetic features of *The Prelude*, its autobiographical idiom, and its brilliant use of varieties of landscape for the expression of mood and idea, are anticipated to some extent in earlier poetry. Milton's sparing but significant self-inclusions as poet in the text of *Paradise Lost*, Dryden's confessional passages in *The Hind and the Panther*, Pope's use of Horace for (among other purposes) fashioned self-portrayal, offer some precedent for Wordsworth's practice in *The Prelude* but (as previously noted) something less than a steadily evolving tradition. A stronger tradition, perhaps, is that of political landscape-writing from *The Faerie Queene*, through Milton and Dryden among others, to Pope's *Windsor Forest* and the scenes of *The Vanity of Human Wishes*. Yet considered even in this light Wordsworth's poem seems rather a sudden departure than the product of a long and steady evolution.

Literary history, I think, may often accord with the history of larger political and social questions. There is no steady sense of long-term progress in the period here explored. There was, for example, no long-term approach towards a republican idiom of thought, which some would consider a mark of progressive thinking. Republicanism is encountered in the age of Milton, as it is in the early Wordsworth, but monarchy does not seem to be being thrust to the edges of the political arena. Only in the boys' card-game in the early *Prelude* are we given an image of redundant kingship: Britain was then on the threshold of its most successful century of monarchy. Again, the ideas of revolution and of long-term progress, certainly present in Wordsworth's mind, were interrogated in *The Prelude* in a way, and a depth, in which a work of art can assess an idea from abstract philosophy. They are interrogated in the light of a notion of the divine. The world of *The Prelude* is not the world of a secular vision. Neither is the imaginative world of Blake, who also penetrated the concept of revolution without recanting what had been at the heart of his hunger for change. The paradigm of continuity and crisis may seem only too obvious a mode of cultural diagnosis in 1994, but it does appear that crises are rarely desired by those who produce them—what is usually desired is a gain without rupture—and that in periods of crisis political and social change is more acceptable than in stable times. Radical programmes generated in crisis, however, do not always stay the course; sometimes they are abandoned as rapidly as they were taken up.

A final point: again a mark of discontinuity rather than evolution. In the political consciousness of Wordsworth and Blake we notice what is hardly to be found in the great pro-republican poet of the seventeenth century who meant so much to them both. We see, especially in Wordsworth, the individual figures of common people, for example a hunger-bitten girl tied to a heifer as it grazed, or a girl, near a mountain beacon, bearing a pitcher, who seemed 'with difficult steps to force her way | Against the blowing wind'.[11] Seen from the outside, it will be said, by the *spectator ab extra* (as Coleridge put it). But in the world of *The Prelude* these are not marginal figures. Connecting within the text of the poem, they are together instinct with significance. They are bearers of the future, whatever the future will bring.

[11] *The Prelude* (1805), ix. 511–34, xi. 306–15, discussed in Ch. 7 below.

PART I

Dryden and the 1690s

I

Dryden's Later Plays and Poems

THIS chapter will discuss political allusion and bearing in Dryden's four later dramas after *Don Sebastian*, especially the neglected later play *Love Triumphant* (1694), and three crucial poems, 'To My Dear Friend Mr. Congreve, On His Comedy *The Double Dealer*' (1693), *Alexander's Feast; Or the Power of Musique* (1697), and 'The Character of the Good Parson', published in *Fables Ancient and Modern* (1700). It will not explore in detail the depositing of Jacobite allusions in *The Satires* (1693) nor the interweaving of Jacobite theme in *Fables Ancient and Modern* as a whole. To continue our comparison of Milton and Dryden 'After the Revolution', however, it is both necessary and rewarding to consider Dryden's later works other than his *Aeneis* and *Don Sebastian*.

I

Don Sebastian's intensity of political allusion is less common in Dryden's later post-revolutionary drama, though each play more or less pointedly performs in the political arena. With his *Amphitryon* (performed at the latest by the end of October 1690, and composed perhaps before the news of King James's reverse at the Boyne reached London on 13 July) he did a particularly brilliant thing. He chose a double-identity comedy, descending to him from the well-known texts of Plautus and Molière, and lightly pointed his version so that in a play where mysteriously there appear to be two military commanders, two masters, two husbands, competing for the same identity, and two servants for another, a comic pertinence is achieved to times of political uncertainty and divided loyalty. Further, the comic treatment of the gods, whereby the false Amphitryon is in fact Jupiter, and the false Sosia Mercury, allows some generally sceptical reflections on the working of providence as it is understood from the way of the world.

The political signals which alert this contemporary awareness, while not dominating the comedy, do build up into a salient and significant sequence. ''Tis our Part to obey our Father . . .' (1. i. 15)[1] says Mercury to Phoebus, of Jupiter, sounding a broadly patriarchal note, though possibly also alluding to various ennobled bastards of two royal brothers. 'He stood upon his Prerogative' (1. i. 25),[2] Mercury pursues, still speaking of Jupiter, and when Jupiter first descends and breaks in on the conversation he remarks:

> Much good may do you with your Politicks:
> All Subjects will be censuring their Kings.
>
> (1. i. 58–59)[3]

With free and easy knowledge of the world Mercury and Phoebus pursue their political conversation in the presence of Jupiter, sporting with some dangerous issues of current and recent history:

PHOEBUS. Since Arbitrary Pow'r will hear no Reason, 'tis Wisdom to be silent.—

MERCURY. Why that's the Point; this same Arbitrary Power is a knock-down Argument; 'tis but a Word and a Blow; now methinks our Father speaks out like an honest bare-fac'd God, as he is; he lays the stress in the right Place, upon absolute Dominion: I confess if he had been a Man, he might have been a Tyrant, if his Subjects durst have call'd him to account: But you Brother *Phoebus*, are but a meer Country Gentleman, that never comes to Court; that are abroad all day on Horse-back . . . are drinking all Night, and in your Cups are still rayling at the Government: O these Patriots . . .

> (1. i. 131–43)[4]

Dryden takes no side here, but nothing could be more plain than that the play enters into relations with the political awareness of its audience.

What, then, is made of these relations, aesthetically speaking? Dryden's choice of comic fable ensures that these and other political remarks are not just isolated thrusts. They are directed towards a central uncertainty conspicuously but not exclusively comic. In a

---

[1] John Dryden, *Works*, ed. I. E. N. Hooker, H. T. Swedenberg, *et al.*, 20 vols. (Berkeley and Los Angeles, 1961–), xv. 231.
[2] *Works*, xv. 232.
[3] *Works*, xv. 233.
[4] *Works*, xv. 235; James A. Winn, *John Dryden and His World* (1987), 446.

dialogue between Amphitryon and Sosia, in the admirable subplot, the former remarks: 'That one shou'd be two, is very probable!' and his servant responds: 'Have not you seen a Six-pence split into two halves, by some ingenious School-Boy; which bore on either side the Impression of the Monarchs Face? now as those moieties were two Three-pences, and yet in effect but one Six-pence—' (III. i. 95–9).[5] That coins bore their maker's image through the land is something we remember from *Absalom and Achitophel* (l. 10). Sosia's ingenious similitude suggests a simple monetary reduction of the dilemma of two masters, *de facto* and *de jure*, but reminds too of the 'Counterpart' rings in *Don Sebastian* ('A heart divided in two halves was plac'd') which, when joined as symbolizing the union of the parents, spelt the division of Sebastian and Almeyda, a tragic paradox. In *Don Sebastian* that ring was the clarifying object which proved the nature of the central relationship; in *Amphitryon* the search for such clarifying objective proof is comically prolonged as each piece of knowledge which ought to be peculiar to the true Amphitryon and Sosia, turns out to be known to their impersonators, being gods. This culminates when the special scar on Amphitryon's arm, from his recent combat with his enemy in battle, proves to be magically on the arm of Jupiter too. As the corrupt judge Gripus, charged with the task of recognizing the true Amphitryon, puts it,

> I have beheld th'appearance of two Suns;
> But still the false, was dimmer than the true;
> Here, both shine out alike.
>
> (V. i. 120–2)[6]

In these lines some of the tragedy latent in a situation which Plautus's Mercury had openly proclaimed to be tragicomedy ('Faciam ut commixta sit: sit tragicomoedia' l. 59) finds expression. It concerns above all Amphitryon and his wife Alcmena. While the former, a hero back from the wars, slowly comes to face the probability that his hitherto loving and faithful wife has betrayed him, Alcmena finds herself in the position of Sebastian and Almeyda: she has sinned unknowingly, in taking a stranger to her bed. As she expresses her predicament, immediately before Jupiter reveals his deceit,

---

[5] *Works*, xv. 257.   [6] *Works*, xv. 306.

> I know not what to hope, nor what to fear.
> A simple Errour, is a real Crime;
> And unconsenting Innocence is lost.
>
> (v. i. 390–2)[7]

These lines, as those of Gripus quoted above, seem to emerge from the dangers and uncertainties of civil war, and Alcmena particularly holds together, at the centre of the play, the linked values of love and loyalty. As in other of Dryden's later dramas, the dramatic focus is upon people in conflict or bewildered in situations where not only values, but even the facts, are uncertain. In connection with what Alcmena and her husband undergo, the sceptical presentation of fate in this drama also comes into focus:

> PHOEBUS . . . what is Fate?
> Is it a blind contingence of Events?
> Or sure necessity of Causes linck'd,
> That must produce Effects? or is't a Pow'r
> That orders all things by superior Will?
>
> (I. i. 96–100)[8]

Jupiter's answer that fate is simply what his own omnipotence has done cuts no ice, and his further claim that he is about to beget a Hercules who will conquer monsters and redress human wrong provokes the *sotto voce* remark of Mercury to Phoebus: 'Ay, Brother . . . and our Father made all those Monsters for *Hercules* to conquer . . .' (I. i. 128–30).[9] This exchange has implications for the final speech of the self-proclaimed 'Impostour God' in which Jupiter reverts to his revelation that from the 'auspicious Night' of his sexual pleasure a Hercules shall come to save the world. Dryden activates none of the Christian accretions of Hercules—as used, for example, by Milton in his sonnet 'Methought I saw my late espoused saint': a champion sired by this god promises to be a distinctly unhelpful saviour. In a little dry dialogue Dryden has given the whole view of the world which *Paradise Lost* and *Samson Agonistes* were written to dispel. The play, at least, appears completely agnostic as to the morality of the divine, and this in turn makes it hard to assent to a Jacobite reading of Jupiter's last speech, even though it does rehearse various panegyrical gestures used in

---

[7] *Works*, xv. 315.   [8] *Works*, xv. 234.   [9] *Works*, xv. 235.

Threnodia Augustalis and *Britannia Rediviva*.[10] Implicit political scepticism seems more evident (whatever Dryden's own personal hopes), and this scepticism may be thought also to involve the amusing contract scene between Mercury and Phaedra, immediately preceding. Here all the provisos 'to be tack'd to this Act of Settlement' (v. i. 374–5)[11], surely mock the recent parliamentary settlement of William and Mary on the throne.[12] In its last act the play takes a shrewd, worldly look at three contending forms of political sanction, patriarchalism, contract, and protection (seeking to recognize her true husband by the love he shows, Alcmena has been spurned by the jealous Amphitryon, deceived by the fulsome promises of Jupiter). As the god in the machine soars away, mankind is left hurt, angry, and in the dark.

II

Dryden's romantic musical play *King Arthur* (performed to the music of Purcell early in June 1691), takes us further still from Milton's post-revolutionary idiom than *Don Sebastian* or *Amphitryon*. It was stated by Dryden to have been composed as his last service to Charles II in 1684, and 'many beauties' had to be removed from the writing 'not to offend the present times'.[13] In the absence of a 1684 text one may be tempted to treat this claim as a blind; at all events Dryden admits to revision, and if some changes were designed to accommodate, others may have been meant to explore. At all events, with the civil war continuing in Ireland, *King Arthur* happens to dramatize two rival claimants to the throne of Britain, at the end of Arthur's long campaign to drive back Oswald, the Saxon invader from Kent. As in *Don Sebastian* two religions are also in conflict, Oswald fortified by the cruel religion of Woden, Arthur inspired and supported by the ultimately but not instantly overwhelming religious power of the Christian Merlin. Dryden stated in

---

[10] Winn, *John Dryden*, 446–7.
[11] *Works*, xv. 317.
[12] The Clark Dryden, *Works*, xv, is silent on this line.
[13] *The Works of John Dryden*, ed. Sir Walter Scott, revised and corrected by George Saintsbury, 18 vols. (Edinburgh, 1882–93), viii. 153. *King Arthur, Cleomenes*, and *Love Triumphant* have not been edited since Scott-Saintsbury. While I give page references to Scott-Saintsbury, I have corrected my quotations by the first editions.

his Dedication that Mary II herself had 'been pleas'd to peruse the manuscript of this opera' and to give it 'her royal approbation'.[14] This must mean that the text was considered by the poet to bear dual political application, as Winn has suggested.[15] It all turns on who is the invader. From a Williamite viewpoint it would be easy to see Oswald as James, beaten back after a long campaign but not yet done for, and his characterization: 'Revengeful, rugged, violently brave',[16] might remind of the total career of James though, as Winn suggests, it could apply to William too. From the Jacobite viewpoint William had been the invader, and here Arthur's long campaign against Oswald becomes a Jacobite vision of future necessity. The apparent hospitality of the text to rival partisian interpretation is an undoubted feature of *King Arthur*, and wonderfully appropriate to its dedicatee, Halifax, whose *Character of a Trimmer* had eventually been published in 1688.

There is no doubt, of course, that the play endorses Arthur, though it falls short of condemning Oswald as an outright tyrant. Arthur, supported by Merlin, is the example of might and right combined in service of the true religion. When we grasp this we see that *King Arthur* is not a totally trimming text. The theme of sexual conquest, a crucial political metaphor here as in all Dryden's post-1688 plays, points to the commitment of the drama. The blind Emmeline, beloved of Arthur, is seized by the defeated Oswald for political reasons.

OSWALD. Passions in Men Oppress'd, are doubly strong.
  I take her from King *Arthur*; there's Revenge:
  If she can love, she buoys my sinking Fortunes:
  Good Reasons both: I'll on.

(II. ii)[17]

The ladies at once cry out 'a Rape! a Rape!' and the term passes into the political exchange between Arthur and Oswald:

ARTHUR. I blame ye not, for loving *Emmeline*:
  But, since the Soul is free, and Love is choice,

[14] *Works of John Dryden*, viii. 136.
[15] Winn, *John Dryden*, 448–9.
[16] *Works of John Dryden*, viii. 142.
[17] *Works of John Dryden*, viii. 160.

You shou'd have made a Conquest of her Mind,
And not have forc'd her Person by a Rape.
OSWALD. Whether by Force, or Strategem, we gain;
Still Gaining is our End, in War, or Love.

(II. ii)[18]

While both Williamites and Jacobites used the image of rape in their mutual accusations, it was used by the Jacobites as a metaphor for wrongful conquest.[19] Oswald thus begins to conform to the Jacobite stereotype of William. A further point concerns the spirit, Philidel, the Ariel of the play. Originally a devil in the service of Grimbold and Woden, Philidel introduces himself to Merlin in lines reminiscent of the Panther's halfway station in *The Hind and the Panther*:

> The last seduced, and least deform'd, of Hell;
> Half-white, and shuffl'd in the Crowd, I fell.

(II. i)[20]

But in practice Philidel has abandoned a trimming role, refusing to obey an order to hurt Christians. This conversion carries him to political support of Arthur, and it is of interest that the small party of Anglican Non-Jurors, having refused to acknowledge William *de jure*, had been displaced from their benefices a month and a half earlier.[21] They had now become witnesses of religious truth and political right, and Dryden was in due course to pay tribute to them in his 'Character of the Good Parson from Chaucer', in his *Fables*. As Winn points out, however, the character of the convert Philidel almost certainly bears some autobiographical significance.[22] Abused as 'Renegado' and 'Apostate' by his old party, Philidel becomes a double agent, praising his foes (when necessary) in order to serve his new faith. In this role he restores the sight of the faithful blind Emmeline, and saves Arthur from falling prey to the enchantment of the false Emmeline. If Dryden in his new situation considered that 'flattering one's enemies may

---

[18] *Works of John Dryden*, viii. 162.
[19] Howard Erskine-Hill, 'Literature and the Jacobite Cause', in Eveline Cruickshanks (ed.), *Ideology and Conspiracy: Aspects of Jacobitism, 1689–1759* (Edinburgh, 1982), 49–50; id., 'Pope: The Political Poet in His Time', in Leopold Damrosch (ed.), *Pope: New Critical Essays* (Oxford, 1988), 123–8.
[20] *Works of John Dryden*, viii. 152; cf. *The Hind and the Panther*, i. 341–6.
[21] John Evelyn, *Diary*, ed. E. S. De Beer, 6 vols. (Oxford, 1955), v. 48–9.
[22] Winn, *John Dryden*, 450.

ultimately allow one to reveal the truth to one's friends',[23] it is appropriate indeed that his apologia in the form of Philidel should be part of the text of *King Arthur*. As a matter of biography there can be no doubt that Dryden thought William the time's wrongful invader. To recognize these things is to see the deeper drift of the drama. Dryden had more than one audience in mind. Perhaps too he wished to draw the larger audience to the insights of the smaller.

Seeing and saying (or not saying) truth is certainly the subject of *King Arthur*, as well as its practice. Dryden framed a romantic drama out of Gothic, perhaps Spenserian, enchantment and chivalric fairy tale, all that Milton latterly despised, but used it to convey the bewilderment and unreality of change of state. The characteristic landscape is one of obscurity, disease, and danger, 'lowland damps | And noisome vapours from the foggy fens', 'rivers | Or dreadful downfalls of unheeded rocks'.[24] Its characteristic metaphors are knowing without sight, and seeing without knowledge. Hidden forces are at work. A war could be won and yet the fruits of war lost. A war has been won and yet the future be full of woe. After the patriotic songs and lovely pantomime of the happy ending, Arthur casts an unenchanted glance into futurity, his words to Merlin seeming to recommend accommodation while acknowledging a deeper grief:

ARTHUR. Wisely you have, whate'er will please, reveal'd,
   What wou'd displease, as wisely have conceal'd:
   Triumphs of War and Peace, at full ye show,
   But swiftly turn the Pages of our Wo.
   Rest we contented with our present State;
   'Tis Anxious to inquire of future Fate.

(v. i)[25]

III

It is interesting that it was *Cleomenes, The Spartan Hero* (performed in April 1692) which got Dryden into trouble with the authorities.

[23] Ibid.
[24] *Works of John Dryden*, viii. 149, 153.
[25] *Works of John Dryden*, viii. 199; as Scott noticed, 'Dryden's discontent with the existing circumstances glances out'.

The play is less fraught with contemporary allusion than *Don Sebastian* but attempts no dual application like *King Arthur*. A tragedy with a single action, it is as close to the austerely classical as Dryden ever gets, though the final act (partly executed by Southerne) must be forgiven him. As usual, too, Dryden had a classical defence ready: it was all based on Plutarch and the poet could produce a well-affected noble witness that he had thought of dramatizing this story seven or eight years earlier.[26] But the traditional assault also remained: as Sir Edward Coke had put it at the trial of Sir John Hayward, 'to quo animo and to what end . . . he selecteth this (only) bloody story (out of all the rest)'. In this case Queen Mary had the Lord Chamberlain prevent performance but Laurence Hyde, Earl of Rochester and uncle to the Queen was able to interpose, and the play was acted only a week late.[27] Whether or not Shadwell or some other enemy of Dryden caused this difficulty, it could not be denied that there seemed to be a basis for objection. For Cleomenes is the warlike but exiled King of Sparta, trying to raise support from the 'friendly' but treacherous court of Egypt to regain his throne. Not only was King James now back in France, but all his forces in Ireland were now defeated, or withdrawn, some into military service under the French King. The tragedy opens with the words of Cleomenes himself:

> Dejected! no, it never shall be said,
> That fate had power upon a Spartan soul:
>
> (I. i)[28]

It is hardly surprising that the authorities did object. At a glance it seemed plain that a parallel was intended and if, without investigating too deeply, they turned to the end, there they found Cleomenes and his few supporters attempting an armed *coup d'état* in Egypt. This seems to show what would most strike a wary censor, hostile critic, or not too penetrating audience: as in the case of *Don Sebastian*, it was broad similarity of situation in certain leading features. Calculating public response to the datum of the drama, as opposed to what the shaping art of the playwright was to make of

---

[26] Winn, *John Dryden*, 453.
[27] Ibid.
[28] *Works of John Dryden*, viii. 275.

it, must have been almost impossibly hard, especially in a situation volatile with personal enmity. A closer consideration of *Cleomenes* would have shown that the very last thing Dryden was doing in this play was inciting to Jacobite rebellion.

When Coenus arrives with news of the reception in Sparta of its conqueror, Antigonus, Cleomenes expects to hear of violence and outrage, ransacked houses, polluted temples, 'And dreadful shrieks, as in the act of rape' (I. i).[29] On the contrary:

COENUS. The Soldiers march'd, as in Procession, slow;
And enter'd *Sparta* like a Choir of Priests,
As if they fear'd to tread on holy Ground.
No Noise was heard; no Voice, but of the Cryer,
Proclaiming Peace, and Liberty to *Sparta*.

(I. i)[30]

Shortly after this Antigonus dies, urging on his troops in another war: 'And, in a purple vomit, poured his soul'—we note the Virgilian gesture of Dryden's line. In so far as Dryden's audience saw Cleomenes as a James, and Antigonus as a William, as initially they might, the tragedy might seem to endorse the conclusion which Cleomenes himself draws:

If this indeed be true,
Then farewell, *Sparta*.

(I. i)[31]

While, of course, the allusion to the now not very warlike James is intensely idealizing, there was enough in common between the dramatic and the historical situations to keep the political interest alive. Befriended by the previous King of Egypt, Cleomenes is long ignored by the new King, Ptolemy. When summoned, it is only to serve Egyptian ends. Like James in France, Cleomenes has soldiers loyal to him in the service of his country of exile. With these he could be useful to the Egyptian court; or he could become a threat. The first scene between Ptolemy and Cleomenes (II. ii),[32] in its

---

[29] *Works of John Dryden*, viii. 283.
[30] *Works of John Dryden*, viii. 285.
[31] *Works of John Dryden*, viii. 284–5; Saintsbury plausibly conjectures that this utterance is the source of the words which Scott gives to Prince Charles in *Redgauntlet* when he hears of the clemency of George III: 'If this be so, then all is utterly lost'.
[32] *Works of John Dryden*, viii. 293–9.

accurate assessment of the mendicant role of kings in exile, pre-figures much that was to come in eighteenth-century Jacobite po-litics and poetry. Dryden sees that the Jacobite cause may become only a card in the game of power politics played by the host country. *Cleomenes* also handles the Jacobite image of conquest as rape in a rather new way. The early account of the peaceful conquest of Sparta anticipates a later scene in which Cassandra, mistress of Ptolemy but now in love with the Spartan Hero, invites him to admire a masterpiece by Apelles depicting the rape of Helen from Spartan Menelaus by Paris. The modern Spartan despises the paint-ing because of the immorality of its content, also perhaps because of its insult to Sparta:

CLEOMENES 'Tis scurvy still, because it represents
A base, dishonest Act; to violate
All Hospitable Rites, to force away
His Benefactor's Wife:—Ungrateful Villain!
And so the gods, Th' avenging Gods have judg'd.
CLEANTHES. Was he a *Spartan* King that suffer'd this?
Sure he reveng'd the Rape.
CLEOMENES. He did, my Boy,
And slew the Ravisher.
CASSANDRA. Look better, Sir; You'll find it was no Rape.
Mark well that *Hellen* in her Lover's Arms:
Can you not see, she but affects to strive:

(II. ii)[33]

Cassandra shows the painting to hint her own willingness to sail away 'with a Poor Fugitive Prince',[34] but the political implications are pretty clear: peoples as well as women are sometimes willing conquests. As the plot unfolds, with Cleomenes resisting Cassan-dra's temptation, it becomes increasingly plain that the Spartan Hero is a hero without a cause. He and his family are put to the test of imprisonment and starvation by Cassandra, and survive without dishonour or degradation. Finally released and threatened with execution, their men successfully beat back the forces of the Egyp-tian King in the name of 'Liberty and Magas' (Ptolemy's younger brother) but, as Cleanthes puts it:

33 *Works of John Dryden*, viii. 302.
34 *Works of John Dryden*, viii. 303.

'Tis all in vain: we have no further work:
The People will not be dragg'd out to Freedom.

(v. ii)[35]

This hero and Cleomenes thus agree to die in a kind of near-suicide pact: each kills the other.

In its picture of redundant physical heroism and peoples self-enslaved *Cleomenes* has much in common with the vision of the later Milton. Yet God had need of a physical as well as spiritual hero in Samson—and then again Cleomenes certainly does not lack moral fortitude. But the conclusion is surely surprising from the hand of Dryden. Perhaps the near-suicide is admirable in a pagan setting, not carrying the freight of sin it did for Christian Don Sebastian. Perhaps the political values are also pre-Christian, yet divine right patriarchalism was supposed to derive from the dawn of time. It must be surprising to find Dryden's Spartan Hero engaging in a *coup* against the reigning, legitimate monarch, in the name of 'Liberty and MAGAS'.[36] What appears to have happened is that heroic virtue, tried intolerably by political disappointment, sexual temptation, and physical suffering, breaks out into the readiest opportunity for martial action, in a politically dubious cause. But if there is criticism of Cleomenes here, it is not adequately expounded—there is no Alvarez to conduct a moral diagnosis—and we are now in the problematic Act V. What may seem more clear is that *Cleomenes*, like *Don Sebastian*, both idealizes and writes out of history the heroic title-bearer to a crown. It is a Jacobite play in its vision, concerned with brave and determined men and women in a Jacobite-like predicament, but certainly not forwarding any Jacobite recommendation. It seeks to lay the cause honourably to rest, one might think, rather than keep it alive. It is after all Dryden's first play after James II's clear defeat, and this conclusion may accord with the fact that Dryden, in desperate financial straits, was at this time seeking support through Dorset from Mary II herself.[37]

[35] *Works of John Dryden*, viii. 359.
[36] *Works of John Dryden*, viii. 353.
[37] Winn, *John Dryden*, 451; see Dryden's letter to Mrs Steward, 7 Nov. 1699, in John Dryden, *Letters*, ed. C. E. Ward (Durham, NC, 1942), 123.

IV

Yet, even in the dangerous medium of public entertainment, *Cleomenes* was not to be Dryden's last word on the current affairs of state. It would certainly not be so in his non-dramatic verse. A change seems to come about in his attitude which may, perhaps, be most readily understood in terms of contemporary culture and the public news. Before turning to Dryden's poem 'To My Dear Friend Mr. Congreve' (December 1693) and his last play *Love Triumphant* (plotted and partly written by May 1693, performed in January 1694), it is worth considering the atmosphere of the time as recorded in the pages of Evelyn's *Diary*. Both poem and play, especially perhaps the latter, may be thought to yield their interest to a political approach.[38]

On 30 January 1694, 'Being the Anniversary of the Martyrdom of K. Charles I', Evelyn was to hear a young man preach 'an excellent discourse' on 'the Excellency of Kingly Government above all other, deriving it from Adam, the Patriarches, God himself, That it was originally in the Primogeniture, & so in a Manner continued in the Father over his children even thro the Ro: Emp: 'til *Justinian*'. The preacher 'Shewed the unnaturalnesse of subjects to destroy their owne King, especially such a King as was this Martyr' . . . 'Many passages in this Sermon, neerely touching the dethroning ['our' deleted] K. James, not easily to be answered' (v. 165–6). This entry shows very well the political and religious character of Evelyn's mind, though neither a Catholic nor a Non-Juror. It shows the continuing power of political patriarchalism over a mind of his generation, and suggests that what he reacted to in the public news over the previous two years—the period when *Love Triumphant* was in gestation and composition—will have been what impressed itself on the more committed Dryden. A few details may be noted here. On 28 February 1692 Evelyn noted William's dismissal of Marlborough '(who so ungratefully left his old Master K. James)' from all 'his greate places' (v. 90); on 20 March he visited the Jacobite Earl of Peterborough to see a picture of the young Prince of Wales just brought out of France (v. 92); on 17 April he notes James

---

[38] Winn remarks that '*Love Triumphant* invites no particular political reading . . .' and has little to say about it. He is right, however, to see that it was 'Self-consciously out of style' and 'deliberately old-fashioned' (*John Dryden*, 471).

II's letter to the Privy Council 'informing them of the Q: being ready to be brought abed'—Princess Louisa Maria was born to King James and Queen Mary in June (v. 96–7). A week later Evelyn records 'Greate talke of the French Invading; & of an universal rising' (v. 97) and follows up, on 5 May: 'The Reports of an Invasion being now so hott, alarmed the Citty, Court & People exceedingly' (v. 99). On 29 May he complains that the Restoration of Charles II was not celebrated in church, as by law required (v. 102). He resoundingly records the naval victory over the French at La Hogue (v. 101) and sorrowfully notes the final fall of Namur to the French, on 26 June (v. 106–7). On 12 February 1693 he briefly notes the public demonstration of what was certainly the most explosive issue in current political apologetics: '(Dr. Burnets [Bishop of Salisbury] book burnt by the hangman for an expression of the Kings title by Conquest, caused by a complaint of Jo: How a parliament member: little better than a madman:)' (v. 131). Burnet's *Pastoral Letter . . . to the clergy of his diocess* (1689) and Charles Blount's *King William and Queen Mary Conquerors* (1693) were condemned to be burned by the House of Commons, led by the hot-tempered member John Grubham, for arguing that William and Mary owed their thrones to conquest. On 14 May 1693 Evelyn noted rumours of a standing army to be created 'under colour of a descent' (i.e. of an invasion), of a declaration by the French King '& another of K. James's with an universal pardon, and referring the composing of all mistakes &c to a Parliament' (v. 140); eleven days later he followed up: 'A Declaration or Manifesto from K. James, so written as many thought to be very reasonable: and much more to the purpose than any of his former' (v. 141). It is not claimed that this is an exhaustive list of Evelyn's public comment for the period, nor that Evelyn knew everything, nor, of course, that his reactions were identical with those of Dryden. These entries do show, however, that to an intelligent and well-informed observer the future might seem quite open politically, and that different events might tug the sympathies two ways, where the great dynastic issue of the day was concerned.

It seems that in 1693 Dryden found his post-revolutionary political equilibrium. The forcing away of James II in 1688 and his military defeat in Ireland by 1692 would seem to have prompted, respectively, *Don Sebastian* and *Cleomenes*. King James's subsequent Declarations, as noted by Evelyn, made it clear that his cause could still be well presented, and continued to be a serious political force in the Continental conflict of war and diplomacy, though defeated for the moment in the British kingdoms. Jacobites at home now awaited the outcome of the war abroad. Dryden's decision to convey his continuing political beliefs and values in a commendatory poem to a play by the brilliant young Whig Congreve was in no way demanded by the occasion, and might have been deterred by the censoring of his Prologue to *The Prophetess* (May 1690), with its bitter sarcasms against the new Williamite establishment and the war. The present poem, however, was more deeply meditated, and altogether more comprehensive in its historical and cultural thought. In its themes of paternity and succession it is a patriarchal poem, concerned with loyalty between different ages and generations. It was also the public announcement of a very practical literary alliance, between the most famous writer of his day, though vulnerable in religion, politics, and oncoming old age, and the young Williamite, likely to secure favour from the new regime. In times of civil conflict an ally on the other side is of value. Writers are no exception to this rule. In the event of a second Restoration, Congreve would have as much to gain as Dryden now. Dryden's retrospect on English writing before and after the civil wars, expressed in part through the images of the Doric and Corinthian columns, recognized the different phases of an evolving culture, strength and grace, vigour and skill, necessary to the achievement of the greatest art. The idea of succession is thus implicitly invoked, as opposed to that of mere replacement or supplanting: what is recommended, and what Congreve himself is said to exemplify, is a receiving from what went before, a learning and a growing from it. Equally, in this paradigm, it is the part of the old to recognize and support the salient achievements of the young:

> Thus old *Romano* bow'd to *Raphael*'s Fame;
> And Scholar to the Youth he taught, became.
>
> (ll. 39–40)[39]

'Old *Romano*', a good term for a poet of Dryden's age and Roman aspiration in a poem praising Congreve as 'the best *Vitruvius*' (l. 15), though it involves a factual error, well conveys that sense in

---

[39] Guilio Romano was in fact the younger contemporary of Raphael. It is worth noting that each was also active in architecture.

which Dryden felt both premature and belated in relation to the younger writer. Nothing is more clear, however, than that Dryden is attempting to bridge over the disruptions of 1688–92 in the literary world. If the state deposed its 'old *Romano*' in favour of the hostile and inferior Shadwell, the older poet could himself recognize his true successor in the young Congreve.

All this has skirted around the recent dispossession and supplant-ing of a king in the political foreground, but political allusion now comes unmistakably to the fore:

> Oh that your Brows my Lawrel had sustain'd,
> Well had I been Depos'd, if You had reign'd!
> The Father had descended for the Son;
> For only You are lineal to the Throne.
> Thus when the State one *Edward* did depose;
> A Greater *Edward* in his room arose.
> But now, not I, but Poetry is curs'd;
> For *Tom* the Second reigns like *Tom* the first.
>
> (ll. 41–8)

Thomas Shadwell and Thomas Rymer now represent the Williamite regime in the realm of letters; it would be better represented by the equally Williamite Congreve. And Dryden, after all, in a concilia-tory and telling gesture, does not choose a literary successor from his own side in the conflict. He chooses merit and has sought alliance. Thus his recognition of Congreve fortifies his following judgement in his recognition of his *de jure* King. And as Edward III succeeded Edward II, so (one notes some implicit criticism of James) the royal line will return with a greater James, the Prince of Wales, one day to be James III.

A month later *Love Triumphant; Or, Nature will prevail, a tragi—comedy* was performed.[40] Like many of Dryden's plays *Love Triumphant* opens in the aftermath of battle. Veramond, King of Arragon, his armies led by his warlike son Alphonso, and aided by Garcia, King of Navarre, is victorious over 'fierce Ramirez' the Castilian King (I. i).[41] Alphonso has indeed bested the older Ramirez in single combat, taken him prisoner, but restored his sword. At

---

[40] In view of the extreme neglect of this play, and the fact that it was certainly premeditated by Dryden as his last full-length work for the theatre, I hope a fairly full account of it will be forgiven.

[41] *Works of John Dryden*, viii. 381.

once there is tension between Veramond, arrogant in victory, and Alphonso, his chief means of success. This first emerges in Alphonso's duty to defer to his father and sovereign, his fastidious sense of honour concerning his royal prisoner, and the controversial issue of the entitlements of conquest. Pressed by Veramond for a more emphatic assertion of triumph the young Alphonso responds with a sombre reflection on the uncertainty of the world:

> If more be wanting on so plain a Theam,
> Think on the slippery State of Humane Things,
> The strange vicissitudes, and suddain turns
> Of War, and Fate recoiling on the Proud,
> To crush a Merciless and Cruel Victor.
> Think there are bounds of Fortune, set above;
> Periods of Time, and progress of Success,
> Which none can stop before th' appointed limits,
> And none can push beyond.
>
> (1. i)[42]

Antagonism now breaks out between Veramond and Ramirez who, though a prisoner, takes the initiative in promising terms. Veramond rebukes 'this boldness to his conqueror',[43] and the boldness of his son in proposing to ransom the conquered. 'Fool,' he declares, 'dost thou know the value of a Kingdom?'

ALPHONZO. I think I do, because I won a Kingdom.
VERAMOND. And know'st not how to keep it.
RAMIREZ. What claim have you? What Right to my *Castile*?
VERAMOND. The Right of Conquest; for, when Kings make War,
No Law between two Soverigns can decide,
But that of Arms, where Fortune is the Judge,
Soldiers the Lawyers, and the Bar the Field.
ALPHONZO. But with what Conscience can ye keep that Crown,
To which, ye claim no Title but the Sword?
VERAMOND. Then ask that question of thy self, when thou
Thyself art King. I will retain my Conquest.[44]

There could scarcely be a more sharply relevant political exchange than this, in early Williamite England, with the flare-up of the conquest debate hardly a year before. An allusion in Veramond to

---

[42] *Works of John Dryden*, viii. 385.
[43] Ibid.
[44] *Works of John Dryden*, viii. 387.

William (or the William men such as Burnet and Blount acclaimed) and in Ramirez to James is clear; but more interesting is the position of Alphonso (played by the great Betterton), torn between duty to an arrogant royal father, and a valiant though unfortunate royal foe. Alphonso becomes more interesting still when Dryden invokes another theme from his earlier drama: that of incest. The sin which settled like a fateful cloud upon the legitimate princes Sebastian and Almeyda is knowingly in prospect here as Alphonso and his sister Victoria come to realize their love for each other. This is enacted with some subtlety in a couplet scene (II. i) set in Victoria's bed-chamber, Alphonso leaving his copy of Ovid turned down at the Epistle of 'th' unhappy *Canace*.[45] As Victoria's growing suspicion is confirmed, and Alphonso reads aloud from the Roman poet, Dryden achieves an extraordinary sense of a purely literary doom becoming alive and present. In this situation our dislike of the proud Veramond is necessarily qualified as he proposes a regular alliance between Victoria and Garcia. The compassion and honour of Alphonso, sympathizer with the fallen Ramirez, is now contaminated. He can only oppose the plan with his own incestuous love. In a stylized exordium he utters the paradoxes of his predicament:

> Oh Dear *Victoria*! cause of all my Pain!
> Oh Dear *Victoria*! whom I would not gain!
> *Victoria*, for whose sake I wou'd survive!
> *Victoria*, for whose sake I dare not live!
>
> (II. i)[46]

As the agonizing paradox of *Don Sebastian* is formally recalled, one wonders whether the Princess Victoria has not been named symbolically.

Act III opens with a Song of Jealousy which extends the idea of tyranny from the public conduct of Veramond to Alphonso's hatred of Garcia:

> *Thou Tyrant, Tyrant Jealousie*
> *Thou Tyrant of the Mind.*
>
> (III. i)[47]

---

[45] I am grateful to Dr Richard A. McCabe, of Merton College, Oxford, for his comments on this scene. See his study, *Incest, Drama and Nature's Law 1550–1700* (Cambridge, 1993), 286–91, and ch. 9 generally.

[46] *Works of John Dryden*, viii. 405.

[47] *Works of John Dryden*, viii. 417–18.

In a clear allusion to *Don Sebastian*, Alphonso now resolves to depart:

> Hither I came to take my latest leave
> Of dear *Victoria*, then depart for ever;
> And buried in some solitary Cave,
> Forgetting and forgotten, end my Days.
>
> (III. i)[48]

But through the guilty copy of Ovid the incestuous love, though unconsummated, is discovered. Veramond calls Alphonso 'a stranger to my blood' and Ximena, his Queen, finds in these words her cue for the revelation which could heal all these conflicts. In *Don Sebastian*, as Alvarez proved, incest was committed, though in ignorance. Ximena's revelation is the reversal of that. She shows that Alphonso is the son not of Veramond but Ramirez. The curse on love and loyalty is thus lifted—Nature has prevailed, Veramond's strange hostility to his victorious son, the son's sympathy with the defeated Ramirez, and his love for Victoria, all now seem intelligible and blameless.

> ALPHONZO. O Joyful News! Oh Happy Day; too good
> To end in Night—My Father, and my King!
> [*Runs to Ramirez, kneels to him, and kisses his hand*]
> My Soul foreknew you, with a sure presage
> Of Native Duty, and Instinctive Love.
>
> (III. i)[49]

But Dryden has not produced this Act III revelation as the easy resolution of his plot. Angered rather than pleased at the new situation, resentful at his Queen's well-meant conniving, jealous that now, if Alphonso weds Victoria, he will inherit a double crown, Veramond imprisons Ramirez, banishes Alphonso, decrees that Victoria shall still wed Garcia, and that together they shall rule Castile.

> Bid her prepare her self to Wed Navarr:
> Whether by force or by consent, I care not.
>
> (III. i)[50]

---

[48] *Works of John Dryden*, viii. 421.
[49] *Works of John Dryden*, viii. 426.
[50] *Works of John Dryden*, viii. 429.

Aided by Carlos, captain of the subplot, Alphonso secures a loyal regiment to release Ramirez and reclaim Victoria. As Act III turns into Act IV Victoria begs Garcia not to press his suit, and Victoria's sister Celidea comes to the fore as the princess truly in love with him. None of the emotions aroused falls into the pattern of the available happy ending. As Ximena tells Garcia,

XIMENA. You cannot Wed *Victoria* but by force:
And force can only make her Person yours.

(IV. i)[51]

The post-revolutionary theme of rape and conquest is still in play. But armed force now comes from another quarter: Alphonso and his troops master the situation at the moment of the marriage ceremony, Garcia to be beaten in single combat but spared, Veramond seized and disarmed, Alphonso stipulating: 'use no Violence to his Royal Person'.[52] From the opening scene the drama has attended to the patriarchal ideal, Veramond embodying the authority of king, father, and husband. This authority underlies, and is certainly not identical with, the arrogant claims he makes in the name of military conquest. He has higher authority than a tyrant, though he behaves like one. This truth comes to bear in a further couplet scene between Victoria and Alphonso, in which she, while affirming her love, will not accept his vows without her father's blessing. Alphonso calls her 'sovereign here',[53] but she, no Mary II, recognizes that she cannot be the free and sovereign Queen during the life of her royal father. Force, now on the side of Alphonso and Ramirez, cannot alter that. It is probable that the two dutiful princesses, Victoria and Celidea, are displayed in implicit contrast to the unfilial daughters of James.

The released Ramirez enters to confront a son almost as doomed as when apparently in incestuous love. He has no hesitation as to the solution: force and revenge.

> *Garcia* shall Dye, and, by his Death, remove
> The cause of Jealousie, and Injur'd Love;
> The King himself, th' ungrateful King, shall fall;
> Of all our Ills the cursed Original.
>
> (IV. ii)[54]

[51] *Works of John Dryden*, viii. 438.
[52] *Works of John Dryden*, viii. 440.
[53] *Works of John Dryden*, viii. 422.
[54] *Works of John Dryden*, viii. 446.

Alphonso reacts against this ferocity with the old divine-right image, beloved of James VI and I, of the king as a shepherd:

ALPHONZO. What have the People done, the Sheep of Princes,
That they shou'd perish for the Shepherd's Fault?

(IV. ii)[55]

but, at the pitch of desperation, is ready to assassinate Veramond and take his own life. Ramirez, protesting in his turn against such violence, proposes that Alphonso should restore him to his throne and then treat with Veramond for Victoria. Alphonso says it would be too late. Victoria's duty appears the obstacle to every solution. Ramirez now withdraws Alphonso's recently successful troops but encamps outside the capital. A herald announces a pardon to all rebels, and Carlos, in a suggestive remark, says: 'Then farewell *Ramirez*; ev'n trudge on by your self, for there's an end of my Expedition; I will lay down my Arms like a Dutiful Subject; and submit to his Majesty, when I can rebel no longer' (IV. iii).[56] Ramirez sounds very like James in these words, but in Dryden's fable Carlos is the true subject of Veramond.

Act V finds Veramond again about to force the marriage, and Victoria owning her duty to him while insisting on its limit with her life. Alphonso enters to them, unarmed and desperate, to offer his life to Veramond. Unknown to any there Ramirez is present in disguise. Hearing no tumult in the city Veramond, in a hushed moment, decides to take Alphonso's life. Urged on by Ximena, Celidea, a figure who has steadily grown in character and prominence since the opening scene of the play, now has her supreme moment, as a favourite child of Veramond, in pleading for mercy. (Her name, probably symbolic like 'Victoria', seems to suggest 'a musical sound' or 'a loud clear voice, as of an oracle'.)[57] She speaks, 'most equitable judge' as Veramond calls her (V. ii),[58] the moral of the whole play. All this is far from static: the whole outcome of the play depends on it. In a fine dramatic effect her judgements move from genuine reproof of Alphonso and Victoria to defence in the guise of accusation. In no word does she judge Veramond, her king

---

[55] Ibid.
[56] *Works of John Dryden*, viii. 450.
[57] I am grateful to Professor Michael White, of the University of Arizona, for his convincing suggestion as to the meaning for Dryden of the name 'Celidea'.
[58] *Works of John Dryden*, viii. 470.

and father; but the power of her implied judgement is overwhelming. Thus she finally melts the tyrant in him, and brings on that comprehensive reconciliation which has been in receding prospect so long. As in an old tale still, the redeemed Veramond rounds off the play, Cymbeline-like, in a procession to the temple:

VERAMOND. Just like the winding up of some Design,
  Well form'd, upon the crowded Theatre;
  Where all concern'd surprisingly are pleas'd;
  And what they wish, see done. Lead to the Temple:
  Let Thanks be paid; and Heav'n be prais'd no less
  For private Union, than for publick Peace.

(v. ii)[59]

The usually perceptive Scott was unremitting in his condemnation of this play.[60] By the standards he brings to bear even Shakespeare's final plays would fall. He has no sense of the avowed artificiality of its romance-like, tragicomic, idiom, nor sympathy with Dryden's evident desire to give his last play a retrospective dimension, recuperating the couplet, for example, for scenes of paradox and dilemma. He does not see how the formal style, in both plotting and verse, is used to bring forward moral and political problems, nor how the subplot, less ebullient than in *Don Sebastian*, counterpoints the main plot with which it is linked by Carlos, in its concern with true and false suitors, paternity, and possession. It seems to me that he much underestimates the power of the dramatic verse.

But what are the politics of *Love Triumphant*? Dedicated to the Catholic convert and evidently Jacobite Earl of Salisbury in a preface which strongly hints this commitment,[61] Dryden's last play displays patriarchal authority grounded in Nature. Force, whether of armed conquest, or the vindictive or jealous assertion of legitimate authority, is exposed as an evil. The extreme romantic denouement endorses Christian passive obedience to legitimate authority even when behaving tyrannically. What of particular applications? There are more applications than resemblances, but *Love Triumphant* continues the trend of Dryden's later drama away from a multiplicity of specific political allusions. As in *Cleomenes*—or

[59] *Works of John Dryden*, viii. 474.
[60] *Works of John Dryden*, viii. 367–70. *Dramatic Works*, ed. George Saintsbury (Edinburgh, 1882).
[61] *Works of John Dryden*, viii. 377.

Samson Agonistes—the dramatist relies on the political implications of his dramatic fable. There is no usurper in *Love Triumphant*, but Veramond was ready to take over Castile by conquest and depose its true king. Veramond is the William figure, and the play offers a romantic vision of his conversion. Ramirez is the James figure, valiant and imperfect, proposing, at one point, a course of action no better than the tyrannous designs of Veramond. But in *Love Triumphant* the curse is lifted from the Jacobite predicament. Brought down in the metaphor of incest in *Don Sebastian*, it is exorcized here. In this play the royal Jacobite role passes through all its historical phases into its hoped-for future. Ramirez, defeated in battle, presumed deposed by some, regains a measure of power through the assistance of others, withdraws from the centre of conflict, and, in the last scene, emerges from disguise, the hidden king returned, to bless a series of loyal alliances. Carlos's remark, realistic enough as a comment on England in the mid-1690s, 'Farewell Ramirez, even trudge on by yourself . . .', is answered by the conclusion of Dryden's magnanimous theatrical romance: a Christian political fable affirmed in the prospect of an end to the Continental wars, and a European treaty which might secure something for the Jacobite cause in a general peace.

V

The treaty when it came, however, was the Treaty of Ryswick, signed 20 September 1697, and long expected.[62] What finally brought the settlement about were probably the new opportunities opening up for France in Poland and Spain. But while William's campaign in 1696 had achieved little,[63] the treaty was a tribute to his sheer determination as a political and military leader, including his personal courage and capacity to choose good generals. Louis XIV now recognized William and Mary, while continuing to give refuge to James II whose *de jure* status was still recognized socially. Meanwhile Dryden had been pressing on with his Virgil translation. On 17 February 1697 he begged Chesterfield to accept the Dedication of the *Georgics*, acknowledging that he had delayed long 'in hopes of his return, for whom, and for my Conscience I have

[62] Evelyn, *Diary*, 27 Sept. 1696, 31 Jan. 1697, 12 Oct. 1697 (v. 259, 263, 267).
[63] Ibid. 27 Sept. 1696 (v. 260).

suffered, that I might have layd my Author at his feet', and that 'Gods time for ending our miseries is not yet'.[64] The whole translation was thus to have been dedicated to the restored James. The pervasiveness of Jacobite and Williamite allusion in Dryden's *Aeneis* may be readily traced. Despite the balancing of the roles of royal exile and providential invader in that poem, the turn of events, in confronting Dryden with the probability of a triumphant homecoming for William, now prompted him to invoke a different personification of conquest.

On 3 September 1697, in a letter to his sons containing frank anti-Williamite allusion,[65] Dryden announced: 'I am writeing a Song for St. Cecilia's feast . . . this is troublesome, & in no way beneficial'.[66] There are two later anecdotes: Bolingbroke's that he found Dryden one morning 'in an unusual agitation of spirits' having written his new ode overnight; and Johnson's that he spent a fortnight composing and correcting it. Dryden certainly told Tonson that when he wrote it he thought the ode 'the best of all my poetry' 'but being old I mistrusted my own Judgment'.[67] This ode was *Alexander's Feast; Or the Power of Musique* (first performed, to music by Jeremiah Clarke, on 22 November 1697). It seems clear that, after the dutiful tone of his letter to his sons, something in the composing of the ode took him by surprise. Bolingbroke's whole story can hardly be accepted, but what could have caused Dryden 'unusual agitation of spirits' was the idea that he might break with the common pattern, exemplified by his own *Ode to St. Cecilia* (1687), to write a narrative ode—a narrative ode of a particularly daring kind, one that would on a great public occasion, in the very season of William's returning to London a conqueror, retrieve that great Jacobite theme, illegal conquest, in the story of the greatest conqueror of antiquity, Alexander, of whom it was said that he mastered the whole world and failed only to master himself.[68] The

[64] Dryden, *Letters*, ed. Ward, 86.

[65] 'I am of your opinion that by Tonsons meanes, almost all of our Letters have miscarryed for this last yeare. But however he has missd of his design in the Dedication [of Dryden's Virgil]: though he had prepard the Book for it: for in every figure of Eneas, he has causd him to be drawn like K. William, with a hookd Nose'. Dryden had of course hoped to dedicate his *Virgil* to King James.

[66] Dryden, *Letters*, ed. Ward, 93.

[67] *Poems* ed. James Kinsley, 4 vols. (Oxford, 1958), iv. 2058.

[68] See e.g. Erasmus on Alexander in his *Institutio Principis Christiani* (1516), trans. L. K. Bovis (New York, 1936; repr. 1965), 245–6; Ruth Smith, 'The Argument

choice of Alexander as the focus of his ode would mean a good deal to the Non-Juring and Jacobite circles of the 1690s. Ever since the arrival of William Non-Juror pamphleteers and controversialists had made use of a series of biblical, classical, and English precedents to convey their sense of the new situation. Prominent among these was conflict between Alexander the Great, Darius, King of Persia, and the Jewish High Priest Jaddus, as recounted by Josephus, which turned on the recognition of force against title.[69] The instance of Alexander was used by these Non-Jurors not only as a precedent but, sometimes, a coded allusion to William. Some of William's supporters, however, called him an Alexander in quite straightforward praise. For example, 'The ROYAL Triumph of Britain's Monarch', a song later collected by D'Urfey which looks as if it were composed to celebrate the Battle of the Boyne, opened as follows:

> New Pyramid's raise,
>   Bring the Poplar and Bayes,
> To Crown our Triumphant Commander;
>   The French too shall run,
>   As the Irish have done,
> Like the Persians, the Persians;
> Like the Persians, the Persians,
> Like the Persians before Alexander.[70]

Seizing on these the Jacobite pamphleteer William Anderton, in his Remarks on the Present Confederacy (1693) derisively announced: 'Since our Boobies will be thought to have made a wise Choice of their King, as they call him, and he must be a great Champion, let him be drest up with all the imperfections of Alexander, with whom they are pleased so often to compare him' (p. 25). In the same year Anderton was executed for high treason in the publication of Jacobite pamphlets: he was hardly obscure.[71]

---

and Contexts of Dryden's Alexander's Feast', Studies in English Literature, 18 (1978), 465–90.

[69] Erskine-Hill, 'Literature and the Jacobite Cause', 50–1.

[70] Wit and Mirth: Or Pills to Purge Melancholy, Edited by Thomas D'Urfey (1719–20), introd. Cyrus L. Day, 6 vols. in 3 (New York, 1959), vi. 99. The next stanza refers to the Boyne, and the final one to Queen Mary as still alive.

[71] Mark Goldie, 'The Revolution of 1689 and the Structure of Political Argument', Bulletin of Research in the Humanities (Winter 1980), 530.

There is, in Dryden's focus on a great champion, his setting his poem on a great state occasion, his fashioning a political fable which did not require numerous specific allusions, and in his build-up to a destructive and terrible catastrophe, something distinctly Miltonic—the Milton of *Samson Agonistes*. Furthermore, the ode is highly structured. Within the seven stanzas, each with its chorus, an inner five-act pattern conveys the drama between the protagonist, Alexander, and his antagonist, the artist Timotheus. While the opening stanza sets the scene ('"Twas at the Royal Feast . . .'), and the closing one rounds off the narrative and invokes Cecilia, 'Thus long ago . . . At last divine *Cecilia* came . . .'), the five central ones each recount a different and successful effort of Timotheus to display the power of music over the conqueror. They are, perhaps, the five temptations of Alexander in Dryden's fable. The first of these five—praising in rich language and harmony—exalts him to a god. Here the ode may recall the hero Jupiter boasted in *Amphitryon* he would beget. In the second and fourth Alexander is beguiled into the pleasure of wine, and of love. In the final stanza of the five he is fired with the desire for a destructive revenge. In the central stanza he is moved to lament his fallen foe in easy emotion; here, in this royalist ode, Dryden gives *his* equivalent of the executed king at the centre of the 'Horatian Ode' of Marvell. This is the place where contemporary allusion is most clear, and several commentators have sensed the fallen James in the dead Darius:

> He sung *Darius* Great and Good,
>   By too severe a Fate,
> Fallen, fallen, fallen, fallen,
> Fallen from his high Estate
>   And weltring in his Blood:
> Deserted at his utmost Need,
> By those his former Bounty fed:
> On the bare earth expos'd he lyes,
> With not a Friend to close his Eyes.

(ll. 75–83)[72]

---

[72] *Diary*, Cf. Evelyn, Dryden, *Poems*, ed Kinsley, iv. 1430. v. 86 (24 Jan. 1692) on the fall from King William's favour of Marlborough: 'Note this was the Lord who being entirely advanced by K James, the merit of his father being the prostitution of his Daughter (this Lords sister) to that King: Is now disgraced; & by none pittied, being also the first who betrayed & forsooke his Master K: James, who advanced him from the son of Sir Winston Churchill, an officer of the Greene-Cloth'; Winn, *John*

It is its use of Timotheus which is both the triumph, and perhaps, the problem of the ode. Starting off from the bardic role of celebrating the ruler and singing his deeds, exalting him to deity, Timotheus, by the end of the poem, has effected a quite epoch-making reversal: the artist is now master, the ruler but his instrument. It is a stunning *coup* by the author of *Annus Mirabilis*, *Absalom and Achitophel*, *Threnodia Augustalis*, and *Britannia Rediviva*, though one may perhaps trace back the ode's capacity to mock amidst a splendour of praise—'And thrice He routed all his Foes; and thrice He slew the slain' (l. 69)—to the opening of *Absalom and Achitophel*. Dryden draws too on the familiar trope of the poet as the bestower of fame. Timotheus, as Winn notes,[73] is a composer as well as a performer. The artist had it in his power to create for posterity, for example, a self-indulgent but finally resolute Charles, a 'warlike' James, and a destructive Alexander—or William. Indeed the very present action of Dryden's words, as they were sung on 22 November 1697 at the Stationers' Hall, London, demonstrated that power. *Alexander's Feast*, it seems, is an act of defiance, a writing on the wall at the Feast of Belshazzar, a challenge thrown down in the face of wrongful military conquest, and a vindication of the artist. The catastrophe is especially telling from the pen of the poet who had just completed the English *Aeneid*:

> The Princes applaud, with a furious Joy;
> And the King seyz'd a Flambeau, with Zeal to destroy;
> > *Thais* led the Way,
> > To light him to his Prey,
> And, like another *Hellen*, fir'd another *Troy*.
>
> (ll. 146–50)[74]

This recalls the Trojan story and Augustan myth with the Stuart associations they had for Dryden. (Some have also seen in the concubine Thais a deeply buried allusion to Mary II,[75] but the line

---

Dryden, 495–6; Bessie Proffitt, 'Political Satire in *Alexander's Feast*', *Texas Studies in Literature and Language*, 11 (1970), 1307–16. Robert P. Maccubin, 'The Ironies of Dryden's *Alexander's Feast*', *Mosaic*, 18 (1985), 33–47, interestingly compares Dryden's poem with the St Cecilia odes of the previous decade.

[73] *John Dryden*, 493.
[74] Dryden, *Poems*, ed. Kinsley, iv. 1432.
[75] Proffitt, 'Political Satire in *Alexander's Feast*', *Texas Studies in Literature and Language*, 11 (Winter, 1970), 1037–1315.

certainly recalls the equivocal Helen portrayed in Act II, Scene ii of *Cleomenes*.) Alexander is here seen as beginning again the destructive cycle which involved the tragic endeavour of the Trojans. At this point, however, we confront an unnerving complicity with power on the part of the poet—again, perhaps, reminiscent of the Milton of *Samson Agonistes*. Like *Samson Agonistes*, *Alexander's Feast* is a struggle for power, a wresting of it back from its wrongful possessor. Who causes the firing of Persepolis, in the fable of the ode, but Timotheus? Timotheus, however, is not to be identified with Dryden, though he displays truths which Dryden wished to reveal. Samson's destruction of the temple is, at the critical moment, handed to God for whom, indeed, in the framing of his fable, Milton presumes to speak. Dryden, displaying not a true but a false champion, needs Timotheus as a kind of *alter ego*, a lavish but vindictive muse who will expose Alexander for what he is, and to this extent be an artist with a moral function. But this was an ode for the 'feast' (Dryden's word in the letter to his sons)[76] of Saint Cecilia, not Belshazzar; there is more to Dryden's vision than the vision of Timotheus; and Winn is certainly right to see the muse of revenge transcended by a sacred muse.[77] '*Let old* Timotheus *yield the Prize*'—certainly—but then Dryden's tracks are swiftly and gracefully covered at the very end of the ode, achieving a formal symmetry by civilly feigning that Timotheus was not a moralist, but merely a master of praise:

> Let *old* Timotheus *yield the Prize*,
> *Or both divide the Crown*;
> *He rais'd a Mortal to the Skies*;
> *She drew an Angel down.*

(ll. 177–80)[78]

Alexander's Feast is a sung meditation on the theme of conquest, the grief of defeat, the power of art, and the need of that art, always,

---

[76] Dryden, *Letters*, ed. Ward, 93.

[77] I cannot, however, agree that Timotheus's art 'has no moral dimension' (Winn, *John Dryden*, 494).

[78] Dryden, *Poems*, ed. Kinsley, iv. 1433. I am indebted in this discussion to the late Dr C. P. Macgregor, whose unpublished paper on *Alexander's Feast* I attempt to respond to here. In regard to Belshazzar's Feast, note Daniel 5: 31: 'And Darius the Median took the kingdom, being about three score and two years old.' In Nov. 1697 King James was 64.

for heavenly guidance. It is not a satiric parallel to the political situation of 1697, though Alexander, not a portrait of William, was meant to remind of him, as Darius was of James. Dryden made the application of the ode a little more clear the second time it was published, for it was among the poems, already written, to be enclosed in his labyrinthine *Fables ancient and modern* of 1700. The verbal, thematic, and allusive links within this collection still await full exploration, but William Myers has shown some of the political interconnections.[79] In the Chaucerian imitation 'The Cock and the Fox' the latter's flattery of the former provoke the following monitory lines:

> Ye Princes rais'd by Poets to the Gods,
> And *Alexander'd* up in lying Odes,
> Believe not ev'ry flatt'ring Knave's report,
> There's many a *Reynard* lurking in the Court.
>
> (ll. 659–62)[80]

The allusion must be to the ironic design of Dryden's ode (especially stanza 2) and to the straightforward laudation by Williamites of William as Alexander. Here the recipient of this Alexandering is, mischievously, warned of a plot, and made a good deal more like William than Alexander: 'He had a high Opinion of himself: | Though sickly, slender, and not large of Limb, | Concluding all the World was made for him' (ll. 656–8).[81] *Alexander's Feast* was thus more clearly pointed; at the same time, however, the tone of allusion was changed. And this is characteristic of the *Fables*, the art of which is, in part, to juxtapose yet interlink different modes and moods, heroic, romantic, comic, discursive, lyrical. Through the themes of restoration, kingship, loyalty, love, conquest, abdication, and rape, the Jacobite/Williamite situation appears and disappears tantalizingly, an elusive figure in a various and shifting literary landscape. Enfolded within this dazzling collection, however, is one poem, never separately published, which behind the mask of its title proves to be a perfectly explicit religious and political poem about 1688 and after, which Dryden's 'Padron', Samuel Pepys, urged on

---

[79] William Myers, *Dryden* (1973), ch. 10.
[80] Dryden, *Poems*, ed. Kinsley, iv. 1621.
[81] Ibid.

probably by the prominent Non-Juror George Hickes,[82] recommended Dryden to write: 'The Character of A Good Parson; Imitated from Chaucer, and Inlarg'd'.[83] The poem is at once a Catholic
convert's tribute to the Anglican Non-Juror position in support of
the *de jure* king—a tribute well directed in that it seems to have been
modelled on the moderate and pastoral, deprived, Bishop Ken—and
a summation and rejection of the various arguments of the 1690s
for accepting the Williamite settlement. Since *Alexander's Feast*, like
Samson Agonistes, was a poem of political implication, and since
Dryden's later dramas were not parallels, it is then valuable to have
an explicit diagnosis of the post-revolutionary situation.

It would be quite wrong, however, to read this poem as entirely
political, as 'a poem on affairs of state'. It is a religious tribute,
recognizing in an Anglican clergyman some of the same qualities of
primitive Christianity that the poet had already portrayed in his
Hind. The explicit politics of the poem spring from the practical
Christianity it praises:

> His Saviour came not with a gawdy Show;
> Nor was his Kingdom of the World below.
> Patience in Want, and Poverty of Mind,
> These Marks of Church and Churchmen he design'd,
> And living taught; and dying left behind.
> The Crown he wore was of the pointed Thorn:
> In Purple he was Crucify'd, not born.
>
> (ll. 89–95)[84]

His lack of worldliness and ambition makes his political judgement
the more telling. The Temper, watching with 'envious Eye', brings
on a crisis of state:

> He took the time when *Richard* was depos'd:
> And High and Low, with Happy *Harry* clos'd.
> This Prince, tho' great in Arms, the Priest withstood:
> Near tho' he was, yet not the next of Blood.
> Had *Richard* unconstrain'd, resign'd the Throne:

---

[82] James Kinsley, 'Dryden's "Character of a Good Parson" and Bishop Ken', *RES*
NS 3 (1952), 155–8.
[83] Dryden, *Letters*, ed. Ward, 115.
[84] Dryden, *Poems*, ed. Kinsley, iv. 1738.

1. James Francis Edward, as Prince of Wales, engraving by Peter Van Schuppen, 1692, after the portrait by Nicholas de Largillierre.

A King can give no more than is his own:
The Title stood entail'd, had *Richard* had a Son.

(ll. 106–14)[85]

Richard II's reign remained a precedent for all those who wished to change the dynasty or alter the constitution, and the articles of his deposition had been important on the parliamentary side in the Civil War.[86] His fate had been feared by James II,[87] as by Elizabeth I. Hickes himself had recently recalled the precedent and those who opposed it, in his *Vindication of Some Among Ourselves Against the Principles of Dr. Sherlock* (1692), where he had written:

. . . we must live *according to Laws . . . we have neither Power nor Policy either to depose King* Richard, *or to Elect Duke* Henry . . . *King* Richard *still remaineth our Sovereign Prince* . . . Thus, Sir, spoke that Heroick Prelate in the Court of Parliament . . . For *he chose not* the safer but the juster side, as all good Men ought to do.[88]

This endorsement of the perhaps legendary Bishop Merks of Carlisle was the judgement of one of the two first Non-Juring bishops, appointed by James II in 1693 and consecrated on 24 February 1694. There can be little doubt that Hickes's polemic lies behind this part of Dryden's poem. The lines, of course, recognize a difference between Richard II and James II, not so much that Richard was put to death, while James II was only forced away but—more important for the future—James, unlike Richard *had* a son. The poem exposes the myth of James's alleged abdication more emphatically even than the conclusion of *Don Sebastian*.

The poem resumes its summary of the political arguments:

Conquest, an odious Name, was laid aside,
Where all submitted; none the Battle try'd

---

[85] Ibid. 1739.

[86] See e.g. the use made of this reign in Henry Parker's *Observations on His Majesties Answers and Despatches* (1642), in Howard Erskine-Hill and Graham Storey (eds.), *Revolutionary Prose of the English Civil War* (Cambridge, 1983), 53; William Haller (ed.), *Tracts on Liberty in the Puritan Revolution, 1658–47*, 3 vols. (New York, 1934), ii. 195–6.

[87] See S. W. Singer (ed.), *Correspondence of Henry Hyde, Earl of Clarendon*, 2 vols. (1828), ii. 211. I am indebted for this reference to Professor John Miller of Queen Mary College, London.

[88] Erskine-Hill, 'Literature and the Jacobite Cause', 50–1.

The senseless Plea of Right by Providence,
Was, by a flatt'ring Priest, invented since:
And lasts no longer than the present sway;
But justifies the next who comes in play.
  The People's Right remains; let those who dare
Dispute their Pow'r, when they the Judges are.
  He join'd not in their Choice; because he knew
Worse might, and often did from Change ensue.
Much to himself he thought, but little spoke:
And, Undepriv'd, his Benefice forsook.
  Now through the Land, his Cure of Souls he stretch'd:
And like a primitive Apostle preach'd.
Still Chearful; ever constant to his Call.

(ll. 115–29)[89]

Two details prevent this passage from being a simple description of the post-revolutionary situation. It was true in the case of Richard but not James that 'none the Battle try'd': perhaps it was because there had been war that the Williamite authorities were so jumpy about the argument from conquest. Of course, as Hickes and Dryden certainly remembered, after Richard the legitimate, dispossessed, line eventually returned to the throne with the House of York. Secondly, Ken at least was eventually deprived, though he may have anticipated his deprivation. The 'flatt'ring Priest' is undoubtedly William Sherlock, the antagonist of Hickes and the other continuing Non-Jurors. Sherlockian providentialism appears especially feeble as we look back on it today, and fully deserving Dryden's dismissal. Yet in more surprising circumstances—those, perhaps, dramatized in Marvell's 'Horatian Ode'—one might not think the argument so craven. Dryden's political analysis, explicit as it is, thus ranges over the recurrences of English history, pointed enough for his own time, and is his latest, clearest, and most Christian response to the experience of political disappointment and defeat.

VII

It is from involvement in defeat that the post-revolutionary works of Dryden arise, as was the case with Milton. Each seeks to explain,

---

[89] Dryden, *Poems*, ed. Kinsley, iv. 1739.

explore, and generate a vision of the future. Neither poet comes to a clear accommodation with the new regime. As a matter of biography, Dryden at several points considered an undertaking not to write against the Williamite establishment while, in his literary record, both *Don Sebastian* and *Cleomenes* seem to offer the vision of a tragic but honourable end for a defeated and fated cause. Other remarks, however, in dedications and letters, attest to Dryden's continuing Jacobitism, and this constancy, even optimism, find expression in other works of varying degrees of explicitness—from *King Arthur* at one end of the spectrum to *Love Triumphant* and 'The Good Parson' on the other. As Peter Brown has recently pointed out,[90] Jacobite hope and contemporary political allusion seem to rise again in Dryden's mind in 1693—perhaps after the shock of James II's military defeat had been assimilated. This is the year of Dryden's epistle 'To My Dear Friend Mr Congreve . . .' with its evident Jacobite allusion.

There was perhaps a similar accommodation in Milton's works. We do not know with certainty when Milton began or ended the ten-book *Paradise Lost*.[91] If Aubrey was right to say that it was started about two years before the Restoration and finished about three years after, the poem may be thought to respond to the fall of Cromwellian monarchy as well as to the return of Charles. Milton's reaction to the defeat of the final republic (whether by covert agreement or no) was to retreat from overt engagement, and work, from biblical subjects of the most seriously shared concern to all, through implication. That the implication is there, there is enough that is explicit, especially at the level of general political ideas, to be reasonably sure. In *Paradise Lost*, Milton had taken the notions of monarchy and rebellion as categories of thought sharable between himself and his Restoration audience, using one to express the unitarian monarchy of God, the other to attest to the allure and prestige of evil as apparent champion but ultimate betrayer of the

---

[90] Peter M. Brown, 'Statecraft and Controversy in the Drama of John Dryden', M.Litt. diss. (University of Cambridge, 1989), 194–200.

[91] 'He began about 2 yeares before the king came-in, and finished about three yeares after the king's restauracion' (Aubrey, *Brief Lives*, 2 vols., ed. A. Clark (Oxford, 1898) ii. 69). Parker sees Milton having begun *Paradise Lost* 'during the closing years of the Commonwealth' and seems to envisage it as having in some measure changed its meaning during the course of composition, as a result of the Restoration (*Milton, A Biography* 2 vols. (Oxford, 1968), i. 593).

poet's political hopes. The hypothesis that the outline of Oliver Cromwell's career is to be discerned in that of Satan—that Satan is 'the devils' Cromwell'—is consistent with this view. The pervasiveness in the poem of all kinds and senses of kingship, together with the absence of a patriarchal account of its origin, attests to the educative function which M. A. Radzinowicz has seen as so important a part of its political life.

If there is no political accommodation in this there is a kind of adjustment to what we may suppose were some of the major public assumptions of the readership. Other kinds of adjustment are to be seen in works such as Dryden's *Amphitryon*, *King Arthur*, and the *Aeneis* translation. *Amphitryon* brings both sides together in recognition of a shared bewilderment, and *King Arthur* does so by seeming to admit what were in fact contrary political applications—something Dryden had contrived locally, though not structurally, in *Don Sebastian*. In his *Aeneis*, however, Dryden perfected his adjustment to a politically polarized readership. Where Milton explains defeat through a Christianization of Virgilian epic, Dryden reads his times in the light of the *Aeneid*, seeing both James (in the earlier part of the poem) and William (in the later) in the Virgilian protagonist. He thus prompted his readers into an active and compassionate effort to understand the often paradoxical, often tragic, nature of historical process and human endeavour.

Dryden's vision in the late dramas moves towards and then beyond defeatism, while Milton had seemed to develop a new defiance in the two major poems published in 1671. *Paradise Regained* is intransigent, *Samson Agonistes* a challenge and threat. In *Samson*, particularly, new energies seemed to emerge from the ruins of the old republic to encounter and confront new constraints. In all his post–1660 works Milton created his own image as individual author with a particular history, using the features of his own career, its ideals, goals, blindness, and defeat, as metaphors for wider experience, to be sure, and in no sense unmediated autobiography, to appeal always to his reader's awareness of 'The Author John Milton',[92] so as to point the political implications of his work.

---

[92] As the title-page of *Paradise Lost*, the title-page of the 1671 volume containing *Paradise Regained* and *Samson Agonistes*, *and* the separate title-page for *Samson*, bear the announcement: 'The Author John Milton' (J. M. French (ed.), *Life and Records of John Milton* 5 vols. (Rutgers U.P., 1949–58), iv. 445; v. 29).

(Thus even in *Paradise Regained*, where the 'author' nowhere appears save in the pseudo-Virgilian claim of identity at the start, the reader is in no doubt as to the contemporary relevance of Christ's rejection of imperial Rome.) Another aspect of Milton's self-created authorial image, fortifying his strategy of political implication, was its high humanist character. Though writing in English Milton, in his choice of form, style, and allusion, proclaimed himself a citizen of the high cultural realm of Buchanan, Tasso, Grotius, and Galileo. Knowing his own powers he could assume this role without false pretence. This classical quality was not just in his choice of forms, however, nor in his exact judgement of how they could be charged, but in the skill with which he measured his response to the new England he so vehemently opposed. *Paradise Lost, Paradise Regained*, and *Samson Agonistes*; and no more. How could there have been more? They were like three different, powerful, blows, each delivered with perfect judgement and timing.

Dryden, by contrast, is prolific in quantity and variety. He lacks the classical features of Milton, and, as a matter of biography, could not have held his own as Milton did in the Florentine academies. He never travelled abroad and, learned as he was in the Latin and Greek classics, his literary output was largely shaped by the English and French poetry of the high Renaissance and Baroque. This meant in practice that Dryden was open to a greater variety of forms than the late Milton. The early Milton might possibly have written something like *King Arthur*, the late Milton never. If Dryden ever achieves anything like classical form in a complete, original, work it is perhaps in *Amphitryon*; it is somehow typical of his life that, ill and needy, he turned to Southerne to help him complete on time his 'classical' tragedy of *Cleomenes*. Almost too fertile in idea and effect in *Don Sebastian*, Dryden the old magus soon paced himself to produce, Merlin-like, a long series of theatrical and poetic shows which explored the problems of change of state and tenaciously rehearsed the themes of *de jure* kingship and wrongful conquest. More drawn than Milton to specific and often satirical comment on the times, Dryden developed techniques of deliberate equivocation and indirection, which served both as protection and a way of responding to the real complexity of the historical situation. He never offers a portrait of the times, or a parallel, though he often plays on his audience's expectation of one. Like Milton, but discursively and indeed copiously, he builds up his reader's sense of him as an author with a certain history,[93] something which often prompts that reader to catch the correct political implication of the work. It is also striking that Dryden evidently loved what the high humanist Milton deliberately presented himself as despising: chivalric romance. This is the Dryden of *Don Sebastian* with its affinities with the narrative of courtly adventure; of the fairy tale and pantomime-like *King Arthur*; and of that 'Later Play' *Love Triumphant*: the Dryden who included *The Knight's Tale* and *The Flower and the Leaf* in his *Fables*, and expanded the term 'fable' to comprehend narratives drawn from Homer, Ovid, Chaucer, and Boccaccio, not to mention poems in different forms than these. In the end, it seems to me, Dryden's attraction to romance softened his sense of political alienation, accommodated him, not to the principles of the new regime, but to the perils and surprises of the time, and, perhaps, helped him to a more magnanimous view of historical change, rupture, and revolution, than is afforded by the last published works of Milton.

This shall be the last point of our comparison. It is made most tellingly by considering the ends of *Samson Agonistes* and of *Love Triumphant*. Milton affords no vision of conversion and reconciliation in his tragedy; it is Dryden's management of the tragicomic form of *Love Triumphant* which can convey something like a Christian spirit. A similar contrast strikes us if we consider the conclusions of *Don Sebastian* and *Cleomenes*. If fatal love brings down the heroic Samson and the heroic Sebastian, how differently Almeyda is treated from Dalila! Dryden uses the relative freedom of his non-biblical source to involve Almeyda as much as Sebastian in the tragic grief of their unwitting sin. Dalila is only a temptress, Almeyda equal with Sebastian in tragic love and loss. Samson recovers from his fall to be God's weapon of destruction: bearing his burden of sin Sebastian withdraws from the world of love and power 'To live alone to Heav'n'. Milton's drama looks to a holy but historical triumph; Dryden's to a holy retreat. In a pact of heroic pagan friendship Cleomenes the Spartan, and Cleanthes the brave Egyptian, agree to kill one another. In so doing they leave undestroyed a corrupt king, a treacherous mistress, a circumspect and

---

[93] This was well recognized in Alan Roper's important book, *Dryden's Poetic Kingdoms* (1965), but has received fresh emphasis in Annabel Patterson's *Censorship and Interpretation* (Madison, 1984).

worldly minister, and a people content with slavery. In the most secular and modern of his last plays, *Amphitryon*, Dryden shows pity for the bewildered Alcmena, tricked into infidelity, whom he has departed from precedent to move into the centre of experience of his drama.

Only *Alexander's Feast*, as we have seen, shows a measure of Milton's vindictive spirit, consummating a bond between poetry and power. The choral ode which turns the conqueror back to destruction has something of the paean of triumph in the final choric ode of *Samson Agonistes*, which celebrates the destruction of the Philistine foe. The feast of Dagon becomes, for a spell, the feast of Samson: only after Timotheus, Milton-like, has had his full rein, does Alexander's feast, Timotheus's reign of power, revert to the Feast of St Cecilia. Both *Samson Agonistes* and *Alexander's Feast* turn to the divine at the end. As poet Milton need say no more, but Dryden, characteristically, though as some may feel anticlimactically, concludes his literary response to the revolution in affairs of state with 'The Good Parson'.

PART II

Pope and the Question of Jacobite Vision

2

Early Poems to *The Rape of the Locke*

FROM the viewpoint of an intelligent Roman Catholic household the reign of James II seemed, even in retrospect, a providential convergence of right and might. The hereditary crown, descending by law within the ancient constitution of the three kingdoms, was worn once again by a supporter of the old religion, the true, dispossessed Church. Further, any Roman Catholic concerned also with the relation between rule and writing, noticed that the greatest poet of 'the last age'[1] had converted to the old faith during James II's short occupation of the throne, thus displaying an extraordinary espousal of faith, rule, and art at their highest level. This image is likely to have lived in the mind, even when qualified by political considerations, recognized by Dryden at the time,[2] as to how James had misplayed his never very strong hand, how he had antagonized the Anglican establishment, or how he had (in the terms of Charlwood Lawton[3]) wrongly resorted to the royal prerogative to bring in his doomed scheme for a civil comprehension of the different Churches of England, Ireland, and Scotland. To these shrewder considerations there has then to be added crude charges that James sought to be a papist tyrant, to violate the liberties of his subjects, and, worst nightmare of all, to return from their secular proprietors to the Old Church those monastic lands acquired by the gentry and nobility under Henry VIII. But, more than by any of these thoughts, the positive image of James II's reign was shaken by the military blow of the Scottish, Irish, and Continental victories of William III. Hope and right had thus met failure and defeat in the ways of the world. At this point the Roman Catholic minority felt as Protestant and Catholic royalists had felt during the high tide of Cromwellian success earlier in the century. Yet Charles II had been peacefully

---

[1] Joseph Spence, *Observations, Anecdotes and Characters of Books and Men*, ed. J. M. Osborn, 2 vols. (Oxford, 1966), 484; i. 207.
[2] Dryden to Etherege, 16 Feb. 1687 *Letters*, ed. C. E. Ward (Durham, NC, 1942), 27; *The Hind and the Panther*, iii. 427–1288; *Works*, iii. 173–200.
[3] BL Add. MSS 40621, fo. 245v.

restored. The moral of this was certainly drawn by the Roman Catholic community, as shown, for example, by the 'Memoire Sommaire' among the religious and political papers of the Belson family:

Mais apres tant d'examples que l'histoire d'Angleterre fournit il y a tout suiet de croire que la nasion, comme elle a deja fait deux depuis 37 ans retournera a ses anciennes Loix et ses veritables Maitres, car on peut supposer que cette derniere revolution ayant le meme principe que les precendentes, estant fondee sur le renversement des mesmes loix, elle finira aussi de la mesmes maniere, Alors les Protestans sentiront l'inutilité de tous les traitez avec l'Usurpateur qui deviendront semblable a tous ceux qui avoient esté concluds avec Cromwel.[4]

Coming as it does from a Roman Catholic milieu, such a diagnosis suggests what must have been considered, if not concluded, in the household of the young Alexander Pope. In some ways it is rather extreme: it makes no bones about equating William III, a prince of the Stuart dynasty, with 'l'Usurpateur' Cromwell. On the other hand, it does not explicitly invoke a particular providence to restore the ancient laws and the true masters. It seems rather to rely on expectation of a cyclical pattern within affairs of state. In so doing it resorts to a widespread, indeed probably dominant, habit of thought about history, available and attractive to Catholic and Protestant alike. The career and writings of Pope can be plotted against this prediction of a return to the old masters and the ancient constitution. The interest in doing so today connects with the academic rediscovery of Jacobitism as the most notable development peculiar to eighteenth-century studies in recent years. Much remains to be discovered, no doubt, and much to be settled, but the vigorous new historical controversy itself suggests that Jacobite principle and feeling are no longer marginal issues. Certainly a discredited but long-lingering picture of the eighteenth century must finally be discarded: that according to which a generally acclaimed public event, the revolution of 1688, led to an inexorable secular and constitutional advance towards the American and French Revolutions and the 1832 Reform Bill.[5] Lockeian contractualism no more expressed the consensus of the nation than did civic human-

---

[4] Berkshire Record Office, D/Ebt Q71/2.
[5] Herbert Butterfield, *The Whig Interpretation of History* (1931).

ism, though each was a major, controversial, strand in political thought. Patriarchalism and providentialism were not less strong than before: they may have been stronger.[6]

Seen in their political aspect, Pope's works may be divided into two parts, before and after what was for him the most dangerous political crisis of his life: the Atterbury Plot of 1722. Before and after this divide Pope deploys a poetry of obliquity and innuendo which he inherited from the last twelve years of Dryden, but in the transitional 1729 *Dunciad*, still more so in the Epistles and *Imitations of Horace* that follow, he blends with his more personal tones a national and oratorical manner. He then becomes one of the strongest voices to articulate a nation-wide campaign of opposition to Britain under the Hanoverian establishment. Pope's earlier work, by comparison, notably *The Rape of the Lock*, is circumspect, exploratory, delicate, yet wide in implication. In these chapters I shall discuss something of these two areas of Pope's work in turn, reserving for the following chapter a consideration of his Epistle *To Augustus*.

I

As we attend to the repercussions of 1688 in the poetry of the later seventeenth and earlier eighteenth centuries we can recognize a range of work differing according to its more or less overt relation to that event. It has elsewhere been shown how Dryden could use ancient epic to explore the experience of the post-revolutionary situation, not through a consistent parallel, but in a more free and circumspect manner. Looking at Dryden's and Pope's earliest imitations of Homer, it is worth asking what governed their choice of episodes apart from bending the bow of Ulysses, showing what they could do by selecting a high and exacting moment from Homer, which certainly was one motive. Dryden's 'Last Parting of *Hector* and *Andromache*. From The Sixth Book of *Homer's* Iliads' (published in *Examen Poeticum* in 1693) may have been a trial run for a later project in the translation of ancient epic, but probably also, as

---

[6] J. C. D. Clark, *English Society, 1688–1832: Ideology, Social Structure and Political Practice during the Ancien Regime* (Cambridge, 1985), 42–56, discusses this matter fully. George Watson, 'The Augustan Civil War', *RES* NS 36: 143 (Aug. 1985), 321–37, has much that is relevant to these issues.

Robin Sowerby has suggested,[7] an allusion to James II, his Queen, Mary of Modena, and their male heir the infant Prince James. Two momentous partings seem likely to have been in Dryden's mind: the first when, as James faced the incoming forces of William, he secretly sent his wife and son ahead of him as refugees to France; the second when, leaving Mary and James behind, he set off from France on his initially successful Irish expedition against William. It must be allowed that Dryden would have been hard-pressed to find another episode from ancient epic which so peculiarly recalled recent history; certainly no encounter of one adversary against another on the field of battle would have done so well. Here the fidelity of King and Queen as pledged to their child, the hope of their kingdom, is set forth in a tragic leave-taking. Homer and English history seem to join as Hector takes off his helmet and blesses his son:

> Parent of Gods, and Men, propitious *Jove*,
> And you bright synod of the Pow'rs above;
> On this my Son your Gracious Gifts bestow;
> Grant him to live, and great in *Arms* to grow:
> To Reign in *Troy*; to Govern with Renown:
> To shield the People, and assert the Crown:
> That, when hereafter he from War shall come,
> And bring his *Trojans* Peace and Triumph home,
> Some aged Man, who lives this act to see,
> And who in former times remember'd me,
> May say the Son in Fortitude and Fame
> Out-goes the Mark . . .
>
> (ll. 156–7)[8]

That Astyanax is heir to a kingdom and shall (in Hector's hope) 'Reign in *Troy*' is all Dryden's addition to Homer.[9]

In the light of this, and of Dryden's Virgil, it is interesting to consider Pope's early Homeric episodes. Pope's youthful epic, *Alcander, Prince Rhodes*, (he later told Spence[10]) was about 'a prince driven from his throne'. The '*Episode* of Sarpedon, Translated from

---

[7] Robin Edward Sowerby, 'Dryden and Homer', Ph.D. diss. (University of Cambridge, 1975), 221–3.

[8] John Dryden, *Poems*, ed. James Kinsley, 4 vols. (Oxford, 1958), ii. 850.

[9] Cf. *Iliad*, vi; *Alexander Pope*, ed. John Butt *et al.*, vii. *The Iliad of Homer* (1967). This point is made by Robin Sowerby in 'Dryden and Homer', 222.

[10] Spence, *Observations*, 37; i. 17.

the *Twelfth* and *Sixteenth* Books of *Homer's Iliads*' (1709) and 'The Arrival of *Ulysses* in Ithica. Being part of the XIIIth Book of *Homer's Odysses*' (1713) take up the relevant themes of doomed resistance, exile, and return. In the first, by linking Sarpedon's successful sortie in Book XII with his death in Book XVI, Pope constructs an episode out of Homer which above all conveys heroic defeat. It may be thought to dramatize before all else an heroic ideal of the aristocracy who, because they enjoy the best that the world affords, and are honoured and obeyed by their people, own a duty, indeed a character and calling, to brave death on the field of battle. The poem reflects back on a recent decade of civil war in which (again from a Catholic and Jacobite viewpoint) the action of a Dundee (praised by Dryden)[11] or a Sarsfield might seem not unworthy of Homeric example:

> Why on these Shores are we with Joy survey'd,
> Admir'd as Heroes, and as Gods obey'd?
> Unless great Acts superior Merit prove,
> And Vindicate the bounteous Pow'rs above:
> 'Tis ours, the Dignity They give, to grace;
> The first in Valour, as the first in Place:
> That while with wondring Eyes our Martial Bands
> Behold our Deeds transcending our Commands,
> Such, they may cry, deserve the Sov'reign State,
> Whom those that Envy dare not Imitate!
> Cou'd all our Care elude the greedy Grave,
> Which claims no less the Fearful than the Brave,
> For Lust of Fame I shou'd not vainly dare
> In fighting Fields, nor urge thy Soul to War.
> But since, alas, ignoble Age must come,
> Disease, and Death's inexorable Doom;
> The Life which others pay, let Us bestow,
> And give to Fame what we to Nature owe,
> Brave, tho' we fall; and honour'd if we live;
> Or let us Glory gain, or Glory give!
>
> (ll. 33–52)[12]

[11] Dryden, *Poems*, ed. Kinsley, iv. 1777; Dryden's lines are a translation of the Latin epitaph written by Archibald Pitcairne (1652–1713), the Jacobite physician and poet.

[12] *The Twickenham Edition of the Poems of Alexander Pope*, general editor John Butt, i. *Pastoral Poetry and An Essay on Criticism*, ed. Emile Audra and Aubrey Williams (London, 1961), 450–1.

This famous passage of translation has been admirably discussed, by R. A. Brower above all.[13] Its combination of the Homeric with the Virgilian in diction and attitude, its incorporation of a reflective Renaissance Neo-Stoicism found in Chapman, all play their part. Pope, however, acknowledged Denham's version of this speech, which indeed pointed the way to Pope's aphoristic patterning, while throwing a few of his decisions into relief. While accepting 'transcend' from Denham Pope is the first to speak of Glaucus's 'Soul'. He replaces Denham's 'Glorious Folly' with 'Lust of Fame' and, rejecting the more secular aristocratic ethos of 'A common Sacrifice to Honour fall' redeems the notion of 'Glory' by saving it for his own final line. Homer sanctions the use of 'glory' there but, as a result of Pope's previous choices of words, 'Glory' in his hands seems to reach for a spiritual meaning. Not surprisingly, perhaps, Pope's presentation of a chieftain facing death in a cause apparently doomed to defeat, attains something of the tone of Christian martyrdom.[14]

'The Episode of Sarpedon' appeared with Pope's *Pastorals* in *Poetical Miscellanies: The Sixth Part* (2 May 1709). He therefore appeared as a poet of epic as well as pastoral vein in his first substantial publication. The epic vein was continued in his 'First Book of Statius His Thebais' published in 1712 but composed, perhaps, considerably earlier. This poem and 'The Arrival of Ulysses' explore further Pope's *Alcander* theme, the first setting forth the fate of a country in dispute between two rival dynasts, one in possession, the other in exile poised to assert his right;[15] the second yielding a vision of a prince, long exiled, almost mystically restored to his native shores. The importance of such a moment, for what Douglas Brooks-Davies terms 'emotional Jacobitism',[16] need hardly be urged. Two moments in this second, neglected but wonderful poem may be touched on here. First (a very contemporary

---

[13] R. A. Brower, *Pope: The Poetry of Allusion* (Oxford, 1959), 107–13.

[14] 'Glory', in Pope's version, is held back until its double appearance in the last line of the passage. (Note also the use of 'transcend' in l. 8). See Julian Ferraro, 'Political Discourse in Alexander Pope's *Episode* of Sarpedon: Variations on the Theme of Kingship', *MLR* 88: 1 (Jan. 1993), 15–25.

[15] *TE* l. 409–46; J. M. Aden, *Pope's Once and Future Kings* (Knoxville, Tenn., 1978), 89–90; Howard Erskine-Hill, 'Literature and the Jacobite Cause', in Eveline Cruickshanks (ed.), *Ideology and Conspiracy: Aspects of Jacobitism, 1689–1759* (Edinburgh, 1982), 53.

[16] Douglas Brooks-Davies, *Pope's Dunciad and the Queen of the Night: A Study of Emotional Jacobitism* (Manchester, 1985).

note) the importance for a prince in exile of an ally and royal host—Dryden explored this situation in *Cleomenes*. Here Ulysses, not at first recognizing the coast on which he wakes, wrongly accuses Alcinous and the Phaeacians of perfidy:

> Some juster Prince perhaps had entertain'd,
> And safe restor'd me to my Native Land.
>
> (ll. 82–3)[17]

Then, secondly, the goddess Pallas persuades him that he really is on the shores of Ithica, and he is able finally to give thanks for his return, and see a future in which his son will inherit his right:

> All hail! Ye Virgin Daughters of the Main;
> Ye Streams, beyond my Hopes beheld again!
> To you once more your own *Ulysses* bows,
> Attend his Transports, and receive his Vows,
> If *Jove* prolong my Days, and *Pallas* crown
> The growing Virtues of my youthful Son,
> To you shall Rites Divine be ever paid,
> And grateful Off'rings on your Altars laid.
>
> (ll. 240–7)[18]

Possible wordplay on 'Rites Divine' may be borrowed from l. 7 of Dryden's *Aeneis*. The whole episode is, of course, more mystical than the 'Episode of Sarpedon' involving a restoration in sleep and a visitation by a goddess in disguise. By the time it was incorporated into his *Odyssey* translation, if not before, Pope was aware of the Christian allegory according to which Ulysses really dies (his sleep on a ship of death) and awakens in Heaven.[19] Too classical to admit anything of such an interpretation into his own version, Pope nevertheless suffuses his picture of a political restoration with the emotions of a religious vision.

II

Pope's choice of Homeric episodes for early translation is, in my judgement, politically suggestive. Harder evidence of his political

---

[17] *TE* i. 468.
[18] *TE* i. 473–4.
[19] *The Odyssey of Homer Books XIII–XXIV*, ed. Maynard Mack, Norman Callan, Robert Fagles, William Frost, and Douglas Knight (1967); TE x. 7 n. 116.

orientation is certainly required, however, and this may be supplied by poems of another sort. The more explicit mode of the formal 'poem on affairs of state' is needed. Once, very early in his youthful career, Pope appears to have published such a poem:

> Behold, Dutch Prince, here lye th'unconquer'd Pair,
> Who knew your Strength in Love, your Strength in War!
> Unequal Match, to both no Conquest gains,
> No Trophy of your Love or War remains.

David Nokes, whose attribution of this epigram to Pope may give us Pope's first published poem, notes that when Pope annotated it with the initials 'A.P.' in his copy of *State Poems* (1705) he also cancelled the second couplet, containing the clumsy and incorrect third line.[20] In either form, however, what we have here is a satirical epitaph on Queen Mary (wife of William III) and Marshal Luxemburg who died in the same year, 1694. The lines invite William to behold the futility of his efforts, both military and sexual. He has no heir of his body for the throne he conquered; neither, the poem alleges, do the achievements of Marshal Luxemburg, the great general of Louis XIV, leave William any trophy of military success. If the poem reads like an outburst of precocious, angry, feeling, it is of great interest in the way it brings together the military and sexual connotations of 'conquest' in a reflection upon William III. Concepts and images thrown up in the immediate debate after 1688 recur here, and not for the last time, in this early work of Pope.[21]

Let us turn now to some of the most celebrated early poems of Pope, the *Pastorals* and *Windsor-Forest*. Not primarily political poems, the pastoral eclogues do, in occasional allusion, assume a clear political position, of an orthodox and royalist kind. The riddle in 'Spring' opens with the question:

> Say, *Daphnis*, say, in what glad Soil appears
> A wondrous *Tree* that Sacred *Monarchs* bears?

---

[20] David Nokes, 'Lisping in Political Numbers', *Notes and Queries*, NS 24 (June 1977), 228–9. However, Margaret Smith, in the *Index of English Literary MSS*, iii. 1700–1800, ed. Margaret M. Smith and Alexander Lindsay, 76–7, stops short of endorsing the attribution.

[21] Howard Erskine-Hill, 'Alexander Pope: The Political Poet in His time', *Eighteenth-Century Studies*, 15: 2 (Winter 1981–2), 123, 129–31.

The allusion of the Royal Oak, in which Charles II hid after the Battle of Worcester, is followed up by a more subtle counter-riddle:

> Nay tell me first, in what more happy Fields
> The *Thistle* springs, to which the *Lilly* yields?

(11. 85–6, 89–90)[22]

The first couplet conveys an uncontroversial Civil War royalism. The second, heraldic, sees that since the Union of England and Scotland in 1707 the Fleurs-de-Lis on the Royal Arms of England have retreated, as it were, before the Thistle.[23] This is also a way of saying that the kingdoms of England and Scotland, united for the first time under Queen Anne, have prevailed against France in the field of battle. The point to notice here is that many Jacobites opposed the French wars. The exiled court, as a matter of policy, did not recognize the Union.[24] So far as the *Pastorals* are concerned, therefore, Pope gives royalist rather than Jacobite signals.

Between the publication of the *Pastorals* and 'Episode of Sarpe-don' in 1709 and *Windsor Forest* in 1713 there occurred the re-markable affair of the trial of Dr Henry Sacheverell on account of his recent sermons. Sacheverell was a popular preacher, but it still seems surprising that a well-established Whig administration should have been so concerned at his preaching of obedience to the higher powers, non-resistance, and the danger from 'False Brethren' within Church and State, that they should impeach him in a show trial for high crimes and misdemeanours. The point here is that the trial turned almost entirely on interpretation of the 1688 Revolution. Not only were the debates of the 1690s revived, including the great issues of resistance and conquest, but specific works were alluded to which repudiated that image so often accompanying the charge of conquest: the image of rape. Charles Blount, in his *King William*

---

[22] *TE* i. 69.

[23] *TE* i. 39–40. But note that though Queen Anne revived the Order of the Thistle, it was James II and VII who founded it. It is remarkable that the emblem of the thistle, with its motto: 'Nemo me impune lacessit' is a recurrent illustration in Pope's *Dunciad* in his 1735 folio *Works*: ii. 14, 19, 35, 49. See Maynard Mack, 'Pope's Pastorals', *Scriblerian*, 12: 2 (Spring 1980), 87–8. See also Brooks-Davies, *Pope's Dunciad and the Queen of the Night*, 156–7.

[24] See the discussion of this, and of the Order of the Thistle, in Bruce Lenman, *The Jacobite Risings in Britain, 1689–1746* (1980), 88–9, 39; also Mack, 'Pope's Pastorals', 87–8.

and Queen Mary Conquerors (1693) had argued that these rulers owed their throne to conquest over James II, in the interest of the people. This 'Licentious Pamphlet', though a pro-Williamite work, had been condemned by Parliament to be burnt by the common hangman, as Sacheverell pointed out in his Sermon against 'False Brethren'.[25] In the *Reply* immediately published it was asserted that:

in his [William's] proudest Tryumph (pardon the Barbarity of that Epithet) he would have taken it very disdainfully to have been saluted with the Address of the Thief to *Alexander*, viz. to be Entituled that *Greatest of Robbers*, however otherwise glorious Name, a Conqueror. No; thanks to Heaven, a softer and gentler Coronation Glory, *Oblation* and *Gift*, not *Rapine* and *Violence*, incircled that Brow.

Non Rapit Imperium Vis tua, sed Recipit.

The writer goes on to repudiate the very words which seem to have been so often used, and denies that William is '*Third William*, the *Second Conqueror*'.[26] William himself is likely to have been alert to the need to deflect the charge of conquest and the image of rape. At his triumphal entry into The Hague, after his victory in Ireland, the second great arch bore the pictures of '*Europe* Distressed' and of '*Neptune* Ravishing' with the respective mottos: 'Snatch the Wretched from the Ravisher' and 'Defend My Right'.[27]

All this, brought back to mind by the Sacheverell Trial, is vital background to *Windsor Forest* and *The Rape of the Lock*.[28] The *Tryal* itself says nothing bad about 1688, naturally. The whole conflict is about the terms in which it could be commended. Sacheverell and his defenders subtly exonerate it from the charge of conquest since this would imply a precedent for resistance. Of course they do not appeal to contract. There has therefore been non-resistance to the supreme powers and no question of victory by arms. This left intact the great Protestant and Church of England

[25] *The Tryal of Dr. Henry Sacheverell, Before the House of Peers, For High Crimes and Misdemeanors . . .*, (1710), 57–8.

[26] *An Account of Mr. Blunt's late Book, Entitled, King William and Queen Mary, Conquerors . . .*, (2nd edn., 1693), 5–6.

[27] *A Description of the Arches erected at The Hague, for the Reception of William the Third . . .* (1691); *The Harleian Miscellany*, 8 vols. (1744–6), v. 368–9.

[28] *The Tryal of Dr. . . . Sacheverell . . .*, 77, 79; Geoffrey Holmes, *The Trial of Dr Sacheverell* (1973); J. P. Kenyon, *Revolution Principles: The Politics of Party, 1689–1720* (Cambridge, 1977).

doctrine of '*Absolute*, and *Unconditional Obedience* to the *Supreme Power*, in *all* things *lawful*, and the utter *Illegality* of *Resistance* upon any *Pretence* whatsoever'.[29] The Whig managers of the trial openly expressed their suspicion that it was upon the authority of this doctrine that Sacheverell and his like hoped to bring in the Pretender. They quite ignored the confusion in 1689 as to how the Revolution was to be justified, and the general convergence on that intellectually unsatisfactory ground: acceptance of the new princes *de facto*, acceptance of the old king *de jure*. Instead they adopted what had then been a minority position. They admitted resistance in 1688, and, if the opening speech for the prosecution can be construed as expressing the whole case, justified it on the Lockeian ground of James II having broken 'an Original Contract between the Crown and the People'.[30] If we read the main body of Sacheverell's sermons, we infer that this was the view he suspected to be covertly held by many in government and the Church. If they thought he wanted to bring in the Pretender, he thought they wanted to make kings by parliamentary vote, or even bring in a republic. Sacheverell seems to have wanted to smoke out the 'False Brethren' and there is a sense in which he succeeded in the very terms in which he was impeached. As has always been accepted, the verdict of guilty coupled with the mild punishment, gave Sacheverell the moral victory.[31]

Pope's *Windsor-Forest*, his chief poetic model, Denham's *Cooper's Hill*, and the Sacheverell *Tryal*, are three texts all concerned with the idea of conquest. In a brisk survey of the possible origins of government, Sir John Hawles in the *Tryal* touches on conquest by allusion to Nimrod the hunter-king:

If it [the origin of government] was Patriarchal, as some have asserted, it was as ancient as *Adam*; if it was introduc'd by Conquest, then it's Date was no higher than *Nimrod*; if it was by Compact, then I can't say when it began; but this is certain, that it was as ancient as the *Roman* People . . .[32]

Appropriate to their rural settings, the two poems approach the idea of conquest through the activity of hunting. Pope, but not Denham, remembers Nimrod in this context:

[29] *The Tryal of Dr. . . . Sacheverell . . .*, 56–7.
[30] Ibid. 34.
[31] Holmes, *The Trial of Dr. Sacheverell*, 229–32.
[32] *The Tryal of Dr. . . . Sacheverell*, 97.

Proud *Nimrod* first the bloody Chace began,
A mighty Hunter, and his Prey was Man.

(ll. 61–2)[33]

Each poet uses hunting as a focus of a morally and politically enlightening double vision. In *Cooper's Hill* the latter part of the poem is dominated by the hunting of the stag: the one sustained narrative sequence of the poem. Introduced as the pastime of 'the king' (or 'our *Charles'*), and so concluded, this hunt shows the hunter hunted before the end. With 'conspiring feet', 'Like a declining States-man, left forlorn', 'And as a Hero', the stag, like the king, fights for his life in the end, and longs for the 'mortal shaft' from some nobler foe.[34] It is a stunning metaphorical volte-face within the structure of the extended simile, and aptly captures that human and political crisis when a king raises the standard of war within his own kingdom. Elsewhere in *Cooper's Hill*, the implicit issues are brought out: Magna Carta is recalled, and the distinction between 'Tyrant and Slave' and 'King and Subject' clearly made. The image of the river, unswollen by rains, and undammed by men, finally adjudicates between the oppression of kings and the oppression of the people.[35] *Windsor-Forest* takes up the notion of '*Third William*, the *Second Conqueror*', either from the reply to Blount's pamphlet quoted above, or the general usage to which the reply responded. In Pope the whole overt presentation of conquest is pushed back to a dark age prior to Magna Carta. Implicitly, however, as has long been suspected and proposed,[36] a *double entendre* runs between William I and II, those conquerors, hunter-kings, and Nimrods, and William III. Parliament's reply to Blount clinches the point. What Pope believed his readers would see in 1713 (and had prudent reasons for not spelling out) he wished to make clear to them after 1736, when he recorded the rejected reading: '*Oh may no more a foreign masters' rage | With wrongs yet legal, curse a future age*'.[37] The presence of the 'Dutch Prince' of Pope's early lampoon can be felt here. In relation to the *Tryal*, *Windsor-Forest* takes the charge

---

[33] *TE* i. 155
[34] *Cooper's Hill* (1642 version), ll. 241, 267, 273, 313, 317–19; *Sir John Denham, Poetical Works*, ed. T. H. Bankes Jr. (New Haven, 1928), 80–5.
[35] *Cooper's Hill*, ll. 331–2; ed. Bankes, 85.
[36] J. R. Moore, '*Windsor-Forest* and William III', *MLN* 66 (1951), 451–4.
[37] *TE* i. 159.

of conquest at the Revolution, which the Whigs alleged to lie between the lines of Sacheverell's Sermons, and embodies it in a myth of dark age conquest. Contrast between the happy age of Anne and the conquering era of William III is emphasized and simplified by the long lapse of time the poem now interposes between the two. Pope is thus able to associate William III with dark age barbarity. The poem ignores, on the other hand, the notion of justifiable resistance of despotism by which the Whigs now sought to explain the Revolution. While both *Tryal* and poem emphasize present happiness under Anne, Pope quite ignores the link alleged by the Whigs between the Revolution and a happy present. Indeed when the poem speaks explicitly of the period between the execution of Charles I and the accession of Anne it simply assimilates it into a scene of civil war:

> A dreadful Series of Intestine Wars,
> Inglorious Triumphs, and dishonest Scars.
>
> (ll. 325–6)[38]

'Inglorious Triumphs' may be aimed especially at the 'Glorious Revolution'.

As Pope brings Nimrod into his poem, so he makes use of the image of rape, in the sense of a violent and sometimes sexual robbery: a conquest. After the example of Nimrod and under the 'haughty *Norman*'

> The Fields are ravish'd from th'industrious Swains
>
> (ll. 61–5)[39]

Later, in a more noticeable departure from Denham, Pope adds the Ovidian myth of Lodona, virgin huntress of deer who becomes the victim of sexual pursuit by Pan. Just as, in a moment of Ovidian horror and excitement, Pan's shadow reaches her and she feels his hot breath on her neck, she prays in desperation to Cynthia and is transformed into a chaste stream, the River Lodden which, near Pope's home at Binfield, flows into the Thames, the free river of English history. Rape has been averted, at a cost.

All this is the darker side of what the mythologized landscape of *Windsor-Forest* discloses. The sunny side, at present, just about

---

[38] Ibid. 180.
[39] Ibid. 155.

predominates, but the two are subtly related. The beauty of the opening scene, leading into the Georgic richness of cultivated plains, the joyful pastime of rural sports, and the final oration of a personified Thames, in prophecy not just of a British peace but a world peace—all this affords a vision of plenty, harmony, and activity. Particularly impressive in a poem which has looked at various forms of slavery, bondage, and oppression, are the lines in which the Thames prays:

> Oh stretch thy Reign, fair *Peace*! from Shore to Shore,
> Till Conquest cease, and Slav'ry be no more . . .

(ll. 407–8)[40]

for Thames's Oration, of course, welcomes the Tory Peace with the Treaty of Utrecht. The treaty offered the right of trade with the Spanish Indies which involved, as more informed minds would appreciate, other forms of slavery than had been known in Britain. Over these creative and peaceful currents Queen Anne presides: indeed she produces them. 'Peace and Plenty tell, a STUART reigns' (l. 42) acknowledges her early in the poem; 'At length great ANNA said—Let Discord cease!' does the same towards the end. Her presence as an Augustan, peace-giving power is important because, as we soon come to feel, the cheerful sportsmanship and hunting of the central sequence of the poem has a darker implication. The netting of pheasants parallels the triumphant seizing of a town in military campaigns abroad, and we have already been given a victim's view of military triumph. The shooting of the pheasant matches, in tragic sympathy, the end of the doomed stag in *Cooper's Hill*. The connections of hunting and war, war and tyranny, are never forgotten. The poem's second invocation of Queen Anne intervenes crucially between ending civil war in Britain, and ending the long European wars abroad. Spatially and temporally, the Thames is the connecting form of the poem, finally articulate in his Oration. At a deeper level, perhaps, the metamorphoses of hunter and hunted, and the hunter hunted, conveying the ambiguity of human living, is the moral form of the poem. But here, where Queen Anne touches this precariousness, or ambiguity, she turns it so as to 'bring the Scenes of opening Fate to Light' (l. 426). It is worth

---

40 Ibid. 192.

speculating about the role of Queen Anne in the eyes of a man from a background like Pope's. Each side in the *Tryal* paid tribute to her happy reign, but in his Sermon against False Brethren Sacheverell had referred to her in a strange way: 'this *Good, and Pious Relict* of the *Royal Family* sits now Happily upon the *Throne* of her Great *Ancestors*' (*Tryal*, 48), a locution which his defence equated with saying that Anne was 'last of the Lineal Descent' of the family (198, 204). In fact the preacher's words are sufficiently peculiar to suggest equivocation, and this points to the uncertain position of many Tories and potential Jacobites at this time. The Act of Settlement in 1701 had given the throne (after any children of Anne) to the House of Brunswick which, closely allied to the Stuart family though it was, was certainly not a line of Stuarts. Pope's first tribute to Anne, then, at first sight an ordinary loyal gesture, seems to have implications for the future. On the death of the now childless Anne there would be another Stuart available to rule Britain, one whose title (save for the sort of parliamentary intervention denounced by Sacheverell) was clearly superior to hers.

This brings me to my last point about *Windsor-Forest*: its dedication to George Granville, Lord Lansdowne. More than a Tory statesman closely associated with the Peace, he was an Anglican Jacobite. As a young courtier when James II was on his throne, he had been devoted to Mary of Modena. Under William and Mary he withdrew from public life. He was imprisoned for Jacobite conspiracy in 1715, pardoned in 1717, but deeply involved in the conspiracy of 1722. Lansdowne was evidently among those who thought that the Act of Settlement could be set aside, who perhaps hoped that James III would embrace the Church of England, and that Anne herself would assist the senior line of the Stuarts to succeed her on the throne after her death. Well might Pope urge Granville to 'bring the Scenes of opening Fate to Light' (l. 426). Taken together, the polemic against rapine and conquest, the presentation of war and peace, and the nature of its tributes to Granville and Queen Anne, make *Windsor-Forest* a crypto-Jacobite poem.

III

One of the remarkable things about the Sacheverell *Tryal* is the degree to which, at this time, implication and innuendo were credited in public discourse. Moral victor though he may have been, Sacheverell was found guilty of high crimes and misdemeanours, and all on the basis of what he never explicitly said. It is as though Dryden's post-revolutionary poetry of innuendo were now officially recognized as a mode of expression by act of state. The milieu of *Windsor-Forest* and *The Rape of the Lock* was not only one in which conquest, resistance, and the Peace were the great controversial issues of the day, but in which it was becoming more and more difficult and dangerous to express certain views of the past, and certain visions of the future. More and more, the writing of political poems was a tightrope walking act, an acrobatic display on a high wire. The quarrel between the two papist families of the Fermors and the Petres—a social event of some obscurity and, one may think, more fictionality—afforded Pope the opportunity to translate these leading issues into a world of social comedy, with the two-canto *Rape of the Locke* (composed by September 1711, published 20 May 1712).

However in debt to recent French and English mock-heroic, *The Rape of the Locke* recalls particularly by its title Tassoni's *La Secchia Rapita* (1622), a mock-heroic poem on a modern historical and political subject;[41] Shakespeare's *The Rape of Lucrece*; and Claudian's *De Raptu Proserpinae*. The probable allusions of Pope's title are nicely balanced between the playful metaphor in Tassoni, the actual rape in Shakespeare with its consequence for the Kings of Rome, and the mythological rape in Claudian with its associations of seasonal death and rebirth. Pope's poem, for its part, is more full of allusions to current political life than really necessary for an heroic-comical poem paralleling a silly social quarrel with the events of ancient epic. What the modern reader can easily forget is how easily political affairs could in this period be translated into amatory form. Thus in an unpublished poem by Daniel Baker, 'Arabella, 1689', probably written during the reign of William III, three kings become three princesses, each beloved as a beauty.[42] Charles II becomes Carolina, gentle and cherished, who on her death is succeeded by Arabella, proud and arbitrary. The story of Arabella

---

[41] Ibid., ii. 108.

[42] BL Add. MSS 11723, 299–302. I am indebted to Alun David of Corpus Christi College, Oxford, for drawing my attention to this significant poem. On Baker, see Alun David, ' "A Tragic Scene of Endless Woe": Daniel Baker's *History of Job*', *Critical Survey* (1991), 208–14.

exactly parallels that of James II, and the narrator of the poem, finally unable to bear Arabella's high-handed ways, privately sends for Henrietta, a 'foreign Princess', upon which Arabella 'Convey'd her self away' and Henrietta, who came 'To conquer, not to treat', occupies 'the Throne' and is soon resented as much as Arabella had been. Henrietta represents William of Orange. This fable of rival loves soon reaches for unmistakably political language, so that, apart from the examples just cited, we hear of infidelity to oaths, passive obedience, 'lawful' Queens, the meeting of a 'Convention', the alleged abdication of Arabella, and so forth. The speaker of the poem, lover of the three ladies, stands perhaps for England, or possibly the established Church (Baker was an Anglican clergyman). The poem concludes, not with recognition of a problem solved, but of a dilemma deepening:

> This taught some of the Passions, when
> Their heat was o'er, to wish again
>   For her that had the Right;
> But Duty some engag'd, and some,
> Because their hopes are crost, become
>   True Pentinents for spight.
> What now, alas! what shall I do?
> The charge imposed by the New
>   Will certainly undo me:
> Nor dare I call home my old Love,
> Lest former wrongs should make her prove
>   More cruel yet unto me.
>
> (pp. 301–2)

The relevance of Baker's poem cannot turn on any question of influence but lies in its demonstration of how a contemporary could write of the dynastic crisis of 1688 in social and amatory form. Its clear line of political allusion differs from the more oblique and complex systems of *The Rape of the Lock*, but it is a further piece of evidence bearing upon the milieu of Pope's poem. A later amatory work, one actually invoked in the text of *The Rape of the Lock*, has a similar bearing. This is Mary De La Riviere Manley's *New Atalantis* (1709), a sensational romance which mentions real people, including real rulers, under a variety of fictional names. Twice in the first two Parts is the 1688 Revolution narrated, through transparent disguises, and is later alluded to by sardonic use of its Whig designation 'Glorious' (Part I, 41–2; Part II, 135–7, 185). The year 1688 and its aftermath is the historical backdrop to the highly charged amours of this work. Indeed the episode of Berintha and the Baron at cards (Part II, 123) may be among the sources for Pope's Belinda and Baron, the latter of whom remembers Mary Manley's work at his moment of triumph:

'As long as *Atalantis* shall be read . . .'

(iii. 165)

The significance of these works is their demonstration of how contemporaries could write of the dynastic crisis of 1688 and its aftermath. *The Rape of the Locke*, another amatory poem, has nothing like the clear line of allusion spun out by Baker, yet it is more full of references to high politics. We hear not only of 'the Glory of the *British Queen*',(i. 77), 'great *Anna*' who takes tea and Counsel (i. 71–2), but of how '*Britain's* Statesmen oft the Fall foredoom | of Foreign Tyrants, and of Nymphs at home' (i. 69–70), of how '*Coffee*' 'makes the Politician wise, | And see thro' all things with his half shut Eyes' (i. 97–8), how 'Steel cou'd the Works of mortal Pride confound, | And hew Triumphal Arches to the ground' (i. 139–140), and how 'th' Egregious Wizard shall foredoom | The Fate of *Louis*, and the Fall of *Rome*' (ii. 181–2). These lines seem to conjure up quite a contemporary political world, with the Queen and a nymph at its centre. Then again, Pope's title recalls the still current political image of rape, and it is worth remembering who or what was alleged to have been ravished, in those crude lampoons of the 1690s which used this word. 'Rape' need not mean sexual rape, but it had usually been a simple virgin, 'made a mere whore, by a vote of the state | Cause she freely her maidenhead did abdicate', or 'a Girle' raped by a 'Dutch Boor' paralleled to 'Ye whole Nation', ravished by one who also 'buggers an Earl': again, allegedly, William III.[43] William's Triumphal Entry into The Hague represented the female figure of Europe as rescued by him from the ravisher.[44] In 1704, in *An Address to our Sovereign Lady*, a poem certainly known to Pope, Queen Anne herself is in the position of the girl or the nation suffering rape:

[43] *Poems on Affairs of State*, gen. ed. George de F. Lord, v, ed. W. J. Cameron (New Haven, 1971), 159, 153–4 (BL Sloane MSS 2717, fo. 98r).
[44] *Harleian Miscellany*, v. 369.

Why Madam, You're Ravisht, Your Queenshipp's Invaded . . .[45]

(l. 15)

The Rape of the Locke seeks to be a comic and polite poem, and so the crude, direct, sexual metaphor is delicately attenuated from the invasion of virginity to the theft of a love-lock. Nevertheless, in the nicer terms of the poem, Belinda is in a similar position to the raped girl of the lampoons or Queen Anne herself in *An Address To Our Sovereign Lady.*

These suggestions concerning *The Rape of the Locke* in historical context are not meant to displace the received image of the poem as dealing with reputation and sexual attraction in fashionable society, and with confusion in a proper scale of human values as perceived through brilliantly comic invocations of an epic world. Pope's poem does not proceed like *Absalom and Achitophel.* Rather I hope to restore a political dimension occluded and forgotten when the poem came to be read as almost pure social comedy. This aspect of the work is, as it were, a vein in its stone,[46] a motif in its delightful yet serious harmony. Among other consequences of this is that political allusion must here make its own way in a comic world:

> O wretched Maid (she spreads her hands, and cry'd,
> And *Hampton's* Ecchoes, wretched Maid! reply'd)
> Was it for this you took such constant Care,
> *Combs, Bodkins, Leads, Pomatums*, to prepare?
> For this your Locks in Paper Durance bound,
> For this with tort'ring Irons wreath'd around?
> Oh had the Youth but been content to seize
> Hairs less in sight—or any Hairs but these!
> Gods! shall the Ravisher display this Hair,
> While the Fops envy, and the Ladies stare!
> *Honour* forbid!

(ii. 13–23)[47]

What the Lock is to Belinda suggests something like the constitution of the kingdom, guarded alike by documents (proclamation and law), and by punishment and torture (ll. 17–18). Both '*Ravisher*'

---

[45] *Poems on Affairs of State*, vi, ed. F. H. Ellis (New Haven, 1970), 620. Pope was convinced this poem was by Congreve (618).

[46] I am indebted to Professor Maynard Mack for this image, suggested by him during a discussion of the political aspects of *The Rape of the Lock.*

[47] *TE* ii. 132.

and 'Honour' were words with a political role; so, since 1660 and
now again in Jacobite discourse, was the word 'Restore':

> Restore the Locke! she cries; and all around
> Restore the Locke! the vaulted Roofs rebound.
> Not fierce Othello in so loud a Strain
> Roar'd for the Handkerchief that caus'd his Pain.
> But see! how oft Ambitious Aims are cross'd.
> And Chiefs contend 'till all the Prize is lost!
>
> (ii. 148–53)[48]

Here are reflections back from the world of affairs of state but in the
foreground, in all Pope's shining invention, is the literal action of the
poem, even if penetrated, at times, by the Politician with 'his half
shut Eyes'. Our aim should be to see the poem in full with our eyes
open. The relation to which we need to be alert is suggested by the
parallel conclusions of The Rape of the Locke and the accompanying (and undeniably historical and political) version of Statius, in
Lintot's Miscellany. In each case a brilliant comet, of 'blazing hair'
(Statius, l. 844), 'a radiant Trail of Hair' (Rape, ii. 173), warns of
historic events to come: 'The change of sceptres, and impending wo'
(Statius, l. 842), 'The Fate of Louis and the Fall of Rome' (Rape, ii.
182). The two poems reflect back and forth from one to another:
their initial proximity suggests the political dimension of The Rape
of the Locke.[49]

---

[48] Ibid. 136.

[49] The nature of Pope's earliest publications has been somewhat neglected. Thus,
he did not at first publish his Pastorals alone, but, in the same volume, his 'Episode
of Sarpedon'. He surely wished to show that he could master epic as well as pastoral
modes. Here the contiguity of his Statius version and The Rape of the Locke is, I
suggest, meant to be noticed.

3

The Rape of the Lock to The Dunciad

I

WHEN Pope published the five-canto version of *The Rape of the Lock*, on 4 March 1714, a reader who remembered the *Miscellany* poem would at once have noted three changes. A system of spirits had been added to the fable, apparent as early as Canto I, line 20. In keeping with this metaphysical expansion an underworld sequence, the visit to the Cave of Spleen, now dominated the aftermath of the rape with some 93 lines of further narrative. And now, immediately before the rape, another new narrative sequence, the card-game at Hampton Court, casts its own new light on the central act of the poem. The game of Ombre was, of course, a part of Belinda's social world. Pope also remembered, however, a tradition of card-game poems, in which the game was often Ombre, and which dealt explicitly with the world of high politics. Such a poem is *The Royal Gamesters Or, the Old Cards New Shuffled for a Conquering Game*, which discusses the European wars of 1702–6.[1] In this poem nations and rulers are mentioned by name, and particular cards are assigned to them at one time or another. In 'Le Nouveau jeu de L'ombre, 1707', a MS card-game by or belonging to Basil Kennett,[2] there is sometimes wordplay where, for example, a king means a king as well as a card. In this game colour, the distinction between Hearts and Diamonds (red) and Spades and Clubs (black), appears

---

[1] *Harleian Miscellany*, i. 173–6.

[2] BL Lansdowne MSS 927, fo. 86. I am grateful to I.D. McKillop who informed me of this MS in response to my question about political card-games. It is Howard H. Schless, however, who in *Poems on Affairs of State*, iii (1968), 225–36, opened the subject of political allusion through card-games in the poetry of this period. See also Howard Erskine-Hill, 'The Satirical Game at Cards in Pope and Wordsworth', in Claude Rawson and Jenny Mezciems (eds.), *English Satire and the Satiric Tradition* (1984), 183–92; Nicholas Roe, 'Pope, Politics and Wordsworth's *Prelude*', in David Fairer (ed.), *Pope: New Contexts* (1990), 189–204. Relevant also is W. K. Wimsatt, 'Belinda Ludens: Strife and Play in *The Rape of the Lock*', in Maynard Mack and J. A. Winn (eds.), *Pope: Recent Essays by Several Hands* (Brighton, 1980), 201–23.

to express religion, Spadille (Louis XIV) being black and Roman Catholic.

Pope's card-game adds some 79 lines of narrative to the central sequence of the poem. From the introduction in which Belinda burns for conquest at Ombre, and in which four kings, four queens, and four knaves, backed by their 'Particolour'd Troops' (l. 43), prepare for battle, the reader expects political implication. When Belinda says: '*Let Spades be Trumps!*' anyone who knew Kennett's game or the assumptions on which it was based, would assume that she was declaring for a French and Catholic alliance. This would be flimsy ground indeed on which to base an interpretation, were it not supported by various other features of Pope's narrative. To say the least this is full of political observation and activity: '*Spadillio* first, unconquerable Lord' (l. 49), 'The hoary Majesty of *Spades*' (l. 56), 'The Rebel-*Knave*, who dares his Prince engage' (l. 59), 'mighty *Pam* that Kings and Queens o'erthrew' (l. 61), 'The *Club*'s black Tyrant' (l. 69), 'Th' embroidered *King* who shows but half his Face' (l. 76), 'the *Queen* of *Hearts*' (l. 88), and 'The *King* unseen' (l. 95) draw from the game a maximum amount of political variety and excitement. When Pope adds the card-game, treated in this way, to a poem already making political allusion and deploying political language, he does so to warn the reader approaching the climactic action of the poem that this act can be seen in a political light. The card-game, in fact, supplies a political context for the forthcoming rape.

There is more to Pope's card-game than this. The text repeatedly incites to political identification. Pope uses the contemporary pack in the style of Rouen,[3] to suggest different monarchs and monarchies. To take an ordinary example from the middle of the game, consider the King of Clubs. He falls victim to the 'warlike *Amazon*' of the Baron as Belinda starts to lose advantage in the war: he is 'The *Club*'s black Tyrant', emphasis is laid on his pride, on his 'Giant Limbs in State unwieldy' and on how he 'of all Monarchs only grasps the Globe' (iii. 65–74). Pope exploits the depiction of the king on the card which gave him the size and the unique detail of the orb. The poet's suggestive transformation is to use the term 'black Tyrant' and, in connection with the unwieldiness of the figure, to turn what might have been 'holds the orb' into 'grasps the Globe'. If

[3] *TE* ii. 391–2.

in English Protestant history any foreign king had been demonized as a tyrant it was the King of Spain. The Spanish monarchy was not only noted for its widespread possessions, but specifically for its huge territories in the new world: 'grasps the Globe' conveys this exactly. We remember that the recent European wars have been the Wars of the Spanish Succession, and recognize that Belinda, in pronouncing Spades as Trumps, has espoused the colour black, the colour of Spadillio. The King of Clubs, like the King of Spades, is one of Belinda's cards at the start of the game. In the war France has been fighting for a dynastic link with Spain.

Similar analysis of political suggestion can be made of the other potentates of the game. Several examples may be briefly considered. The Baron is the master of Diamonds. As the Baron consolidates his advantage,

> Th' embroidered *King* who shows but half his Face,
> And his refulgent *Queen*, with Pow'rs combin'd,
> Of broken Troops an easie Conquest find.

> (iii. 76–8)

Dryden's post-revolutionary works supply a background to this allusion, but the broader and more obvious point is that history had supplied few recent examples of a King and Queen *together* achieving success on the field of battle. William and Mary are the great exception, Mary being Queen in her own right as well as William being King. If colour indicates religion they are, as we would expect, Protestant. Mary II was striking in her beauty and style; with the King Pope again adroitly exploits the card. The King of Diamonds was presented in profile:[4] Pope changes this to 'shows but half his Face', reveals but half his purpose, a shrewd remark on William's original invasion of England, to which 'embroidered' adds the more standard implication that what he did was flattered and falsified. Again,

> The Rebel-*Knave*, who dares his Prince engage,
> Proves the just Victim of his Royal Rage.

> (iii. 59–60)

This episode is not a conflict between the Kings but an attempted *coup* within the same royal family. Again, if we search recent history

---

[4] Ibid. 392.

for a parallel we find one that is obvious: the rebellion of Monmouth, Dryden's Absalom, eldest natural son of Charles II, against
James II, his legitimate brother and King. Unlike William's expedition against his father-in-law, Monmouth's rebellion was put down,
and put down severely. Again,

> The *Knave* of *Diamonds* tries his wily Arts,
> And wins (oh shameful Chance!) the *Queen* of *Hearts*.

> (iii. 87–8)

In the Poems on Affairs of State, King or Queen of Hearts could
mean (as the words suggest) a monarch of popular choice rather
than right.[5] Queen Anne was called 'Queen of Hearts' in a state
poem of March 1704, where the wording refers to the famous
announcement of her first speech from the throne in Parliament: 'I
know my own Heart to be intirely English . . .';[6] a 'Queen of Hearts'
is what a Jacobite would think of Queen Anne, and the 1704 state
poem in which the term occurs is Jacobite in fact. Jacobite opinion
felt more comfortable with Anne, an English Stuart princess, than
with Dutch William, but did not concede Anne's title to the throne.
Here, more certainly, Pope's text makes a historical and indeed
contemporary allusion. Yet the game includes a further allusion,
more pointed still:

> Ev'n mighty *Pam* that Kings and Queens o'erthrew
> And mow'd down Armies in the Fights of *Lu*
>
> .   .   .   .
> Falls undistinguish'd by the Victor *Spade*!

> (iii. 61–4)

The intent of these lines is more clear because of a brilliant and
effective pun. Lu or *Loo* was another card-game, similar to, but
different from, *Ombre*, in which '*Pam*', i.e. the Knave of Clubs, had
a power greater even than the Ace of the Trump suite.[7] But on the
other hand 'Loo' was the name of William III's Dutch palace, often
invoked, angrily or sneeringly, in political lampoons against him, as
witness: '*Windsor*, gutted to aggrandise *Loo*' in *The Mourners*, a
poem ascribed to the Jacobite Bevil Higgons in Pope's copy of

---

[5] See Arthur Mainwaring's *King of Hearts*, POAS v. 83–94.
[6] 'On March 1703', pp. 1–2, in POAS vi. 614; *A Collection of All Her Majesties Speeches* (London, 1712), 4.
[7] TE ii. 389–90.

Poems Relating to State Affairs (1705).[8] The 'Fights of *Lu*' are thus William's wars, and if we are to explicate the reference we need to think of an exceptionally powerful commander who not only 'mow'd down Armies' in William's wars and those further wars with France which followed them under Anne, but who also overturned 'Kings and Queens'. This does suggest a historical person: Marlborough (referred to as 'Le Prince Duc de Marlborough' in Basil Kennett's game).[9] Briefly, perhaps, the most powerful Englishman of the age, Marlborough had, by his desertion of James II in 1688, overthrown at least one King and Queen, and had subsequently become the great and feared general in the wars with France. This *double entendre*, which works so well in the world of cards and that of affairs of state, cannot, in Pope of all poets, be a coincidence. And if these lines constitute a historical allusion, so, surely, do the other instances explored above.

Yet features of inconsistency and ambiguity are involved in the political allusion of the game. Each of the players (even remembering the shadowy third player whom Pope deliberately occludes so as to present a game between three as a contest between two) holds cards of each colour. When Belinda loses the Queen of Hearts she turns pale, losing in her face the very hue she sought to retain in the contest. It is her worst moment in the whole game. Again, the card which produces her final but all too brief moment of triumph, 'The *King* unseen' (iii. 95), is the King of Hearts, here the hidden king, as Don Sebastian or Cleomenes had been hidden kings, kings for the moment obscured in exile without losing their capacity to strike back. James II himself had struck back in this way when, having withdrawn into exile, he had then invaded and seized Ireland. Despite choosing Spades and the colour black, therefore, Belinda tenaciously values all the hearts she holds. This is possibly Pope's point in the politics of his game. Holding the hearts is achieving success. The Queen of Hearts has proved fickle; the King of Hearts wins a brief triumph, before Belinda, beyond the game, is despoiled in a different yet related way, and loses her lock. This argument may be supported by observing that the King of the very suit and colour Belinda originally chooses, the King of Spades, is said to wear a

---

[8] See Bevill Higgons, *The Mourners*, l. 8 (the poem so ascribed by Pope in his copy of *Poems Relating to State Affairs* (1705) (BL pressmark: c. 28. e. 15); *POAS* vi. 362. See too BL Sloane MSS 2717, fo. 94.

[9] BL Lansdowne MSS 927, fo. 86.

'many-coloured Robe' (iii. 58). We have assumed that the King of Spades might allude to James II. If so, 'many-coloured' must refer to his policy to win concessions for Catholics by granting them also to Protestant dissenters: the ambiguity allows James to be expressed by both Spades and Hearts. Anne as Queen of Hearts is a similarly ambiguous figure, *non semper eadem*. One side of her face might be expressed by the 'warlike *Amazon*' who fights for the Baron (iii. 67), for she was certainly a Queen whose armies prevailed on the field of battle. But this means she is expressed by the Queen of Spades as well as the Queen of Hearts. Certainly Anne was seen as both in history.

What sort of political allusion does Pope's card-game supply? In the broadest sense only does it follow the course of historical events. It does so in so far as in the last years of Charles II and the first of James II it looked as if a Catholic and crypto-Catholic, Bourbon and Stuart alliance had the advantage in western Europe: the central country here was France, ruled by the mighty Louis XIV. Belinda seems to choose this particular centre of religion and power in her choice of Spades as Trumps (i.e. Spades as winners). At first her expectations are fulfilled, but in due course the potentates of the other colour and religion gain the advantage. This conforms to the general movement of affairs between 1688 and 1714, but it is hard to see any equivalent to Belinda's final, transient, triumph in its chronological place in that movement. Pope's game does not, then, follow the system of chronological allusion found in *The Royal Gamesters*, or the more famous *Absalom and Achitophel* or Middleton's *The Game at Chess*. Once we look at Pope's order of specific allusions it is clear that he does not follow an actual historical sequence: note, for example, the unhistorical contiguity of the 'Rebel-*Knave*' and 'mighty *Pam*' couplets. Pope's allusive narrative rather follows the tradition of *The Faerie Queene*, *Richard II*, and Dryden's *King Arthur* and *Aeneid* version, which allow multiple reference, dual identification, and fictional sequence. Contemporary allusion does not disclose a single contemporary parallel but uses the resources of a poem repeatedly to remind of recent times while revealing more of the beguiling, slippery, and surprising character of historical succession than a chronicle-like fidelity could do. It has something of the quality of a dream, strange yet familiar. Familiar here is the variety of allusions to recent history, from the Monmouth Rebellion to the War of the Spanish Succession. All the key figures are present, James II in his 'many-coloured Robe', William III 'who shows but half his Face' and 'his refulgent *Queen*', and Queen Anne, cherished but ambiguous '*Queen of Hearts*'. The name of their game is conquest. In commencing to play Belinda 'swells her Breast with conquests yet to come' (iii. 28): amatory and (mimic) military senses of the word are equally in play. Spadillio is (or seems) an 'unconquerable Lord' (iii. 49), while the King and Queen of Diamonds find an 'easie Conquest' (iii. 78), as they did in the England, if not the Ireland or Scotland, of 1688. Strange, on the other hand, is the repeated change of scale, with the operation of Pope's analogy and allusion. Conquest, the word which links military and amatory, is the word which leads us out of the card-game and back into the larger yet smaller world of high society. Pope has already alerted the reader to different games (Ombre and Lu) and different levels; it is now on a different level of symbolic play that the Baron turns Belinda's triumph at Ombre, by a sudden and unexpected revolution in civil conflict, into a conquest and 'Triumph' of his own. Thus the rape of the lock echoes back and forth within the world of the card-game which precedes it. The card-game alerts the reader to the political and historical implications of the rape. What makes the 1714 poem very much not a Whig poem is that neither card-game nor rape is presented as a vision of deliverance. To the Jacobite, and to the Tory who so often shared a Jacobite vision even when he did not take Jacobite action, 1688 appeared an aberrant act, an invasion and desertion even within the family itself, out of the ordinary run of historical events, with more in common with the execution of Charles I than a reverse in the field of a foreign war. Within the social comedy of the poem the rape is seen in this way. It is a bolt from the blue, an almost unheard of violation, and to this extent reveals a Jacobite vision.

The visit to the Cave of Spleen now shifts the focus from this aspect of the rape, but Umbriel returns from the Cave with all he needs to stoke up anger and defiance. How Belinda responds to the rape has political implications of a kind analogous to the various responses in 1688, and the mission of Umbriel adds to these. As in epic and historical worlds, so here, it would have been possible to acquiesce meekly in the violation, taking it, indeed, as the will of the gods or the work of providence. Again, perhaps, diplomacy and bargaining might produce an acceptable outcome. This is tried and fails through the ridiculous figure of Sir Plume. Finally, there is the response urged by Umbriel and Thalestris, dubious influences perhaps, who now insist that a deed of rapine can be answered only by active resistance. This is Belinda's final choice. Each of these attitudes was an attitude to what had happened in 1688: history supplies another not replicated in the text, namely the Whig view of the 'rape' as a rescue from oppression. Pope's initial choice of action and title effectively rules out this interpretation, at least for the present. Belinda, therefore, casts dignity and decorum to the winds to fight for the return of what she values so much. This is by no means a trivial-minded choice, but the immediate consequence affords, perhaps, the most exquisitely comic sequence of the poem. Not only the farcical chaos of whalebone and snuff, but the beautifully funny deaths of Dapperwit and Fopling, place us in that special world of comedy in which what is lost is at once restored. 'But Airy Substance soon unites again' (iii. 152), we remember, and here:

> She smil'd to see the doughty Hero slain,
> But at her Smile, the Beau reviv'd again.

(v. 69–70)

The defiant gallantry of the Baron himself participates in this comedy, but its climax is reached when, at the height of the struggle, the lock is lost. As a result of her decision to fight, therefore, Belinda does not recover her lock, but the Baron does not retain it, as his conquest and trophy, with all the implications that would have had for how society thought about her. It is the poem itself which retrieves the controversial hair and, as no other human agency could do, makes it eternal. The author's 'quick Poetic Eyes' alone see the apotheosis of the lock as it becomes first a meteor and finally a star. The 1714 poem itself thus seems to endorse Belinda's resistance. At the heart of the poem's comic extravagance, the lock is not quite a trivial thing. If Belinda's world appears merely elegant and fashionable by comparison with the invoked epic and recalled historical worlds of the text, still the lock is part of her free beauty and sense of herself, part too of her reputation and honour. As Pope's 1714 text comes to its brilliantly imaginative and comic conclusion, the high politics of the poem, not just the politics of sexual courtship but the way in which amatory relations remind of the conspicuous figures and forms of rule, *The Rape of the Lock* supports the efficacy of resistance to wrong.

Over three years now passed before any change was made to the published text of the poem. During this time great political changes and some literary activity throw light on the eventual form of the poem. On 1 August 1714 occurred that 'eclipse' which Swift wrote of to Pope on 28 June 1715:[10] the death of Queen Anne, 'Queen of Hearts'. What Pope probably hoped for, and may have expected, that Anne, Oxford, Bolingbroke, Lansdowne, and others would 'bring the Scenes of opening Fate to Light' (*Windsor-Forest*, l. 426) and bring about a second Restoration, was prevented by James III's refusal to convert to the Protestant faith, the fact that the Act of Settlement had not been repealed, and that, therefore, George I had been promptly proclaimed. The new king arrived from Hanover in September and soon made it clear that he would not trust the Tories to continue in government. As the months went by the revolution in affairs became more and more dangerous to those who had led or were attached to the former administration. In the same month that George landed in England, *A Further Hue and Cry After Dr. Swift* contained 'An Ode to the Pretender. Inscribed to Mr. Lesley and Mr. Pope'; the poem parodies parts of *Windsor-Forest*, assumes that Pope favours James III, and associates him with the prominent Non-Juror and Jacobite controversialist, Charles Lesley.[11] *Windsor-Forest* was, of all Pope's early poems, the one with the most obvious political tendency. Sometime before Swift left for Ireland in August, however, the Scriblerians noticed something in the reception of *The Rape of the Lock* which amused and concerned them. In response Pope drafted a Scriblerian tract, *A Key to the Lock*, which was shown to Swift and Arbuthnot, and which the latter referred to in a letter to Pope of 7 September 1714. The writings of Scriblerus, he says, lie neglected:

I wish to God they had been amongst the papers of a noble Lord sealed up. Then might Scriblerus have passed for the Pretender, and it would have been a most excellent and laborious work for the Flying Post or some such author, to have allegoriz'd all his adventures into a plot, and found out mysteries somewhat like the Key to the Lock.[12]

[10] Alexander Pope, *Correspondence*, ed. George Sherburn, 5 vols. (Oxford, 1956), i. 301.
[11] J. V. Guerinot, *Pamphlet Attacks on Alexander Pope, 1711–44* (1969), 17–19.
[12] *Corr.*, i. 251.

The letter is notable for its awareness of an atmosphere of political suspicion (the 'noble Lord' is Bolingbroke whose office as Secretary of State had been sealed at the end of August) and of the readiness of some readers to look for allegories in the poem. As in the Sacheverell Trial, reading between the lines was something many expected to do. Political events soon began to move rapidly. Bolingbroke fled to France at the end of March 1715, Ormonde followed in July, when Oxford was imprisoned in the Tower, and Mar left London in August to raise the standard of James III in Scotland. This was done on 26 August/6 September. Meanwhile, in April, Pope had published a *Key to the Lock*. When Swift saw it, at the end of June, he wrote: 'I think you have changed it a good deal, to adapt it to the present times.' This letter of Swift is full of political discussion, confesses his love for Bolingbroke, Oxford, and Ormonde, and notes Pope's boldness in retaining in his *Iliad* Preface (published 4 June) his acknowledgement to Bolingbroke.[13] At this point it was widely suspected that Bolingbroke would take office under James III, but he had not yet made up his mind. He did so in July.

These events and letters reveal the context of *The Key to the Lock*. Political readings of the poem were the cause of concern. The revolution in affairs of state left the author of *Windsor-Forest* vulnerable; if treasonable innuendo were to be detected in *The Rape of the Lock* also, the poet might be much endangered. The tract goes to work, first by the creation of the comic *persona* whose very name (Esdras Barnivelt) suggested Dutch republican bias, and whose profession promised simple-mindedness in literary judgement. Barnivelt is made to seem quite relentless in detecting papist opinion, but behind Barnivelt Pope himself operates with wonderful plausibility in advocating a political interpretation of the poem. Only at the start of the exposition, where Barnivelt asks that his basic premise be conceded, does the whole thing seem utterly ridiculous:

The only Concession which I desire to made, is that by the *Lock* is meant

The BARRIER TREATY.[14]

The Barrier Treaty was of course a great issue of Whig concern in the termination of the wars with France. Everything else in Barni-

---

[13] Ibid. 301–2.
[14] Alexander Pope, *Prose Works*, i. 1711–20, ed. Norman Ault (Oxford, 1936), 185.

velt's exposition is supposed to follow from this. Thus, 'The Game of *Ombre* is a mystical Representation of the late War . . .' (i. 193), but other card-game poems show that this cannot be thought a foolish suggestion. The lines on 'mighty *Pam*' are held to allude to the recent disgrace of the Duke of Marlborough (i. 193), and Belinda 'GREAT BRITAIN, or (which is the same thing) her late majesty' (i. 185). A large number of other particular identifications are proposed, some of which must have struck the contemporary as absurd (Sir Plume as Prince Eugene?) others as possible, given the conventions of some recent literature, for example Arbuthnot's own *History of John Bull*. The effect of the tract is then to mingle absurdity and plausibility together, to the general effect of rendering any political reading of the poem ridiculous. The modern reader can think one or two things about the *Key*: first, that *The Rape of the Lock* had been totally unpolitical, and the pamphlet a *reductio ad absurdum* of an entirely inappropriate response; secondly, that the poem had a political aspect which opened up issues in affairs of state over the last thirty years in a way quite unlikely to recommend itself to the new regime after Anne's death, and that the *Key* mingled something of what the poet had intended with much absurdity in order to turn a curious readership of a very popular poem away from this line of interpretation. It may seem that the *Key* enters into the process of political interpretation too minutely and ingeniously for the former to be likely. Further, the *Key* itself quickly came under sceptical and hostile scrutiny: 'Another [wit] obliges the World with a *Key* to his own *Lock*, in which the *Wards* are all false . . .'.[15] Thomas Burnet, the author of this attack, thus declares that the *Key* is designed to deceive, and since the wards of a key must correspond to those of the lock, the implication is that the poem is also dissimulating. It seems probable, to sum up this phase in the reception of *The Rape of the Lock*, that what we have here is a case of differently calculated readerships. The bearing of the rape of the lock upon the alleged rape of the crown in 1688, with all the political innuendo of the card-game, appealed to a coterie audience, while the social and sexual comedy in which the innuendo was placed had naturally a wide appeal. This was harmless enough—indeed brilliantly contrived—in the milieu of the last years of the Queen. With change of state and a vindictive party regaining the

[15] Thomas Burnet, *Pamphlet Attacks*, 33.

upper hand, those features of Pope's poem which linked popular
and arcane meaning, chiefly the ambiguity of such terms as 'rape'
and 'restore', began to make the author of the poem a political
target. After the period of civil war, and James III's arrival and
departure from Scotland, the attacks on Pope became more menacing. In January 1716 he was included in a 'print' described in a
ballad, grouped with Ormonde, Sacheverell perhaps, and others,
round the figure of James III:

> The next is,—or may my End be a Rope;
> That little High-Church Rhimer, Poet Po—;[16]

and the imputation of guilt by association was not much diminished
by the following suggestion that this poet may have been Prior. In
May was published in a collection of State Poems a discarded
prologue to Addison's comedy, *The Drummer*. Though the imputation of Jacobitism is again present, what is telling here is the
observation that Pope may be alarmed at what readers made of his
works:

> A very POPE (I'm told may be afraid),
> And tremble at the Monsters, which he made.
> From dark mishapen* Clouds of many a Dye,
> A different Object rose to every Eye:
> And the same Vapour, as your Fancies ran,
> Appear'd a *Monarch*, or a *Warming-Pan*
> *The late *Meteor*[17]

This is an interesting response. The design of the *Key* had been to
show that since absurd interpretations could be made to seem
plausible, plausible interpretations were absurd. *The Rape of the
Lock* seems to be the subject: and the prologue is a reply to Pope's
attempt to deflect political interpretation. The allegation is that he
is still nervous at what he has done. Most telling of all is the last line
of the passage which not only responds to the Whig/Jacobite issue,
but takes the reader back to 1688, when the publicly witnessed birth
of a male heir to James II was alleged by some Whigs and Williamites to be the product of a plot to smuggle a male infant into the
Queen's bed in a warming-pan. This poem, which Pope must have

[16] George Sherburn, *The Early Career of Alexander Pope* (Oxford, 1934), 159–
60.
[17] *Pamphlet Attacks*, 35.

seen, could only suggest to him that demonstrations of the ambiguity of interpretation would not save him from censure. Some further step, to save his most brilliant poem from going under the kind of political cloud which had originally darkened the reputation of *Paradise Lost*, would have to be taken.

II

The final major change in the text of *The Rape of the Lock* was unannounced. Republication in Pope's *Works*, 1717, dispersed attention from the mock-heroic poem alone to all Pope's earlier works, and nothing in Pope's new volume declares that now, for the first time, a speech of 34 lines is given to Clarissa in Canto V in which she attempts to persuade Belinda to reconcile herself to the loss of the lock. It would have been possible for a reader familiar with the poem of 1714 to open the *Works*, confirm that the celebrated poem was included, yet never realize that the text had now been changed substantially and in a way crucial to its interpretation. Some, rereading the poem, may have assumed they had simply forgotten a passage which must (they might suppose) have been there since 1714.

This famous speech, '*to open more clearly the* MORAL *of the poem*',[18] has figured prominently in critical discussion. It is all the more important, therefore, to state that no footnote in *Works*, 1717, includes the familiar words just quoted: at this stage Pope offers no comment on the speech whatsoever. In his *Works*, 1736, Pope glossed the addition merely with the words: '*A parody of the speech of Sarpedon to Glaucus in Homer*'. Only after Pope's death, in Warburton's edition of 1751, does the familiar footnote appear, together with its incorrect statement that Clarissa is '*A new Character*'.[19] This error, unconvincingly explained in the *Twickenham Edition*,[20] casts doubt on the authority of Warburton. At least we see that readers of the poem in Pope's lifetime could not have been influenced by this footnote, as modern readers have been.[21]

---

[18] *TE* ii. 199.
[19] Cf. Works (1712), i. 107–12; (1714), iii. 127–30.
[20] See ii. 199 n. 17.
[21] Alexander Pope, *Works* (1717), 148–50; *TE* ii. 199 n. 7, allows the vigilant reader to reconstruct what Pope did, and did not, say. But it is hardly made obvious.

Clarissa's speech is a translation of a translation. Based on Pope's 'Episode of Sarpedon', it brilliantly turns the warrior prince's vision of death on the battlefield into the society beauty's prospect of an afterlife of marriage, age, and death. It adds a sombre tone to what had hitherto been a poem of wit, beauty, and high spirits, and we remember that the 'Episode of Sarpedon' had comprised not only Sarpedon's speech but the account of his death in *Iliad*, xvi. Although in the 1714 text both the Baron and Belinda are in different ways defeated, this is the first time Pope has introduced the feeling of defeat into his poem. Having dwelt on the political implications of *The Rape of the Lock*, to which, indeed, the addition of this speech makes a real difference, I want, before discussing this, first to point out a connection, not previously observed, between Virgil's *Aeneid*, Dryden's version, and the central act of *The Rape of the Lock*. Geoffrey Tillotson, the *Twickenham Edition* editor, stated that Pope's poem *'is about the cutting off of a lock (which, it is allowed, is sufficiently vexing to a girl), but it is also about life and death.'*[22] This is certainly right, and is supported by an analogue not touched on by Tillotson, lines describing the eventual death of Dido at the end of *Aeneid*, IV, in Dryden's translation:

> Then *Juno*, grieving that she shou'd sustain
> A Death so ling'ring, and so full of Pain;
> Sent *Iris* down, to free her from the Strife
> Of lab'ring Nature, and dissolve her Life.
> For since she dy'd, not doom'd by Heav'n's Decree,
> Or her own Crime; but Human Casualty;
> And rage of Love, that plung'd her in Despair;
> The Sisters had not cut the topmost Hair;
> Which *Proserpine*, and they can only know;
> Nor made her sacred to the Shades below.
> Downward the various Goddess took her flight;
> And drew a thousand colours from the Light:
> Then stood above the dying Lover's Head,
> And said, I thus devote thee to the dead.
> This Off'ring to th' Infernal Gods I bear:
> Thus while she spoke, she cut the fatal Hair;
> The struggling Soul was loos'd; and Life dissolv'd in Air.
>
> (iv. 993–1009)[23]

---

[22] *TE* ii, 179, 154 n.
[23] *Works*, v. 483–4.

The connection between this passage and *The Rape of the Lock* is seen not only in the description of the goddess Iris which, with later imitations, is a source for the presentation of Pope's Sylphs (see especially ii. 59–72), but more obviously in the cutting of Dido's lock itself: 'Sic ait, & dextra crinem secat: & una | Dilapsus calor, atque in ventos vita recessit', iv. 704–5, in Ruaeus's Virgil.[24] There is hardly a more famous example in the literature of classical antiquity of the cutting of a lock from the head of a woman. If Pope takes the apotheosis of the lock from the lock of Berenice in Callimachus and Catullus, and from the various stellifications in Virgil and Ovid, the act of cutting itself has its clearest precedent in Dido's death. The parallel works well for the mock-epic. Belinda in her fashionable world is linked with a heroine and a queen injured through love and treated as a sacrifice. The Baron is briefly a mock-Aeneas, going off with the lock as his trophy, as Aeneas, having had Dido as his lover, deserts her to pursue his Roman destiny. What was in the *Aeneid* an act of mercy by the goddess is in Pope's poem an act of rapine by a man. But the Baron's imperial purpose is soon lost in confusion, from which the lock is rescued by the poet. Most important of all is that Virgil's passage completes a tragedy of love and death. The 1714 poem, despite sadder and darker moments, does not remind us of this aspect of life for long. The rape of the hair is an act of high excitement, and the anger of the injured party comic in the first instance. In 1717, however, Clarissa's speech casts a grave, sad, retrospective reflection on the rape and its aftermath, in the light of which we may note, with a sense of new implication, how Pope's own lines on Aeneas, Anna and Dido:

> Not half so fixt the *Trojan* cou'd remain,
> While *Anna* begg'd and *Dido* rag'd in vain.
>
> (v. 5–6)

now lead up to the recall by the Sarpedon speech of a warrior's death on the battlefield. Two heroic deaths are left in the reader's mind, that of Dido and that of Sarpedon.

Sarpedon and Dido after him fall victim to forces more powerful than their own. Troy will fall also after the death of Sarpedon;

[24] Published in Paris in 1682.

Carthage will hardly survive Dido. Within the half-comic but always serious realm of Pope's mock-heroic, Belinda is defeated, like them, in the theatre of her own world. Pope's poem asks us to consider that love involves death of a kind: even the symbolic rape reminds us of sexual consummation, itself a part of 'whatever is begotten, born and dies', the prospect revealed in Clarissa's speech, challenging the seeming immortality of youth, beauty, confidence, and admiration of others. At this level of metaphor the poem takes Belinda beyond her anger at her injury to a consideration of whether she can reconcile herself to live with the wrong done to her. The reader is asked to consider again the question of resistance to wrong, injury, invasion. Clarissa's speech is, in effect, a speech advocating orthodox Anglican obedience to the higher powers. The famous lines bring together the courage of an epic hero and the afterlife of a society beauty, who also needs courage if she is to live in the knowledge of all she has lost. There are *three* points within the circle of Pope's allusion: the Homeric world, Belinda's political world, and Belinda's social world. The Jacobite implications of 'The Episode of Sarpedon' are not erased but transmuted here into all that spells defeat for Belinda. She has lost her lock, her party has lost the kingdom and the war, she will lose her social allure on marriage, she will lose her beauty. In the end the greatest ravisher is not the Baron, not the conqueror, but time and fate: Atropos 'with the abhorred shears' whose meaning is death. Like Sarpedon Belinda needs resolution and a face, or a stance, with which to meet what the world will disclose. Clarissa offers her a solution:

> But since, alas! frail Beauty must decay,
> Curl'd or uncurl'd, since Locks will turn to grey,
> Since painted, or not painted, all shall fade,
> And she who scorns a Man, must die a Maid;
> What then remains, but well our Pow'r to use,
> And keep good Humour still whate'er we lose?
>
> (v. 25–30)[25]

This is certainly a moral, and the increased gravity and emotion of the passage doubtless accounts for the fact that Warburton and generations of subsequent readers have been willing to see in it 'the MORAL of the Poem'. It is nothing of the kind, as is underlined by the facts that Pope does not give it to a new character, nor utters it in an authorial voice, but allows it to be spoken by the most unsuitable person in the poem to speak it: the lady who originally abetted the rape of the lock. This lends the moral speech a measure of falsity. The morality itself may be valuable and realistic, but within the fiction it seems designed to persuade Belinda to let the Baron keep his spoils. One of the ravisher's party, Clarissa continues to support 'her knight' the Baron. Her famous speech is then the moral in the poem, but not of it. It serves to make the 1717 *Rape of the Lock* politically unexceptionable, at first sight, and Pope never acknowledged that this 'MORAL' had been absent from his poem prior to the 1715 Jacobite rising. Yet Pope does not abandon the logic of his 1714 version. With brilliant ingenuity he contrives that the comedy of his poem shall hold out two different kinds of reconciliation. One, explicit within the text, entails complete victory for the Baron, with Belinda reconciled to her defeat and loss. The other, implicit in the poem's concluding action, denies the Baron his triumph at the same time as it denies Belinda the restoration of what she so prizes. It suggests that resistance to wrong, rapine, and conquest need not be futile or fatal, even if it fails. Pope's conclusion both allows something, and denies something, to protagonist and antagonist; and with a special playful generosity it turns the lock into a star, so that, in the heavens at least, the rightful possessor shall be acknowledged—

And mid'st the Stars inscribe *Belinda's* Name!

(v. 150)[26]

The comedy underlying this act of poetic justice, residing in the fact that the contending parties of mortals manage to lose the lock in their strife, does reach back to endorse the wise falsity of Clarissa. 'Keep good Humour still': the poem's conclusion saves the valuable and wise injunction from its compromised source. This is the qualified optimism of Pope's final comic balance.

III

When, in his Epistle *To Arbuthnot* (1735), Pope alluded to his earlier poems as 'pure Description' (ll. 148–50) he was being

---

[26] Ibid. 212.

disingenuous. It is clear that *Windsor-Forest* and *The Rape of the Lock*, though never wholly and directly political like *The Poems on Affairs of State*, have a political aspect, a political vein in their stone. They engage with the leading historical issues of Pope's lifetime. If we seek to characterize this political vein we may say that it is much concerned with defeat and loss through conquest. It does not allude to the deliverance of England from popery and arbitrary government, it does not support contract between prince and people as the basis of rule, it does not endorse the long European war. Nothing in these poems expresses the political vision which the Whig managers of the Sacheverell Trial derived from the events of 1688–9, or which an earlier generation of political historians associated with the Glorious Revolution and the Bill of Rights. Pope's political cast is not Whiggish, therefore, and only courtly in regard to the Tory phase of Anne's reign. If anything delivers England from ill, it is Anne's peace policy in her last years. If, then, Pope's political cast is Tory, does that make it crypto-Jacobite? Not necessarily. Here the literary historian confronts the political ambiguities of Pope's time. Anne's four Tory years nurtured this ambiguity. Some Tories served her in the hope that she would manage to restore the *de jure* royal line. One such was probably the dedicatee of *Windsor-Forest*, Lord Lansdowne. Others hoped to serve the Electoral Prince if he would be served by them. Such were Robert Harley, Earl of Oxford, and Henry St John, Viscount Bolingbroke, driven towards Jacobitism by the hostility of the new King to the court Tories of the former reign. This ambiguity, which began to clear up only after 1714, accords with the tentative and exploratory nature of Pope's poems. Yet 'The Arrival of Ulysses', if political at all, must be a Jacobite dream of restoration; *Windsor-Forest* hopes for a Stuart future of peace and plenty; *The Rape of the Lock* is preoccupied with conquest, loss, and right. These poems do seem to entertain a Jacobite vision.

Does Pope's political vein change in his later years, as the political situation also changes? In answering this question I shall chiefly consider Pope's 'Epistle to Lord Oxford and Mortimer with the *Works* of Parnell' (composed by 25 September 1721, published in 1722), and *The Dunciad* of 1728, 1729, and 1743. However, Pope's later poems have been long recognized as poems of political vision. Unlike the pre-1717 poems, the later poems are the basis for Pope's reputation as almost the first and probably the finest poet of polit-

ical opposition in English literature. Interspersed though they often
are with wit, humour, self-mockery, and self-portrayal, they still
constitute a long-running attack, often specific and practical, but
ultimately historical and mythic, against the long ministry of Walpole, the court which kept him in power, the new financial trends of
the time, and their cultural consequences. Pope here challenged
with great eloquence what looked like and perhaps was a long
national decline into self-interest and short views.[27] In the concluding sections of this chapter, therefore, I shall not labour the orthodox argument about the political importance of Pope's later
poems, but will address myself to the more specific matter of how
far Pope's poetry of opposition is poetry of a Jacobite vision. The
Dunciad will be found the most significant work from this point of
view.

The Epistle to Oxford is a poem we are lucky enough to have in
an early manuscript form. This manuscript contains an early instance of a way of writing for Pope, which, in the *Imitations of
Horace*, would attain extraordinary rhetorical power. This concerns
the first person singular: 'I'. In *The Rape of the Lock* Pope referred
to 'the Muse' (e.g. v. 123, 149): in the manuscript of the poem to
Oxford he refers to 'My Muse', though this is changed with other
features of the earlier version when the poem is published. This is
how Pope originally addressed the fallen statesman who had been
Anne's first Minister during her four last years:

> In vain to Desarts thy Retreat is made;
> The Muse attends thee to the silent Shade:
> 'Tis hers the brave Man's latest Steps to trace,
> Re-judge his Acts, and dignify Disgrace.
> Wait, to the Scaffold, or the silent Cell,
> When the last ling'ring Friend has bid farewell.
> Tho' Int'rest calls off all her sneaking Train,
> Tho' next the Servile drop thee, next the Vain,

[27] See Maynard Mack, *The Garden and the City: Retirement and Politics in the
Later Poetry of Pope, 1731–43* (1969); Howard Erskine-Hill, *The Social Milieu of
Alexander Pope: Lives, Example and the Poetic Response* (1975); Bertrand A.
Goldgar, *Walpole and the Wits: The Relation of Politics to Literature, 1722–1742*
(1976); Howard D. Weinbrot, *Alexander Pope and the Tradition of Formal Verse
Satire* (Princeton, 1982). The debate about Augustus in the 18th cent. also bears on
this subject: see Howard D. Weinbrot, *Augustus Caesar in 'Augustan' England: The
Decline of a Classical Norm* (Princeton, 1978), and, as reply, Howard Erskine-Hill,
The Augustan Idea in English Literature (1983).

> Tho' distanc't one by one th'Oblig'd desart,
> And ev'n the Grateful are but last to part;
> My Muse attending strews thy path with Bays . . .[28]

The shift from 'The Muse' to 'My Muse', especially in the context of the last line quoted, is exceptional as a personal and political affirmation, and unparalleled in any earlier poem of Pope. All the drama of the passage comes from its being a tribute to a fallen statesman: the poet asserts his independent judgement against that of the world. The language of contempt is very strong: note Interest's 'sneaking Train'; the allusions to the 'silent Cell' and 'the Scaffold' are stronger still. The lines assume a world of crisis and martyrdom. Oxford is at the centre of this vision because he had been imprisoned in the Tower after the coming of George I, as indeed had another of Pope's noble dedicatees, Lansdowne. Unlike Bolingbroke who had fled to France, Oxford and Lansdowne risked impeachment and execution for treason though each was eventually released. So much the world saw, and Pope's poem, intended for publication, obviously alluded to this, taking Oxford's release and retirement as a vindication. What the world did not see, though some knew, was that during his time in the Tower Oxford had directed the Swedish Plot in favour of James III which collapsed in 1717.[29] Pope could have known this, though it is not clear that he did. This is important in regard to the line: "Tis hers the Brave Man's latest Steps to trace' which bears the general meaning that the poet will trace the whole life of the fallen statesman until the present, after his fall as well as before. Retirement is as honourable as office. Yet 'latest Steps' suggests active measures rather than simple retirement, and it is possible that this line alludes to Oxford's part in the Swedish Plot. No other salient decisions of Oxford seem to qualify, for it was after Pope had sent his MS version to the Earl that the latter declined a request that he assume the leadership of the English Jacobites. The passage may thus be crypto-Jacobite. In any event the final line, which seems to give poet and statesman an almost messianic role, was revised before publication into a more formulaic praise of retirement ('Ev'n now she shades thy Evening Walk with Bays'); 'latest Steps' remains, the independence of the

[28] TE vi. 239.
[29] Romney Sedgwick (ed.), *The History of Parliament: The House of Commons, 1715–1754*, (1970), i. 63.

2. Medals of (i) King James III and Queen Clementina on the birth of Prince Charles
Edward in 1720, by Ermenegildo Hamerani; (ii) James III, on the occasion of the
South Sea Bubble crisis in 1721, by Ermenegildo Hamerani; (iii) Sir Robert Walpole,
on his elevation to the peerage in 1742, by Laurence Natter; (iv) Prince Charles
Edward, by C.N. or J.C. Roettier, dated 1745, but probably struck in 1748 to assert
the Stuart claim at the time of the Treaty of Aix-la-Chapelle.

poet's voice is more emphatically asserted (l. 36), but 'My Muse' disappears, and we must wait for the Epistle *To Burlington* and the *Imitations of Horace* for Pope to appear in his own poems again *in propria persona.*

To understand Pope's later political poetry it is necessary to understand the events of the next two years. The discovery and collapse of the Jacobite conspiracy led by Pope's friend, Bishop Atterbury, left the poet more exposed to the suspicions of government than he had ever been. The impetuous loyalty of his letters to Atterbury during the latter's imprisonment might easily have increased the danger he was in at this time. But as Atterbury was sent into exile where he became Secretary of State to James III, Bolingbroke, who had held this office during the 1715 Jacobite Rising, but had since abandoned the Jacobite cause, was allowed to return to England. The literary campaign against Walpole which Bolingbroke launched in 1726 with his journal *The Craftsman*, made an enormous difference to Pope and to others of the same sympathy because it was on the face of it loyal to the House of Brunswick. Bolingbroke's repudiation of Jacobitism in his *Letter to Sir William Wyndham* (1718) could not have been more public or explicit. Not everybody believed it, and at a later date both Bolingbroke and Wyndham grew interested in the Jacobite option once more. But, for the present, Bolingbroke built a new opposition not only out of the Hanoverian Tories such as he and Wyndham had become, but also from Whigs out of office and Tory Jacobites. Attacks on the Walpole administration or even the court need not, if under Bolingbroke's aegis, be treasonable. Yet different contributors to Bolingbroke's extraordinary campaign might have very different motives. The prolonged assault on Walpole inevitably affected the reputation of the two kings who kept him in power, and Jacobites in exile were delighted to learn of the growing unpopularity of George I and George II.[30]

As motives differed, so often did the nature of the attack. Telling here is the different character of its three most famous works of literature. John Gay's *The Beggar's Opera* (1728) quite clearly attacks Walpole through the figures of both highwayman and receiver, Macheath and Peachum. Its satiric challenge was recognized

---

[30] Eveline Cruickshanks, *Political Untouchables: The Tories and the '45* (1979), 12.

by contemporary audiences including Walpole himself.[31] While the court comes into the scope of Gay's satire it does so only in the most traditional role, as a greedy and treacherous place. Monarchy has no place in Gay's vision, and beyond the redirection of the anti-Jacobite air, Lillibullero, the work seems quite untouched by Jacobitism. Two years earlier, Swift's *Gulliver's Travels* had had a good deal to say about monarchy. If the political memory of *The Beggar's Opera* reaches back to the South Sea Bubble crisis, that of the *Travels* goes back to Anne and the issue of the Tory peace. The Emperor of Lilliput is the image of a Whig king, the King of Brobdingnag the model of a Tory one. Swift's Tory views emerge in the depiction of these two princes, their aims and values, but the issues of title, right, and succession only appear in the scathing summary of the history of Lilliput in Part I. Swift had several friends who were Jacobite at one time or another. One was Bolingbroke, probably alluded to in the Gulliver of *Travels*, Part I, but without reference to his Jacobite episode. Another was Charles Ford, in whose hand a treasonable passage, now added to modern texts of Part III, was written into the first edition of the *Travels* but never published in Swift's lifetime. This passage refers to an intention, in certain circumstances, 'to kill the King . . . and entirely change the Government'.[32] This could be regarded as a Jacobite addition, though only tenuously. Pope's *Dunciad* of 1728 and 1729 differ from their two predecessors partly in that they are visionary dream-poems, partly in that they are filled with the idea and rituals of royalty. Three levels of royalty, however, mingle entrancingly in Pope's dream-world. The Goddess Dulness is a queen. The various laureate figures are kings of Dulness. Appearing fitfully between these two levels of 'royalty' a real king can sometimes be made out. So it would seem to an eighteenth-century reader of the early *Dunciad* when he encountered the line:

> Beneath his reign, shall E——n wear the bays
>
> (1728: iii. 271)

the proper name being filled out to 'Eusden' in 1729 (iii. 319), for Laurence Eusden had been the Poet Laureate since 1718, so that in

---

[31] John Hervey, *Memoirs*, ed. Romney Sedgwick (1952; rev. edn. 1963), 20 (under 1729).

[32] *Gulliver's Travels*, Part III, ch. 3; ed. Paul Turner (Oxford, 1971), 171, 346.

1728–9 'his reign' certainly seemed to denote the reign of George II more clearly than anything else. It might then have been noted that in both versions the antecedent to 'his' was given in the couplet immediately preceding:

> This, this is He, foretold by ancient rhymes,
> Th' Augustus born to bring Saturnian times:
>
> (1729: iii. 317–18)

and that (a point Pope was later to exploit in his Epistle *To Augustus*) Augustus was the second name of George II. Parallels with Augustus were common in political panegyric.[33]

The readiness of Pope's readers (alerted no doubt by the initials and blanks of his *Art of Sinking in Poetry*) to pick up innuendo can be seen from another example. In a line satirizing the arrival of pantomime at court, Pope, in 1728, wrote:

> Thy dragons ** and ** shall taste
>
> (iii. 251)

The 'Insinuation' of this provocatively empty line prompted Matthew Concanen to protest that 'whoever understands the Measure of the Verse, and compares it with the Context [will see] that the Blanks are to be filled with Names, which of all mortal Names ought to be the most Sacred, and the most exempt from Ridicule . . .'. He warned Pope to fill the blanks with words 'consistent with his Allegiance'. Concanen must have thought Pope intended the names 'George' and 'Caroline'; Edmund Curll suggested 'Kings' and 'Princesses'.[34] Hostile to Pope though these commentators were, they were hardly wide of the mark, since the lost manuscript drawn on by Elwin and Courthope records the early reading: 'Peers and Potentates'. In 1729 Pope filled the blanks safely with 'Magistrates and Peers' and unfairly mocked Concanen and his attention to 'Measure' by alleging that he thought Pope meant 'Kings and Queens'.[35] All the ingredients for the original political reading of *The Dunciad* are found here. 'Allegiance' was at stake, but Pope played with his readers, implanting in their minds the notion of a treasonable jest, only to repudiate it and seem to attribute it to them.

---

[33] Erskine-Hill, *The Augustan Idea*, chs. 7 and 9.
[34] Goldgar, *Walpole and the Wits*, 77–8.
[35] *TE* v. 184.

These instances have been drawn from the great anticlimactic end of Book III, but they are not merely local effects. As early as l. 6 of Book I of the 1728 *Dunciad* Pope calls our attention to a striking innuendo:

Still[†]*Dunce the second reigns like Dunce the first*

the dagger drawing the reader's eye down to the abbreviation 'Dryd.' at the foot of the page. The line remains the same in the *Dunciad* of 1729 and of 1743, save that the italicization which indicates an allusion is dropped. It must always have been pretty obvious that this was a hit at George I and George II, but now that the awareness of poems on affairs of state has faded from readers' minds it is worth showing why. Pope originally drafted a line more obviously confined to poets and laureates: 'And when a Settle falls a Tibbald reigns',[36] and it is clear the accession of George II in 1727 gave Pope a special opportunity to use 'Second' and 'First'. Both Curll and Edward Ward smelled treason in the line, though Curll reasonably enough thought '*Dryd.*' must refer to the dunces in *Mac Flecknoe*.[37] In 1729 Pope might have seemed to deflect political suspicion by giving the true source and actual line from Dryden:

And *Tom* the Second reigns like *Tom* the first

('To My Dear Friend Mr. Congreve', l. 48)

The two lines are close indeed, but the reader who recalls the working of Dryden's poems as it pursues a parallel between the succession of poets and the succession of kings will have no doubt about Pope's political intention. Pope is developing Dryden's late mode of oblique political allusion, and to follow this logic is to associate George I and George II with William III. What William meant to Dryden, in lack of a legitimate title, George meant to Pope. This takes the poem beyond mere satire on a dull court. Though I once hesitated to think so, I have now no doubt that the allusion is finally a Jacobite one.[38]

Recent work supports the analysis. James Sutherland, in the *Twickenham Edition*, volume v, made nothing of the concluding couplet of Book I, save to confirm from Pope's notes that it is drawn from

---

[36] Ibid. 61.
[37] Ibid., n. 6; John Dryden, *Mac Flecknoe*, ll. 31–2, in *Works*, ii. 55.
[38] Howard Erskine-Hill, *Alexander Pope: The Dunciad* (1972), 49.

John Ogilby's *Fables*.[39] It has a very duncelike effect, and readers have been content to rest with that.

> So when Jove's block descended from on high,
> (As sings thy great fore-father, Ogilby,)
> Loud thunder to its bottom shook the bog,
> And the hoarse nation croak'd, God save King Log!

> (i. 257–60)

'Of the Frogs desiring a King', Ogilby's royalist fable, tells how the frogs, having lost their king and been 'turn'd into a State', petition Jove for a new king. Jove throws them down a log, which they soon come to despise. They then beg for a more active king, upon which Jove sends them a stork who preys upon them all. The thudding rhyme of 'bog' and 'Log' comes from Ogilby who ends his line with '*Jove* save King Log'. The same rhyme occurs in the fable 'Of the Frogs fearing the Sun would Marry' where the frogs were associated with the republican Dutch, inhabitants of 'Low-Country Provinces, United Bogs'. Sir Roger L'Estrange in his prose *Fables* (1692, 1699) treated the original fable in the same royalist way. Douglas Brooks-Davies, the first to explicate Pope's allusion, is certainly right to detect in it a Jacobite tendency.[40] The case may be clinched by a poem not mentioned by Brooks-Davies, *The Duumvirate*, evidently written after the Act of Settlement and during Anne's wars:

> The Kingdoms antient Laws they quite forsake,
> And of old England a new Poland make.
> They hunt and fish for Kings, like Aesops Logs,
> In *German Forests*, and in Holland Bogs . . .

> (added italics)[41]

---

[39] v. 94.

[40] Douglas Brooks-Davies, *Pope's Dunciad and the Queen of the Night: A Study of Emotional Jacobitism* (Manchester, 1985), 96–8. Pope was familiar with both Ogilby and the Fables of Sir Roger L'Estrange: see Joseph Spence, *Observations, Anecdotes, and Characters of Books and Men*, ed. J. M. Osborn (Oxford, 1966), 30, 478; i. 14, 204.

[41] Bodleian Library, Oxford, Carte MSS 208, Item 62, fo. 397v. This is a printed poem, perhaps published in France (David Foxon, *English Verse, 1701–1750* (Cambridge, 1975), i. 210 (D 564). David Nairne's Diary (National Library of Scotland, MS 689) shows the poem to have been by John Caryll, the Jacobite Secretary of State, and uncle of Pope's friend (see under 18 Dec. 1705–29 Dec. 1706).

To Pope's contemporary reader, the allusion to the fable and the loud, blockish rhyme, would have had an unmistakably anti-Hanoverian implication.

There was of course the question of how far could Pope go. He chose an idiom of comic obliquity prompting the reader to tease out the poet's intention. He himself seems to have considered ways in which he could reinforce his allusions in the eyes of later readers and of posterity. Thus he actually printed rejected lines from *Windsor-Forest* which served to clarify the anti-Williamite trend of the poem.[42] Thus, perhaps, employing Jonathan Richardson the younger to record early drafts of *The Dunciad*, Pope allowed the following incomplete draft of the opening of *Dunciad*, Book II, to be preserved:

> High on a Bed of State, that far outshone,
> Fleckno's proud seat, or Querno's nobler Throne
> ——exalted sate. Around him bows
> The Laurelld Train & breathes Poetic Vows.
> With Kingly Pride ye genl. Joy he spies
> And marks each Subjects Transport while Lyes.
> His strut, his stare, his stupid Eye they praise,
> And grinning Crowds grow foolish as they gaze . . .[43]

Maynard Mack, who has published and discussed Pope's *Dunciad* drafts, suggests that 'Brunswick' was meant to fill the blank in the third line. Concanen's advice to attend to the 'Measure' and 'the Context' would endorse the proposal. Also supporting this suggestion is the absence of an initial or even an asterisk (in this draft), which suggests danger. Then, since the 'Kingly' '——' is not one of the 'Laurelld Train' but the object of their devotion, the 'Bed of State' and all the other royal references do not seem to pertain directly to bad poets but rather to one who really appropriates royalty. The 'strut' and 'stare' were quite common satiric comments on the early Hanoverians (Pope's earlier thought, 'dead Stare' was perhaps especially suitable to 'King Log'). Finally, Mack confirms his case by quoting lines on George I from Addison's poem *To Sir Godfrey Kneller On His Picture of the King*, a poem which reviews

---

[42] TE i. 159.
[43] Maynard Mack (ed.), *The Last and Greatest Art: Some Unpublished Poetical Manuscripts of Alexander Pope* (1984), 127. I have adopted the revisions of the draft recorded in Mack's transcript.

England's kings from Charles II on from a heavily Hanoverian viewpoint:

> Whilst all his gracious aspect praise
> And crowds grow loyal as they gaze
>
> (pp. 21–2)[44]

This passage, if used, would in the larger structure of the poem have still been about King Tibbald. But within that saving structure Pope did, we can have no doubt, once consider the insertion of a satire on false royalty, and wished to preserve a record of having done so. Those who argue that Pope was an 'emotional Jacobite' (not a politically active Jacobite) may find here a rare example of the content of emotional Jacobitism. Behind the more prudent, circumspect, or ironic locutions, this scathing, indeed hate-filled vision, seems likely to have expressed something of what Pope really felt, but was too prudent to print, soon after the accession of the second Hanoverian King. Too prudent to print, but not perhaps unwilling that posterity should read.

These points of Jacobite implication in the poem link with others which touch, in a markedly sceptical way, on political commitment and action. There is a moment in Book I when the old empire of Dulness and Whig Britain merge, as King Tibbald considers saving the state 'by cackling to the Tories':

> Yes, to my Country I my pen consign,
> Yes, from this moment, mighty Mist! am thine . . .
>
> (A: i. 187–94)[45]

Nathaniel Mist (d. 1737) was the proprietor of the important Jacobite/Tory journals, *Mist's* and *Fog's* (1716–37). But in Book III we hear in a prophecy that the Goddess Dulness 'smiles on Whig and Tory race' and that 'To Dulness, Ridpath is as dear as Mist' (iii. 283–6), Ridpath being a noted Whig journalist. In the refashioned *Dunciad* of 1743 these two moments are brought together in Book I, as King Cibber contemplates embracing 'Party' 'And cackling save the Monarchy of Tories'. He finds Dulness in both Parties and on all

---

[44] Joseph Addison, *Miscellaneous Works*, ed. A. C. Guthkelch (1914), i. 192. This skilful and effective poem is a clear piece of anti-Stuart propaganda.

[45] For an up-to-date account of Mist, see Jeremy Black, 'An Underrated Journalist: Nathaniel Mist and the Opposition Press During the Whig Ascendency', *British Journal of Eighteenth-Century Studies*, 10 (1987), 27–41.

sides, but especially perhaps on the side of 'the Minister' (Walpole) (B: i. 205–14). The near-impossibility of Jacobite action, in the realm disclosed by *The Dunciad*, is lightly touched on in Book IV, where the 'vast involuntary throng' following Dulness includes

> Not those alone who passive own her laws,
> But who, weak rebels, more advance her cause.

> (B: iv. 81)

This is a good analysis of Jacobite failure in practice: the cause had only been compromised by weak rebellion, and enfeebled by the doctrine of Passive Obedience which had originally enjoined loyalty to James II and his heirs. If we turn from the practical to the mythic aspect of a new Restoration, we are perhaps subtly put on our guard by the prominence of 'Ogilby the great' on the shelves of King Tibbald or King Cibber (A: i. 121; B: i. 141). The royalist Ogilby had celebrated the Restoration of 1660 as a new golden age; his handsome folios, the *Homer*, the *Fables*, and the *Entertainment*, filled with learning, lavish illustration, and humdrum verse, might give any poet pause. And indeed, the reader of the 1729 and 1743 *Dunciads* is early warned that Dulness had done something to the ideal of an Age of Gold:

> Here pleas'd behold her mighty wings out-spread,
> To hatch a new Saturnian age of Lead.

> (A: i. 25–6; B: i. 27–8)

Pope's own note points the ambiguity of the term 'Saturnian': golden for poets, but 'in the Chymical language' leaden.[46] Here is the strong point in Brooks-Davies's alchemical reading of Pope's poem: the leaden/golden paradox brilliantly captures the poet's concern with true and false kingship, and what Dulness as a moral and political malaise can do to take the mystery out of the myth of restoration through cyclical recurrence.[47] James II had figured as Saturn in Addison's *To Sir Godfrey Kneller* ('Old Saturn too with up-cast eyes | Beheld his abdicated skies . . .').[48] All this and more is in mind when Pope, in the 1743 *Dunciad*, refashions his lines on the restorer of the golden age:

---

[46] *TE* v. 63.
[47] *Pope's Dunciad and the Queen of the Night*, chs. 3 and 5.
[48] *Miscellaneous Works*, i. 192–3.

> This, this is he, foretold by ancient rhymes:
> Th'Augustus born to bring Saturnian times.
> Signs following signs lead on the mighty year!
> See! the dull stars roll round and re-appear.
>
> (B: iii. 319–22)

The golden name has a leaden echo; the heavenly powers have become a pantomime show.

While the royal references and Jacobite implication of *The Dunciad* open out into history and myth, there is much more to the poem than it has been my purpose to consider here. Many still think of the poem as a satire on bad writers. I suggest that the Grub Street writers and publishers are as much a metaphor for human littleness as objects of satire in their own right, but the poem's concern for the condition of literature is a part of its tenacious Augustan ideal. The twin concerns with writing and rule are traced through those images of a doomed city in Book I, and those prospects of falling civilizations and of the migration of barbarian peoples in Book III. *The Dunciad* is a dream-poem of decline and fall, in which fragments of literary and political contemporaneity succeed one another with dreamlike logic, sometimes contracting our vision and sometimes expanding it. But what, perhaps, gives the political aspect of Pope's poem a special and ironical importance is that the larger movement of the poem itself, as set forth in the preliminary matter and the Arguments to the Books, is itself based on that myth of loss, exile, wandering, and restoration which caused Dryden to find in the first half of the *Aeneid* an apt narrative for Jacobite experience, and which underlies Dryden's 'Last Parting of Hector and Andromache', and Pope's 'Episode of Sarpedon' and 'The Arrival of Ulysses'. It is Pope's *Alcander* theme once again. As we have seen, however, the golden age restored gleams wanly against the darkness of that larger restoration—'Ye Pow'rs! whose Mysteries restor'd I sing . . .' (B: iv. 5)—which will turn a free people to welcomed slavery, 'And make one mighty dunciad of the land!' (B: iv. 602–4).

This climactic moment, when land becomes poem, is succeeded by an unmistakably political passage, which Pope's footnote explicitly links with the tradition of state poems (B: iv. 615–18 n).[49] Speaking of the mighty 'Yawn' of Dulness, the poet declares:

---

[49] *TE* v. 405.

Churches and Chapels instantly it reach'd;
(St. James's first, for leaden Gilbert preach'd)
Then catch'd the Schools; the Hall scarce kept awake;
The Convocation gap'd but could not speak:
Lost was the Nation's Sense, nor could be found,
While the long solemn Unison went round:
Wide, and more wide, it spread o'er all the realm;
Ev'n Palinurus nodded at the Helm:
The Vapour mild o'er each Committee crept;
Unfinish'd Treaties in each Office slept;
And Chiefless Armies doz'd out the Campaign;
And Navies yawn'd for Orders on The Main.

(B: iv. 607–18)

The passage builds up from at first comic detail to the generality of the 'solemn Unison'. Sleep in church and school seems hardly alarming; John Gilbert is most unfairly treated but the poet wants 'leaden' for symbolic reasons; Convocation is mentioned with historical accuracy, for at this time elections to it were regularly held but it was never allowed to meet.[50] From Westminster Hall, through Convocation to the House of Commons, the lassitude rises until, with 'Wide, and more wide . . .' the famous conclusion of *The Dunciad* (which immediately follows this passage) begins to be anticipated. But with 'Ev'n Palinurus' the political character of this prelude to the end is reasserted: Palinurus was obviously the now-fallen Walpole, once publicly praised by that name as the sleepless 'pilot of the realm'.[51] This, the last of *The Dunciad*'s long series of allusions to the *Aeneid*, does a kind of honour to the great Prime Minister and vigilant enemy of Jacobitism. Palinurus did not desert

---

[50] On this little-known point, which shows Pope's political diagnosis as accurate as ever, see Paul Langford, 'Convocation and the Tory Clergy, 1717–61', in Eveline Cruickshanks and Jeremy Black (eds.) *The Jacobite Challenge* (Edinburgh, 1988), 107–122.

[51] *TE* v. 405; *Aeneid*, v. 835–61, vi. 337–83. It is worth recalling the lines of Edward Young:

What felt thy WALPOLE, pilot of the realm?
Our PALINURUS† slept not at the helm;
His eye n'er clos'd; long since enur'd to wake,
And out-watch every star, for BRUNSWICK'S sake:
By thwarting passions toss'd, by cares opprest,
He found the tempest pictur'd in his breast:
But, *now*, what joys that gloom of heart dispel,
No pow'rs of language—but his own, can tell;

the helm but was overwhelmed by the god of sleep and fell from the ship; he would be killed and left unburied on the Italian shore. With Walpole gone, who had in Pope's view ruled rather than served his Hanoverian master (B: iv. 598–604), the political world is left with neither direction nor life. The closing lines of the passage describe a kingless realm. The false Augustus has been swallowed up in Dulness; the true Augustus is signally absent, the hidden king once more.

> His own, which *nature* and the *graces* form,
> At will, to raise, or hush, the civil storm.
> † *Ecce Deus ramum Lethaeo rore madentem, &c. Virg. lib. V.*

Edward Young, *The Love of Fame, The Universal Passion in Seven Characteristical Satires* (1725–8), Satire VII; in *Works* (1762), i. 169.

PART III

Johnson: Poems on Affairs of State

4

The Decision of Samuel Johnson

I

POPE was a phenomenon. Born into the marginal Roman Catholic community when it had lost its chance of power, he won his way by talent, friendship, patronage, and industry to the centre of his country's civilization. There his poems spoke, sometimes, in tones of accommodation, sometimes of rueful self-mockery, but most memorably with the voice of critical and passionate opposition to court and government. This could not have been achieved without the wider culture of opposition—not, at least, without Pope abandoning most of the values and sentiments with which he entered the public world. Hopes for a restoration during the final, ambiguous, years of Anne, and after that the ideological realm of opposition which grew from the decision of the first two Hanoverian kings to proscribe the Tories from office—these offered Pope a world of thought and literary practice in which he could at once remain himself and pursue a poetic vocation.

Johnson's situation was different in almost every respect. Neither a Roman Catholic nor a Protestant Dissenter, Johnson was born and brought up in the established Church of England, in which communion he remained from conviction throughout his life. His father Michael Johnson the bookseller (whatever his personal views) had held public office in Lichfield, and taken the Oaths to George I.[1] Unlike Pope, Johnson was able to enrol at a university, and spent just over a year at Pembroke College, Oxford. Unlike Pope, Johnson's early constraint was lack of means. This seems partly to account for his premature departure from Oxford and thus for his lack of a BA. and an MA. Johnson's early poverty in London may have been exaggerated;[2] but certainly, if he could but achieve a modest prosperity by his literary labours the world would be open

---

[1] A. L. Reade, *Johnsonian Gleanings*, Part IV (1923), 201–3 (Appendix N).
[2] Thomas Kaminsky, *The Early Career of Samuel Johnson* (Oxford, 1985), 85.

to him in a way it had never been to Pope. Nothing in his back-ground of any formal or serious nature could prompt suspicion of political disaffection. Nothing in his early circumstances obliged him to become an opposition writer. The way of the world, and the prompting of human need, invited him to seek patronage by ex-pressing his support for the king on the throne and the government of the day.

These religious and political points are important because, at our present distance from the poetry of the 1730s, it can sometimes seem inevitable that Johnson, in his first major poem, *London* (1738), should have written a satire something like Pope. Boswell notes that, when Johnson and Garrick first came to London in 1737, Pope 'filled the poetical throne without a rival'.[3] In particular the literary scene was dominated by Pope's Epistles and Horatian poems: what more natural than that the *Imitations of Horace* should have spurred Johnson to emulate Pope by an imitation of Juvenal? But this is to oversimplify the situation. It is improbable that Johnson felt a wholehearted admiration for the still papist Pope, with his widely advertised devotion to the widely distrusted Bolingbroke. If Johnson sought poetic fame above all (which might be disputed) he had before him a wide choice of recent examples. He was not obliged to follow Pope. He could in principle have adopted as his model the historical poem exemplified by Thomson's *Liberty* (1736), which his classical learning might have prompted him to think he could outdo, and which he was later to ridicule. Thomson's association with the circle around the Prince of Wales and the Whig opposition to Walpole might have attracted a young poet both critical and ambitious. Or Johnson might have turned to the fable form of the late John Gay, whose last collection had come out ten years before, and whose posthumous *Fables* would appear in 1738. Gay's opposition satire was radical but oblique—and may have given something to Johnson in his *Marmor Norfolciense* (1739). Above all, if the inclination of the young poet were towards formal satire, he might have taken as his pattern the seven epistles of Edward Young's *Love of Fame, The Universal Passion* (1725–8), a collection which in many ways anticipated Pope's satires of the 1730s, evinced a strain of moral independence, but which was

---

[3] James Boswell's *Life of Johnson*, ed. George Birkbeck Hill, DCL, rev. L. F. Powell (Oxford, 1934), i. 128.

devoted to the House of Brunswick, its ministers and advisers. Now a beneficed clergyman of the Church of England, Young might have seemed an appropriate model for the ambitious young Johnson. The fact that he produced satires uneven in quality, having vigour and wit but a bad ear for verse, need have been no obstacle: Johnson could have bettered him in his mode.

Young and Pope, the one the formal satirist of the 1720s and the other of the 1730s, illustrate the range and perhaps the extremes of formal satire which confronted the writer of *London*. A brief retrospect upon this earlier satire will supply a useful context for Johnson's poem and help us to understand, in terms of the 1730s, the decisions that he made.

As it happens, Pope's Epistle *To Augustus*, which was published in May 1737, soon after Johnson first arrived in London, has some links with Satires IV and VIII of *The Love of Fame*. Each poem uses, though in markedly different ways, the *laudes Caesaris* motif or related Virgilian parallel; each poem is addressed to a ruler or a potential ruler. The first, Young's Satire IV, was addressed to Spencer Compton, head of the Prince of Wales's household during the last years of George I. It was thought that Compton would become first minister on the Prince's accession to the throne, and such, plainly, was Young's expectation. Young next wrote the satire always meant to terminate the sequence, that addressed To the Right Honourable Sir Robert Walpole (the two satires on women, V and VI in the completed sequence, were composed later). In these satires Young can write effectively against irreligion, and against parsimony:

> GEHENNO leaves the realm to CHRENES' skill,
> And boldly claims a province higher still:
> To raise a name, th'ambitious boy has got,
> At once a *Bible*, and a *shoulder-knot*;
> Deep in the secret, he looks thro' the whole,
> And pities the dull rogue that *saves his soul*;
> To talk with rev'rence you must take good heed,
> Nor shock his *tender reason* with the Creed:
> Howe'er well-bred, in public he complies
> Obliging friends alone with *blasphemies*.[4]

---

[4] Satire IV, *Works of the Author of the Night-Thoughts* (1762), i. 111.

Young has learned from Dryden (*Absalom and Achitophel*, ll. 604–5), as well as Swift (*A Tale of a Tub*, Section II) to produce this sarcastic attack upon a closet atheist. It is by no means bad satire, and the sixth line anticipates the idiom of Pope in the 1730s. Next Young touches on charity and economic distress:

> He glories in late times to be convey'd,
> Not for the poor he has *reliev'd*, but *made*:
> Not such ambition his great fathers fir'd,
> When HARRY conquer'd, and half *France* expir'd:
> He'd be a slave, a pimp, a dog, for gain:
> Nay, a *dull sheriff* for his *golden chain*.[5]

This, perhaps, is less good (the most effective line is against conquest, not avarice, and the last line is a bit of an anticlimax), but the moral tendency of the satire is such as Johnson could hardly fail to endorse. Young has, of course, a vein of praise as well as of moral sarcasm. Early in the poem Compton is complimented on his political sagacity ('Deep to discern, and widely to survey . . .') while at the end Young invokes the famous Augustan parallel in a laudatory sense:

> Were there no tongue to speak them but his own,
> AUGUSTUS' deeds in arms had ne'er been known.
> AUGUSTUS' deeds! if that ambiguous name
> Confounds my reader, and misguides his aim,
> Such is the Prince's worth, of whom I speak;
> The ROMAN would not blush at the mistake.[6]

In view of the debate about Augustus in the eighteenth century, the word 'ambiguous' may arrest our attention. But moral ambiguity does not seem to be meant: the name is 'ambiguous' because it points to two different men, the Roman *princeps*, and Compton's master George Augustus. If the reader hesitates over which Augustus the poet means (Young insists) the first Augustus would have no grounds for offence. This is an adroit allusion to the line in Horace's Letter to Augustus (l. 267) which speaks of how ill-judged praise may cause embarrassment: Pope would choose the very line as an epigraph to his own version of Horace's poem.[7] There is a clumsy

---

[5] Young, *Works*, i. 118.
[6] Young, *Works*, i. 119.
[7] *TE* iv. 189.

diffidence about all this, but the acceptability of the ending might well depend on what the reader thought about the Prince of Wales. Satire VII has a similar structure. It opens and ends in panegyric while the body of the poem satirizes that lust for fame which seeks fulfilment through military glory. This is a peace poem, and the pacific policy of Walpole and George I in the 1720s provides Young with a standard of judgement as well as an opportunity for praise:

> While I survey the blessings of our isle,
> Her *arts* triumphant in the royal smile,
> Her public *wounds* bound up, her credit high,
> Her *commerce* spreading sails in every sky,
> The pleasing scene recals my theme agen,
> And shews the madness of ambitious men,
> Who, fond of bloodshed, draw the murd'ring sword.[8]

The theme is pursued from the well-known example of Alexander to the scene of a battlefield where the speaker himself, seeing 'A realm of death! and on this side the grave;' is moved to indignation at the prospect (i. 162–3). When Young, 'a ready celebrator,' turns to the monarch on the throne, even an age accustomed to the conventions of panegyric may have noticed a certain excess:

> In BRUNSWICK such a source the Muse adores,
> Which public blessings thro' half *Europe* pours,
> When his heart burns with such a god-like aim,
> Angels and GEORGE are *rivals* for the fame;
> GEORGE, who in foes can soft affections raise,
> And charm envenom'd Satire into praise.[9]

Not a lot can be said about this kind of hyperbole, but we may note that Young is good at incorporating into his praise what are grounds for anxiety and aggression to others. 'Half *Europe*' must (together with Britain) allude to Hanover, whose natural importance for the new dynasty was much resented by those who would have preferred an English king. References to constant sea voyages back and forth to Germany would become a way of alluding to the non-English origin, and to some the illegitimate claim to the throne, of the Hanoverian kings. This is comparable with the satiric claim

---

[8] Young, *Works*, i. 162.
[9] Young, *Works*, i. 168.

that William III had 'Gutted *Windsor* to aggrandise *Loo*';[10] it is code for the view that the king on the throne is a stranger. Converted into a public statement this could be seditious. Thus the outspoken Jacobite Member of Parliament, William Shippen, was sent to the Tower for saying in the House of Commons in 1717 that the King was 'a stranger to our language and constitution'.[11] Near the end of Satire VII Young takes an incident on one of George I's voyages as an occasion for a positive Hanoverian affirmation:

> While *sea* and *air*, great BRUNSWICK! shook our State,
> And sported with a king's and kingdom's fate,
> Depriv'd of what she lov'd, and press'd with fear,
> Of *ever* losing what she held most dear,
> How did BRITANNIA, like ACHILLES, weep,
> And tell her sorrows to the *kindred deep*?
> Hang o'er the floods, and, in devotion warm,
> Strive, for Thee, with the surge, and fight the storm?[12]

The King had been nearly drowned in a storm off Rye on his return from a Hanover voyage. This leads to the passage on Walpole as a Palinurus sleepless at the helm, which would give Pope so good an opportunity for reply in Book IV of *The Dunciad*. Pope certainly knew these poems of his acquaintance Young, being explicitly addressed in Satire I, and there invited to continue the seventeenth-century tradition of moral satire from Donne to Rochester.[13] At the time when this invitation was issued Pope was preparing a quite different sort of poem, *The Dunciad*, but his satires of the 1730s show that in general moral judgement he had quite a lot in common with Young. The two great differences are poetic quality and political orientation. Pope's satires are more perfectionist, resonant, and imaginative. Again, nothing like Young's praises of the House of Brunswick and its ministers can be found in Pope. Pope *could* write lavish praise, to Harley, to Atterbury (in private letters), and to Bolingbroke, but goes less far than Young with *his* 'Angels and GEORGE'. What is more, Pope's strongest praise is for opposition figures. Young's panegyric was not so extraordinary for the time,

---

[10] *Poems on Affairs of State*, ed. G. de F. Lord *et al.*, vi (New Haven, 1970), 362.
[11] Romney Sedgwide (ed.), *The History of Parliament, The House of Commons, 1715–54*, 2 vols. (1970), ii. 422.
[12] Young, *Works*, i. 168–9.
[13] Young, *Works*, i. 80.

but to the opposition culture he must have seemed a sycophantic Whig.

Pope's Epistle *To Augustus* can certainly be seen as a special response to *The Love of Fame* and its invitation to him. Pope's poem takes, or seems to take, from its Horatian original the same pattern which had underlain Young's Satires IV and VII: praise at the beginning and end, satire in between. But, as everybody knows, Pope takes the mode of hyperbolic praise (so ostentatious in Young) and swells it further till it tips over into irony. What is more Pope brings off this ironic *coup* with the help of a political implication. Young's serious peace poem in Satire VII is answered by Pope's praise of an Augustus who opens 'all the Main' (l. 2) and whose enemies 'wonder'd while they dropp'd the sword!' (l. 399). Then, running with apparent casualness through the body of the Epistle is the theme of Britain's earlier military glory: 'Edward and Henry, now the Boast of Fame' (l. 8), 'We conquer'd France . . . ' (l. 263), 'Old Edward's Armour beams on Cibber's breast!' (l. 319),[14] and this keeps the reader in mind of the opposition charge that Walpole's peace policy betrayed Britain's liberty, independence, and commercial interests.

With equal apparent casualness, interspersed in the knowing and familiar literary discourse which forms the body of the poem, are some remarks of more drastic implication:

> But Britain, changeful as a Child at play,
> Now calls in Princes, and now turns away (ll. 155–9)

The tone is of one that sees the way of the world, the simile of the changeful child plays the whole thing down, and yet that phrase 'turns away', in the present tense, suggests that this Augustus might be sent back to Hanover for good. James II, though hardly called in like George, had certainly been turned away. Might it not all happen again? This trembles on the verge of sedition. All the poet could have said in his own defence, if challenged, was that he advocated nothing but simply observed how Britain had changed. This might have some effect, but would hardly give an impression of loyalty. At a later but related point in the poem Pope advances further into danger. Pope's tribute to Swift:

---

[14] *TE* iv. 229, 195, 217, 223, 209.

> Let Ireland tell, how Wit upheld her cause,
> Her Trade supported, and supply'd her Laws;
> And leave on SWIFT this grateful verse ingrav'd,
> The Rights a Court attack'd, a Poet sav'd.

(ll. 222–4)

In some potentially seditious ballads the word 'court' was at this time represented as 'c——t' as a transparent evasion.[15] To charge the 'court' with a violation of rights was very strong, and, according to the Jacobite John Barber, writing to Swift after the publication of the Epistle, the lines were discussed at the Privy Council when the possibility of arresting and interrogating Pope was considered. The fact that this allusion to the crisis of Wood's Halfpence occurred in a former reign and not that of George II allowed the Council to pass the matter over.[16] The link with the earlier passage is that in the eyes of the more ideological Whigs (as expressed, for example, in their prosecution of Sacheverell) James II had been turned away for the violation of the laws and liberties of his subjects. Pope's tribute to Swift seemed to present George I, and his court, in the same light.[17]

There is a mystery about Pope's Epistle *To Augustus*. While the opening and closing ironies implicitly recognize in George Augustus a ruler falling short of the original Augustus, in power, intelligence, and wisdom, the addressee of the main literary part of the poem, penetrated with political allusion though it is, is assumed to have the intelligent interest in English literature of Pope himself, and perhaps to favour the older English writers as Augustus had preferred the older writers of Rome. The implied hearer of Pope's discourse is, perhaps, a necessary fiction: ruler, patron, friend, lover of English poetry. While he may have been based on one or more of Pope's actual friends—the second Earl of Oxford, creator of the Harleian Collection, would be a good candidate—he is really the missing Augustus we have already noticed in connection with Pope's *Dunciad*.[18]

---

[15] *TE* iv. 213–4; for a Jacobite ballad, see Cambridge University Library, Syn. 3 73. 2.

[16] *TE* iv. 213.

[17] Geoffrey Holmes, *The Trial of Dr Sacheverell* (1973), 131–2; J. P. Kenyon, *Revolution Principles: The Politics of Party, 1689–1720*, (Cambridge, 1977), 134–6.

[18] See Ch. 3 above.

II

Johnson could have written excellent satire dedicated to King George and Walpole. If he sought his readiest way to rise in the world he would have been well advised to do so. Young had shown how.

For some reason Johnson rejected Young's example. What about the more recent example of Pope? That was all very well, but Pope would hardly have published *To Augustus* when he was young and vulnerable. Yet Johnson chose the more dangerous course in his first published poem. Different as *London* is from anything from the pen of Pope, it shares with Pope a recognizable opposition and political standpoint. Johnson springs fully armed upon the stage as warrior of the opposition. *London* is an eloquent and energetic denunciation of a capital city and land allegedly decadent. Old glory is forgotten, old freedoms abandoned, old integrity ignored. It is a vision Johnson shared with *The Craftsman* papers, Pope's 1730s satire, and other writings of the opposition culture. This vision certainly involved Tory and Whig politics (not to be confused with modern party systems), but was far from being confined to them: it voiced a fear that Britain, through its specific contemporary politics, had betrayed itself and been betrayed into decline and fall within the large cyclical patterns of history. At the centre of this vision is the matter of military achievement, past glory, and present incapacity. This can be traced forward from *To Augustus* into *London*. Both Pope and Johnson mention Edward III and Henry V ('Edward and Henry'), and Pope's line: 'Old Edward's Armour beams on Cibber's breast' is picked up and expanded on by Johnson:

> Illustrious EDWARD! from the Realms of Day,
> The Land of Heroes and of Saints survey;
> Nor hope the *British* Lineaments to trace,
> The rustic Grandeur, or the surly Grace;
> But lost in thoughtless Ease, and empty Show,
> Behold the Warrior dwindled to a Beau;
> Sense, Freedom, Piety, refin'd away,
> Of FRANCE the Mimic, and of SPAIN the Prey.
>
> (ll. 99–106)[19]

---

[19] Samuel Johnson, *The Poems*, ed. David Nichol Smith and Edward L. McAdam, Jr. rev. J. D. Fleeman (Oxford, 1974), 73.

Johnson's l. 104 corresponds more closely to Pope than to the
cue-lines in Juvenal, iii. 67–8,[20] but what strikes the reader is the
way in which the compressed wit of Pope's line has been opened out
into a stately if indignant reflection upon what 'The Land of Heroes
and of Saints' had become. Loss of values, loss of memory, loss of
identity, form the poetic drama of the passage, which reaches a
point of contemporary political grievance only with the final line
(and paragraph's end). It is clear that the specific political judgement, opposition advocacy of war with a resurgent Spain, together
with all the allusions to Britain's warlike past, are present to convey
a deeper anxiety: that Britain, sunk into self-interest and inertia, is
losing its capacity for effective public action.

Linked with *London's* concern about action and inertia is a series
of cryptic references with dynastic implication. As the opening lines
of Johnson's imitation introduce the idea of a retreat from the
capital to some remote region of Britain, Thales, we are told, will

> . . . fix'd on CAMBRIA's solitary Shore,
> Give to ST. DAVID one *true Briton* more.
>
> (ll. 7–8)[21]

The italics of the original edition (unfortunately erased in the mod-
ernized text of the Yale Johnson but restored by J. D. Fleeman) give
a notable emphasis, especially in a couplet in which we find the
proper names 'Cambria' and 'David' unitalicized. Thus, early in the
poem, the retreating Thales, parallel of Juvenal's Umbricius, is
designed as a figure of unfashionable integrity. Further, as Fleeman
points out, the words seem to allude to the journal, *The True Briton*,
conducted by the second Duke of Wharton in 1723–4 in defence of
Bishop Atterbury during the latter's trial for Jacobite conspiracy in
the House of Lords. Johnson's persona in his crypto-Jacobite tract
of 1739, *Marmor Norfolciense*, would be styled 'Probus Britanicus',
True Briton.[22] The proceedings ended with Atterbury being sen-
tenced to exile, whither Wharton would soon follow him. Each of
these men were at that time Protestant Jacobites, though Wharton
would later convert to the Catholic faith. Each was a strong oppo-

---

[20] Samuel Johnson, *Works* vi, *Poems*, ed. E. L. McAdam, Jr., with George Milne
(New Haven, 1964), 53.

[21] *Poems*, 68.

[22] *Complete English Poems*, ed. David Fleeman (Harmondsworth, 1971), 197;
Johnson, Works, x. *Political Writings*, ed. Donald J. Greene (New Haven, 1977), 22.

nent of Walpole. The probability that Johnson was reminding some of his readers of *The True Briton* is strengthened by the way the double allusion to exile is made at the very point we hear of Thales's retreat. A second cryptic reference catches our attention early in Thales's speech: it is a line with two blanks (l. 50) and as such unique in the poem:

> Some secret Cell, ye Pow'rs, indulgent give.
> Let—live here, for—has learn'd to live.
>
> (ll. 50–1)[23]

The cue-lines in Juvenal (ll. 29–30) name 'Arturius' whom the relevant note in Dryden's *Juvenal* had designated: 'Any debauch'd wicked Fellow who gains by the times' (*Poems*, ii. 693). But Johnson's line, it has been noticed, closely paraphrases Boileau: 'Que George vive ici, puisque George y sait vivre' (Boileau, *Satires*, i. 34) and seems to incite the reader who notices this to insert the name 'George' for 'Arturius' in the blanks.[24] The blanks function as a warning of a dangerous meaning. The parallel with Boileau, though *he* meant no one in particular by 'George', confirms an allusion to the monarch on the throne. 'Let him live here, since he has found out a way to live here,' Thales is saying, 'I am getting out.'

In the manuscript of *London* in the Hyde Collection, 'Orgilio' (l. 208) is found to be 'Sejano': in any imitation of a Juvenal satire that is bound to be suggestive (cf. Juvenal Satire X. 54–113). Were it but a slip, and not the trace of an earlier conception, it would show that Johnson was at some stage thinking of the Orgilio of the poem not only as the epitome of pride and wealth but as a corrupt minister whose downfall would come. The lines on Orgilio (in Juvenal, Satire III, Asturicus) form the chief satiric portrait in *London* but, as the bookseller Charles Hitch would remark, and Johnson himself would recognize, it is 'no picture of modern manners, though it might be true to Rome'.[25] He has not effected a transformation from Roman to English so well as elsewhere in the poem, but the 'Sejano' variant marks how it might have been done, and would be done in *The Vanity of Human Wishes*. As it is the word leaves a trace from Johnson's mind concerning the ruler of London and its land. Sejanus

---

[23] *Poems*, 70.
[24] *Poems*, 70 and l. 50 n.
[25] *Poems*, 77.

had not served an Augustus, but a Tiberius.²⁶ This points us to the end of the poem, where the King just appears:

> Scarce can our Fields, such Crowds at *Tyburn* die,
> With Hemp the Gallows and the Fleet supply.
> Propose your Schemes, ye Senatorian Band,
> Whose *Ways and Means* support the sinking Land;
> Lest Ropes be wanting in the tempting Spring,
> To rig another Convoy for the K——g.
>
> (ll. 242–7)²⁷

In Johnson's original, Juvenal had complained that so much iron was being used for chains that there was hardly any left for ploughshares (ll. 310–11). *London* substitutes rope for iron, execution for imprisonment. The attack continues to be extreme. Like prayers to 'save my country'²⁸ talk of a 'sinking Land' implies an extreme crisis and the need for a drastic solution. It goes much beyond severe commentary on manners in a fundamentally sound establishment. Thales presses his diatribe into a final and extraordinarily scathing irony, and in so doing resorts to unmistakably Jacobite innuendo. Rope is not only needed to hang people with; in the 1730s it is needed to rig the fleet which escorts King George back and forth between Britain and Hanover. This implicitly draws attention to what Shippen had been sent to the Tower for uttering in Parliament: that the King 'was a stranger to our language and constitution'. It is comparable to the charge that William III drained the wealth of England into Holland: something a 'stranger' would try to do. Sir John Hawkins, Johnson's strongly Whig biographer, had no difficulty in recognizing the intent of the passage: 'that in his visits to his native country, the king drained this of its wealth.'²⁹ Further, the term 'tempting Spring', and the ambiguous word 'rig' (if the latter not only means 'prepare' and 'prepare by fraud' but also suggests 'riggish') imply that another motive for the King's Hanoverian visits was to see some of his German mistresses. Like Tiberius (it might have been said) he preferred his pleasures to his capital city. All these charges, the small print of Jacobite innuendo, border on

---

²⁶ See Juvenal, x. 65–113.

²⁷ *Poems*, 80.

²⁸ See Pope's Epistle *To Cobham*, ll. 264–5, and his Epitaph *For Dr. Francis Atterbury*, l. 8; *TE* iii–ii. 36; vi. 344.

²⁹ Sir John Hawkins, *Life of Samuel Johnson, LLD* (1787), 60–1.

sedition, but, despite the aggressive tone of the poem, do not go so far as Pope's line on the *Drapier's Letters* crisis in *To Augustus*. Thales's diatribe is severe, but he does seem to say: 'Let [George] live here, for [George] has learn'd to live.'

There is more to *London* than Jacobite innuendo, however sharply some of Johnson's contemporary readers will have been aware of it, and however Johnson integrated such references into his full text. If Johnson, against all his worldly interests, chose to follow the path of Pope as a satirist, rather than that of Young, he also measured a distance from Pope in certain literary and historical ways. Johnson follows Pope in presenting a formal imitation of a Roman poem, but a satire of Juvenal not Horace. Dryden had advocated combining the two,[30] and, as must have been obvious to Johnson, Pope in the mixed mode of several of his recent imitations had seemed to be moving towards Juvenal. It is as though Johnson perceived this evolution and resolved to overtake Pope on his own course. Naturally, this also had political implications. An imitation of Horace prompted the reader to try the parallel between modern and Augustan; an imitation of Juvenal prompted recollection of those emperors who ruled Rome between Augustus and Trajan. To produce a real, English, imitation of Juvenal 'consisting', as Johnson wrote to Cave in April 1738 'in adapting Juvenal's Sentiments to modern facts and Persons',[31] implied an English decline into corruption comparable with the Roman times presented in Juvenal's satires.

In keeping with this diagnosis and this parallel, Johnson's poem is not conversational as Pope's formal satires predominantly are, but consistently oratorical. In Juvenal, Satire III, Johnson found a text for a poem about departure and exile, a *sermo* of farewell. Further, Juvenal's departing Umbricius affords Johnson the dramatic form of the *sermo*. The voice of Thales is not identical with the voice of the poem; there is also the framing narrative at the beginning and end. That Thales is about to withdraw from London for ever lends weight to his judgement, but that the speaker should on his departure be possessed 'Of dissipated Wealth the small Remains' (l. 20) suggests at least that this speaker is not a model of prudence. He is

[30] John Dryden, *Poems*, ed. James Kinsley (Oxford, 1958), ii. 660–1.

[31] Samuel Johnson, *Letters*, ed. Bruce Redford (Oxford, 1992), i. 16 (Johnson to Edward Cave, Apr. 1738).

'injur'd' and 'indignant', and the exaggerated sarcasms of his diatribe have something of the quality of a performance that seeks to
outdo itself as paragraph succeeds paragraph. While there is such
topical and tonal variety as the Roman original provided, and as is
consistent with the character of the *satura*, Thales's *sermo* mounts
from defiance to defiance. The very name 'Orgilio' (Proud) gives a
more climactic significance to Juvenal's 'Asturicus' while the lines
on the King's convoy (ll. 242–7) which soon follow as the poem
nears its end, are a specific political challenge not found in the Latin
text.

The moment of 'transient Calm' at the beginning, when the narrator and Thales 'kneel, and kiss the consecrated Earth' where
Queen Elizabeth was born effectively contrasts with the rhetorical
energy to come, and with the characters of the virtue which it
defends. This is 'rebellious Virtue', 'the surly Grace' and our 'rugged
Natives', 'surly Virtue' and 'starving Merit': such epithets pervade
the text. The roughness and vigour of Thales's diatribe everywhere
show up the qualities he denounces: the lavish and polished, the
obsequious, servile, and degenerate. This defiant voice is associated
with an indomitable English identity, and made to turn against
foreign influence: the lure of Hanover, the manners of France, and
the commercial greed of Spain. Pope's later satire speaks of these
attitudes and qualities, but Johnson's Thales is master of the very
idiom they demand: it is effectively a new voice of satire:

> Has Heaven reserv'd, in Pity to the Poor,
> No pathless Waste, or undiscover'd Shore?
> No secret Island in the boundless Main?
> No peaceful Desart yet unclaim'd by SPAIN?
> Quick let us rise, the happy Seats explore,
> And bear Oppression's Insolence no more.
> This mournful Truth is ev'ry where confest,
> SLOW RISES WORTH, BY POVERTY DEPREST:
> But here more slow, where all are Slaves to Gold,
> Where Looks are Merchandise, and Smiles are sold,
> Where won by Bribes, by Flatteries implor'd,
> The Groom retails the Favours of his Lord.
>
>   (ll. 170–81)[32]

---

[32] *Poems*, 76–7.

The rhetorical questions range over a Renaissance history of discovery, and of islands familiar or Utopian. Next the pride of Thales comes out with the word 'Insolence': it is not just oppression he resents but the insolence of it. Honour and anger lurk behind the line. The famous line of the passage, which Johnson capitalized, has often been taken as the heart of the poem, and too often wrenched from its rhetorical context. Like all the best political poetry *London* is both generalizing and specific: 'But here more slow . . .' are words we should notice, words which well convey the angry condemnation of Thales. It is worth emphasizing the poetic craft which links the first 'Slow' with 'more slow' and that, alliteratively, with 'Slaves' and 'Smiles'. The weighty *sentence*, with its English/Latinate contrast, is actually embedded in a passage which opens with a resentful and sarcastic attack on resurgent Bourbon Spain, and gives human force to the widely shared concluding vision of a nation self-enslaved. The oft-quoted line, massive in its strength, is an integral part of one political vision and one rhetorical performance. *London* enacts the very courage which it lauds.

The poem is surely an extraordinary poetic exertion, its energy pointed, its depiction shaped, the whole text animated and controlled. Yet as a political poem it has been very dismissively treated. That it uses 'the merest commonplaces of opposition propaganda' is to say no worse of it than one says of 'Pope's great *Epilogue to the Satires*': that is, if these 'commonplaces' were really no more than clichés, were not, on the contrary, serious and widely made accusations against Walpole's Britain, then the shaping spirit of these poets' imagination has achieved a wonderful transformation. Further, to see *To Augustus, London*, and the *Epilogue to the Satires* as great political poetry does not mean we must endorse their vision of Sir Robert Walpole as the whole truth. Even some Jacobites at this time saw Walpole as a minister loyal to his King, as opposed to opposition Whigs who only clamoured for place. Walpole himself never underestimated the Jacobite threat, or 'the merest commonplaces of opposition propaganda' which were levelled against him by so many.[33] Finally, to talk of *London* as 'a haphazard list of the various things connected with London that Johnson dislikes' seems

[33] Donald Greene, *The Politics of Samuel Johnson* (New Haven, 1960), 88, 90–1; *The Commons, 1715–54* i. 68–9.

no very adequate literary critical response to a carefully structured rhetorical text.[34] *London* is not a letter, or a page or two of a journal, but a poem. If political analysis of poetry is going to ignore what poetry does then it will not take us very far. Literary and political analysis must find a way of working together.

II

The political tendency of *London* is confirmed and clarified by two prose satires published by Johnson in May 1739, *Marmor Norfolciense . . . By Probus Britanicus* and *A Compleat Vindication of the Licensers of the Stage*. Each is a Scriblerian fiction whose 'author' is most adroitly managed, especially perhaps in the first of these works, to display the very attitudes Johnson most desires to undermine and attack. At the centre of his concern in each case is a poetic text. In *A Compleat Vindication* this text is Henry Brooke's play *Gustavus Vasa* (1739), just banned from public performance under the Licensing Act in 1737. In *Marmor Norfolciense* it is a poem Johnson himself has supplied, a set of prophetic verses in Monkish Latin supposed to have been carved on a stone unearthed, *deterré* as it were, in a ploughed field in Norfolk. The author includes a translation into modern heroic couplets:

> *To Posterity*
> When'er this Stone, now hid beneath the Lake,
> The Horse shall trample, or the Plough shall break,
> Then, O my Country! shalt thou groan distrest
>
> .   .   .   .
>
> Then o'er the World shall Discord stretch her Wings,
> Kings change their Laws, and Kingdoms change their Kings.
> The Bear enrag'd th'affrighted Moon shall dread;
> The Lilies o'er the Vales triumphant spread;
> Nor shall the Lyon, wont of old to reign
> Despotic o'er the desolated Plain,
> Henceforth th'inviolable Bloom invade,
> Or dare to murmur in the flow'ry Glade;
> His tortur'd Sons shall die before his Face,
> While he lies melting in a lewd Embrace;

---

[34] Greene, *The Politics of Samuel Johnson*, 88.

And, yet more strange! his Veins a Horse shall drain,
Nor shall the passive Coward once complain.

(ll. 1–3, 15–26)[35]

Like the card-game in Pope's *Rape of the Lock* this poem is designed
to recall through cryptic and compressed allusion a series of crises
in high politics. 'Kings change their Laws, and Kingdoms change
their Kings' might apply to many situations, but to the English
reader it would suggest above all the period between 1688 and
1714, and the outbreak of civil discord with the innovations of
James II. The poem evolves as a kind of heraldic beast-fable in
which the Turkish 'Moon' wanes at the aggression of the Russian
'Bear', and the British 'Lyon', once a conqueror of France, grows
powerless before the land of the Fleurs-de-Lis: now the Bourbon
alliance of France and Spain. His sons are mistreated by these old
enemies (the atrocity of Jenkins's Ear, etc) while he himself is
unnerved from action 'in a lewd Embrace'. This 'Embrace' is the
latest inflection of that 'Rape' in terms of which the change of kings
in 1689 had been previously presented. It aims at the alleged corruption of Britain, too selfish to shake off a slavish rule. Some of this
explication emerges from the Author's own clumsy and obtuse
attempts to interpret the poem. The rationale of the satire is that the
Author becomes more baffled as the allusions grow more obvious.
The strange climax of the poem, as the Horse drains away the life of
the enervated Lion, would have been more obvious to the 1739
reader, accustomed to think in heraldic and fabular terms, than it is
to us. The Author perceives the intention here but cannot accept the
implications:

Were I to proceed in the same tenour of interpretation, by which I explained
the moon and the lilies, I might observe that a horse is born in the Arms of
H——. But how then does the horse suck the lyon's blood? Money is the
blood of the body politic.—But my zeal for the present happy establishment
will not suffer me to pursue a train of thought that leads to such shocking
conclusions. The idea is detestable, and such as, it ought to be hoped, can
enter in the mind of none but a virulent Republican, or bloody Jacobite.[36]

The Author is not so stupid that he does not see what the poem has
supplied: the Horse is indeed in 'the arms of H[anover]'. It is, as

---

[35] *Poems*, 87–8.
[36] Johnson, *Works*, x. 42.

Donald Greene points out, 'the badge of the great Guelph house of Saxony, from whom the Hanoverian electors descended . . .'.[37] With something of a seditious humour Johnson has his Author collocate 'virulent Republican' with 'bloody Jacobite'. No doubt the tract does reflect on 'kings in general' but it ought not to be dismissed as 'Politically' . . . 'not very interesting', its targets 'the commonplaces of opposition propaganda'.[38] Unlike commonplace opposition propaganda, the emblem of the Horse draining the blood of the Lion is dynastically anti-Hanoverian. Indeed Johnson seems to come to his targets from a specifically Jacobite direction, for the source of his emblem (though it has not so far as I know been pointed out) appears to be Otto Hamerani's fine Jacobite medal of 1721, or later depictions deriving from it. The reverse side of the medal shows over the Thames the London of St Paul's Cathedral and the new churches, while on the nearer shore a horse tramples upon a struggling lion and unicorn, Britannia weeps, and three men seem to carry away plunder. The motto is 'Quid Gravius Capta'. On the right side of the medal appears the godlike bust of James III in Roman garb, the motto 'Unica Salus'.[39] Hamerani's medal was doubtless conceived as comment on the South Sea Bubble crisis and propaganda for Atterbury's Jacobite plot then going forward. Johnson's *London* shows that these ways of thinking were not out of date in 1738. Thus *Marmor Norfolciense* gives us the side of the medal which is complaint: 'What more grievous captivity?' The other side, which displayed the solution in the absent King, 'The only cure', might be inferred only by those who had seen one of these medals.

Pope's response to these two works is worthy of note. *London* at once aroused his curiosity, but his original enquiries resulted only in the information that the author 'was some obscure man': those who were in the secret probably felt the need for discretion. Pope's comment (as reported by Boswell from Reynolds and Richardson the younger), 'He will soon be *deterré*', may recognize the conspiratorial atmosphere surrounding the anonymous publication of near seditious texts. By the time *Marmor Norfolciense* came out, Pope at

---

[37] Ibid.
[38] Johnson, *Works*, x. 21.
[39] Noel Woolf, *The Medallic Record of the Jacobite Movement* (1988), 83; Paul Kleber Monod, *Jacobitism and the English People, 1688–1788* (Cambridge, 1989), 78–9 and plate 4. See Plate 2 in the present book,

least had uncovered the name of the author and had apparently 'endeavour'd to serve Him without his own application . . .' by writing to Lord Gower, though without success.[40] There are obscurities about this attempt to assist Johnson, but it is interesting that it involved that reputedly Jacobite Tory, Lord Gower. Those with influence in the opposition culture recognized not only Johnson's talent but his political tendency, and knew the most appropriate people to recruit in his cause.

The source of *Gustavus Vasa* seems likely to have been the same book which fostered Johnson's interest in Charles XII of Sweden: Voltaire's *History* of the latter king, the English translation of which was published in 1732, including Latin verses in praise of Charles by the Jacobite Archibald Pitcairne. Voltaire sketches Gustavus's career early in his work, and makes it clear that Charles XII was his descendant.[41] Brooke's *Gustavus Vasa, The Deliverer of his Country* has just about every sign of sedition that a drama of this time could display. That it should have been prohibited from performance under the new Licensing Act is not surprising, and by the standards of the age not unreasonable. The centre-piece of opposition propaganda was its assault on Walpole as a corrupt first minister; Hervey's *Memoirs* show that this was why Gay's *Polly* was banned; Trollio, the corrupt and treacherous chief minister in Brooke's play, would immediately have been seen to touch this sore. This is where the government's objections must have begun. But while Gay's operas, at least, never touched on matters of royalty, Brooke's plot allowed the reader to proceed from corrupt minister to corrupt master. If Trollio lampooned Walpole, the Danish Cristiern, usurper of the Swedish throne, must have seemed to involve George II. Cristiern is the blatant character of a tyrant. Really virulent attack upon the Hanoverian kings usually betokens a Jacobite standpoint of some kind. Trollio and Cristiern together would have been enough to suggest Jacobite sedition. Worse than this, the plot of the play openly revealed an armed rising against Cristiern ending in his overthrow.

---

[40] *Complete English Poems*, ed. Fleeman, 196; Boswell, *Life of Johnson*, i. 128–9, 133–4; J. L. Clifford, *The Young Samuel Johnson* (1955), 211–12.
[41] *The History of Charles XII. King of Sweden. By Mr. de Voltaire. Translated from the French* (1732), 4–9. See p. 185v for Pitcairne's poem.

It is when we turn from these villains to the character of Gustavus the Deliverer of 'his Country' that the political allusion becomes less obvious. Donald Greene has called the play 'a barefaced allegory' of the opposition view of England,[42] and suggested that Gustavus might be either Frederick, Prince of Wales, or James III. Yet in the story Brooke has chosen there is no ground for seeing the deliverer as a son of the tyrant: the play is not really congruent with that pattern of Hanoverian opposition, which sought to set up the eldest son against the father. As 'first Cousin of the deceased King' of Sweden (*personae dramatis*) Gustavus seems to have a hereditary claim to the throne, as Greene notes, but this is not much insisted on in the text of the play. In character and experience Gustavus, the inveterate warrior and inspired leader, hardly resembled either the inexperienced young Frederick, or that dignified gentleman, James III, living in his palace in Rome. Further, the Epilogue to Brooke's play (whether or not part of the original censored text or a prudent addition) equated the 'Deliverer' with 'Nassau'. Bolingbroke in his effort to create a united opposition of Whig and Tory had invoked William III as an instance of a patriot prince, and the House of Nassau had, from one point of view, a good history of deliverance. The means of deliverance also command our attention. The most striking feature of the drama is its conception, less of the hidden king than the concealed commander, of Gustavus rising with the common people of the northern mines and mountains to deliver his country. These 'Mountain peasants' are the 'rustic sons of Liberty', their 'Northern Province' of Dalecarlia provided 'These last Retreats' of freedom: here Gustavus talking in his sleep declares: 'O *Sweden*! O my Country! Yet I'll save thee.'[43] If Brooke's 'barefaced allegory' displays the (alleged) condition of Britain in the 1730s, the quarter from which deliverance comes, from the north and with the assistance not of regular troops but warlike Highlanders, can hardly fail to remind of the 1715 Jacobite Rebellion, at which James III had at least been present and under arms.

It is, however, clear that Gustavus corresponds to no one eighteenth-century figure. The play is not a simple parallel. He represents patriotic virtù, just as Thales in *London* represented rejected inte-

[42] *The Politics of Samuel Johnson*, 99.
[43] Henry Brooke, *Gustavus Vasa, The Deliverer of his Country* (1739), 3, 5, 11–12.

grity. The principle of liberty alone is what activates him, and in his interesting defiance of Cristiern's claim on his obedience, the issue of freedom and oppression is set above any regular title to a crown:

> But if thou think'st
> That Crowns are vilely propertied, like Coin,
> To be the Means, the Specialty of Lust
> And sensual Attribution—If thou think'st,
> That Empire is of titled Birth, or Blood;
> That Nature in the proud behalf of one
> Shall disenfranchise all her lordly Race,
> And Bow her gen'ral Issue to the Yoke
> Of private Domination—then, thou proud one,
> Here know me for thy King—Howe'er be told,
> Not Claim Hereditary, not the Trust
> Of frank Election;
> Not ev'n the high anointing Hand of Heav'n
> Can authorize Oppression[44]

Gustavus is not discounting these claims of title on his own behalf, but denying that any of them can require obedience to oppression. In so doing he puts the capacity to restore natural liberty above all. This is similar to the line of thought to be found in Pope's '1740. A Poem', where he seems to say to a potential patriot prince:

> Be but a man! unministered, alone,
> And free at once the Senate and the Throne;
> Esteem the public love his best supply,
> A ☉'s true glory his integrity
> Whatever his religion or his blood,
> His public virtue makes his title good.

> (ll. 89–96)[45]

It also rehearses the political moral of the English scene in Shakespeare's *Macbeth*. Brooke's play has a Jacobite trend in its diagnosis of Britain's ills, and indeed in its military solution to them, but it is of the libertarian Jacobite vein, which had brought figures such as Charlwood Lawton and Sir James Ferguson round to the cause of James II in the 1690s, and which could still look to the exiled claimant when even few Roman Catholics now defended James II's

---

[44] Brooke, *Gustavus Vasa*, 60–1.
[45] *TE* iv. 337.

decisions on the throne. The cult of northern liberty is affirmed in Brooke's Prologue ('A race of hardy, northern Sons he led, | Guiltless of Courts, untainted, and unread') while his Prefatory Dedication, though denying any contemporary allusion, can quite relevantly defend the text by saying that its subject was taken 'from the History of *Sweden*, one of those Gothic and *glorious* Nations, from whom our Form of Government is derived, and from whom Britain has inherited' 'unextinguishable Sparks of Liberty and Patriotism' (p. iv). Out of the old myth of Gothic freedom, and influenced, no doubt by way of Voltaire's account of Swedish history, Brooke has created a more specific myth of Sweden, composed of natural freedom and military heroism, just the qualities to cure the corruptions of the times.

That Johnson should have satirized the banning of this extreme play, with its cult of northern liberty and its example of military action, is remarkable. Opposition culture offered many opportunities to attack the times without challenging the dynasty on the throne. Yet it is consistent with authorship of *London* and *Marmor Norfolciense*, and of course the Compleat Vindicator is a satiric creation comparable to the Author of *Marmor*. Each is uncritically loyal to a present happy establishment; each has loyalty taken by Johnson to an absurd extreme. The Vindicator is shut up within the show and comforts of the present moment, and just cannot understand why the 'party' of the opposition should talk so much about '*posterity*' and insist so much on 'reason'. His idea is that within the established culture of court and government nobody need ever give a reason for having or doing anything, certainly not a reason connected with posterity.[46] The tract approaches Brooke's play from this satiric angle. By the time it quotes from the Prologue, the notions of heroism and fame (the recognition of posterity) have joined in the figure of Gustavus. Next the Vindicator pitches on the idea of natural liberty 'in th' unlettered mind' and indignantly denies that unlettered minds have anything to do with liberty. Unlettered minds (he explains) are those the ministry most relies on to fill employments of profit, trust, and honour. This unexpected stroke of irony on Johnson's part entirely occludes any serious response to Brooke's libertarian ideas. The tract comes closer to current political

---

[46] Johnson, *Works*, x. 57, 62–3.

awareness and expression when the Vindicator quotes Gustavus's line in his sleep:

O Sweden, O my country, yet I'll save thee. This line I have reason to believe thrown out as a kind of watch-word for the opposing faction, who, when they meet in their seditious assemblies, have been observed to lay their hands upon their breasts, and any out with great vehemence of accent, O B——, O my country, yet I'll save thee.[47]

In the authentic Swiftian manner in which irony mixes some truth with absurdity and falsity, the Vindicator has here recognized a feature of the opposition code—'watch-word' is a good term. To talk of the saving of ones country is always radical and extreme, presupposing a crisis and the need for salvation. (Other kinds of political commentary might speak of guiding, aiding, and enriching: that would be inoffensive.) In his final speech at his 'trial' in the House of Lords, Atterbury had quoted Paolo Sarpi's prayer: 'Save my country, Heaven!' and Pope had in the early 1730s attributed this petition to both Atterbury, in the Epitaph on the Protestant Jacobite leader, and to Richard Boyle, Lord Cobham, who had recently gone over into opposition to the government.[48] The 'Unica Salus' medal had, as we have seen, deployed exactly this trope as a Jacobite response to the real crisis of the South Sea Bubble. At this point *The Compleat Vindication* touches upon the Jacobite diagnosis and the Jacobite emotion; it does not recommend Jacobite action. The tract moves to its end by paying some attention to the alleged corruptions of the time, and by arguing (following earlier *Craftsman* ironies) that 'the productions of our old poets' with all their allusions to 'liberty, natural equality, wicked ministers, deluded kings', etc., should be rigorously censored.

III

It will be noted that in introducing Pope into this discussion of political poetry I paid attention to his Roman Catholic background, while in considering Johnson I have so far ignored completely the question of any attitudes or principles inherited from his home or his

[47] Johnson, *Works*, x. 67.
[48] Howard Erskine-Hill, 'Life into Letters, Death into Art: Pope's Epitaph on Francis Atterbury', *The Yearbook of English Studies*, 18 (1988), 200–20.

early years. The reason for this difference of approach is a controversy concerning Johnson's background and political views, this being connected in turn with the question of the reliability of Boswell, especially on Johnson's earliest years.[49] I have therefore attempted, first, to outline some of the possibilities that were open to Johnson the young poet, and, secondly, to show how deliberately and clearly Johnson chose to follow the political line of Pope. That these early texts of Johnson belong to the culture of the opposition is hardly in dispute, but not all opposition writing was politically the same. A broad distinction should be made between texts which targeted a corrupt minister only, leaving the possibility that the king on the throne was merely deluded, and texts which went out of their way to bring, by innuendo, extreme charges against the Hanoverian kings. The former could be considered Hanoverian opposition, and its complaints could in principle be answered if and when Prince Frederick succeeded his father to the throne. The latter, often implying that the king on the throne was a stranger or a usurper, deploying often a rhetoric of extreme crisis ('Save my country!'), and sometimes seeming to derive from unquestionably Jacobite sources such as the 'Unica Salus' medal, is crypto-Jacobite. The early Johnson appears to belong to this kind of opposition writing. When we read *London* we shall also be wise to remember that political poetry is still poetry, not just the sum of its ideas. Even if its experience, its ideas, and its accusations *were* opposition commonplaces, Johnson charged them with a new literary power. This in turn suggests that to Johnson they were far from weary commonplaces routinely adopted. However inadequately or routinely expressed by others, they were serious ideas to him in the later 1730s, and he endowed them with all the intelligence and eloquence he could command.

With this character of Johnson's early political texts in mind, we should now turn to the earlier, pre-Boswellian biographical record.

---

[49] Greene, *The Politics of Samuel Johnson* (rev. edn. 1989), pp. ix–lxv; Howard Erskine-Hill, 'The Political Character of Samuel Johnson', in Isobel Grundy (ed.), *Samuel Johnson: New Critical Essays* (1984), ch. 10, 107–36 nn.; 'The Poet and Affairs of State in Johnson's *Lives of the Poets*', *Man and Nature* (*Proceedings of the Canadian Society for Eighteenth-Century Studies*), VI (1985), 93–113; id., 'The Political Character of Samuel Johnson: *The Lives of the Poets* and a Further Report on *The Vanity of Human Wishes*', in Eveline Cruickshanks and Jeremy Black (eds.), *The Jacobite Challenge* (Edinburgh, 1988), 161–76.

Here one of the prime documents, known to Boswell only after the publication of his *Life of Johnson*, is the letter of 31 July 1762 to the Earl of Bute recommending Johnson for a pension from the new administration.[50] This anonymous document was probably one of several submitted with the same end in view and there is no sure reason to think that it secured Johnson's pension more than any other representation. It may have been composed by Richard Farmer, Master of Emmanuel College, Cambridge, and written by Edward Blakeway of Magdalene College.[51] If so it came from a circle which knew Johnson well, even though he and Farmer were as yet unacquainted. The composer of the letter wishes to serve Johnson, and sees an objection which he tries to overcome: 'If it be objected that his political principles render him an unfit object of His Majesty's favour, I would only say that he is more to be pitied on this account . . . I am told that his political principles make him incapable of being in any place of trust, by incapacitating him from qualifying himself for any such office—but a pension, My Lord requires no such performances . . .'.[52] What can these remarks mean? This is very categorical and extreme language, and must be saying more than that Johnson is a principled Tory (or Whig). By 1762 the long proscription of the Tories had ended and if Johnson were a Tory that would not make him an unfit object of favour to the new King. The writer rather suggests that Johnson is in some way hostile to the House of Hanover, and when he speaks of principles which incapacitate from qualifying for an office the meaning is completely clear. These phrases were applied to those who had been, or would be, unable to take the Oaths. The anonymous writer is telling Lord Bute that Johnson is a Non-Juror—not necessarily one who had been called to take the Oaths and had refused, but one who if the Oaths were tendered to him would refuse. Sir John Hawkins, author of the first substantial biography of Johnson, discusses the pension in similar terms: Johnson, he says, 'had very little claim to the favour of any of the descendants of the house of Hanover' but, on accepting the pension, 'found himself in a predicament similar to

[50] Marshall Waingrow (ed.), *The Correspondence and Other Papers of James Boswell Relating to the Making of the Life of Johnson* (New York, 1969), 512–15; J. L. Clifford, *Dictionary Johnson* (1979), 263–5, 269.

[51] Bertram H. Davies, 'The Anonymous Letter Proposing Johnson's Revision', *Transactions of the Johnson Society of Lichfield* (Lichfield, 1981), 35–9.

[52] Waingrow, *Correspondence*, 515.

that of Dr. Sherlock, who, at the revolution, was a non-juror to king William, but, after deliberating on his refusal as a case of conscience, took the side that made for his interest . . .'.[53]

Johnson's acceptance of this pension is certainly what brought the question of his political principles into the public sphere. Whereas, before, his known authorship of several anonymous anti-Hanoverian texts was treated by many with a measure of discretion, now Charles Churchill in his anti-Bute satire *The Ghost* (1762–3) could brutally exploit Johnson's apparent inconsistency:

> POMPOSO, *Fame* around should tell
> How he a slave to int'rest fell
>
> .   .   .   .
>
> How to all Principles untrue,
> Nor fix'd to *old* Friends nor to *New*,
> He damns the *Pension* which he takes
> And loves the STUART he forsakes.
>
> (iii. 797–8, 817–20)[54]

Much of *The Ghost* is devoted to anti-Jacobite attack and there is no doubt that 'STUART' alludes to both the surname of Bute's family and the exiled royal line. It is probably significant that it is shortly after this that Anna Seward writes of Johnson having 'imbibed' from her grandfather, master of Lichfield Grammar School and 'a Jacobite', 'his master's absurd zeal for the forfeit rights of the house of Stuart . . .'.[55] Seward and Hawkins agree on Johnson's early Jacobitism, but differ over who was a crucial Jacobite influence upon Johnson in his early Lichfield days, his father or his schoolmaster. Neither is a very good witness: Anna Seward too young, Hawkins too distant. But Hawkins is probably right when he says that many inhabitants of Staffordshire were Jacobite: he considers it a Jacobite region, as did the Jacobite agent James Butler in 1743.[56]

This evidence should be completed by Hawkins's comments on Johnson's early works. In Hawkins we have a witness who knew Johnson long before the pension episode (certainly from 1749 but,

[53] Hawkins, *Life*, 393–4.
[54] Charles Churchill, *Poetical Works*, ed. Douglas Grant (1956), 126–7.
[55] Anna Seward, *Poetical Works*, ed. Walter Scott (Edinburgh, 1810), i, p. lxx.
[56] Eveline Cruickshanks, *Political Untouchables: The Tories and the '45* (1979), 120.

in the opinion of Hawkins's modern editor, probably from 1739).
Hawkins roundly condemns Johnson's early 'political prejudices'
and gives a most interesting account of his views:

He almost asserted in terms [that is to say, formally affirmed] that the
succession to the crown had been illegally interrupted, and that from
Whig-politics none of the benefits of government could be expected. He
could but just endure the opposition to the minister [Walpole] because
conducted on whig principles; and I have heard him say, that during the
whole course of it, the two parties were bidding for the people.[57]

It may be noted from this, not only that Johnson is said to share
the Jacobite analysis of 1688, not only that he was uneasy at the
opposition to Walpole because it was conducted on Whig principles, but also that he was capable of a shrewd democratic analysis of the political oppositions of the 1730s. Hawkins's attitude
to these alleged opinions is one of impatience and distaste. It is
quite different from the attitude of Boswell who, while disavow-
ing such opinion, is sympathetic and fascinated. Hawkins is of
great interest in that he seems likely to preserve the reactions of a
contemporary Whig to Johnson's earlier writings. Thus he says of
London:

The topics of this spirited poem . . . are evidently drawn from those weekly
publications, which, to answer the view of a malevolent faction, first
created, and for some years supported, a distinction between the interests of
the government and the people, under the several denominations of the
court and the country parties: these publications were carried on under
the direction of men, professing themselves to be whigs and friends of the
people, in a paper intitled, 'The Country Journal or the Craftsman', now
deservedly forgotten . . .[58]

On the passage on George II's voyages to Hanover, he recognized
the accusation 'that in his visits to his native country, the king
drained this of its wealth'.[59] On *Marmor Norfolciense* Hawkins
remarked: 'The explanation of the prophecy, which is all ironical,
resolves itself into an invective against a standing army, a ridicule of
the balance of power, complaints of the inactivity of the British lion,
and that the Hanover horse was suffered to suck his blood.' Moving

[57] Hawkins, *Life*, 80.
[58] Hawkins, *Life*, 60.
[59] Hawkins, *Life*, 61.

on from accusation to emblem, Hawkins accurately concluded that: 'The principles it contained were such as the Jacobites of the time openly avowed . . .'.[60]

If Boswell is under suspicion for being too sympathetic to Jacobitism (despite his clear repudiation of it), and too ready to find it in Johnson, Hawkins can hardly be distrusted on the same grounds. Viewing the disputed issues as they may be seen in Johnson's life as a whole, one can hardly fail to be struck by how two biographers of such different sympathy, who knew their subject well from such different times, can be so much at one in discovering a Jacobite orientation in the early Johnson. The evidence of others (the recommender of the pension, Churchill, Anna Seward) supports their diagnosis, and together their testimony supports the foregoing analysis of Johnson's earlier writing.

One further piece of literary evidence, of intrinsic interest and significance in context, is Johnson's tragedy of *Irene* (1736–49), the basic conception of which goes back to the early part of this period. The plot of the play displays major features in common with Dryden's *Don Sebastian*. In each case Christian rulers have been overwhelmed in battle, and an alien people with an alien religion assume command. In each case heroes and heroines from the previous political order survive into the new regime and are confronted by the dilemma of whether to join it, defy it, or to attempt flight. In each case there is a cunning and self-serving minister, willing to foment the incipient conflict to serve his own ends. In each case political opposition is heightened and dramatized by being transposed into religious conflict. Johnson's two Christian ladies, Irene and Aspasia, express the two sides of the consequent dilemma: whether to accommodate or oppose. The two plays—one might add Dryden's *King Arthur* and the Non-Juror Fenton's *Mariamne* (1723)—expose the problems facing those who support the old order.

---

[60] Hawkins, *Life*, 71–2.

5
The Vanity of Human Wishes in Context

I

THE four years after Johnson's publication of *London* were dominated by the opposition's increased efforts to bring down Walpole. He eventually resigned in February 1742. The publication of the banned *Gustavus Vasa* was just one occasion when a large number of opposition figures joined together to support an author's right to express his particular political vision and to deliver a public reproof to the first minister. A glance at the names on that long subscription list shows the interpenetration of political and literary worlds and reveals (in the light of later events) the great variety of motive and hope which urged on the attempt to change the government. The list includes a great literary name, that of Swift, the only person to subscribe for as many as ten copies. It includes the names of great political figures who were also writers and idealogues of the opposition, such as Bolingbroke and Chesterfield, both ambiguous figures. Bolingbroke liked to keep his eye on the Jacobite alternative, while Chesterfield had no hesitation in co-operating with Jacobites at the highest level. In 1740 it was decided to seek James III's order to his supporters in Parliament to vote against Walpole on all occasions, and it was Chesterfield who travelled to Avignon to negotiate the matter with the exiled Duke of Ormonde.[1] In the list also are several Jacobite Tories, such as the Duke of Beaufort, Sir Watkin Williams Wynn, and Sir John Hinde Cotton. All three were among the English magnates who invited Prince Charles Edward Stuart to invade with French support in 1743. Walpole believed Cotton to be 'the Pretender's secretary [of state]'.[2] Another group in the list is of sometime Jacobites now really Tories seeking office, such as Lord Bathurst and Lord Gower. Another is of the

---

[1] Romney Sedgwick (ed.), *The History of Parliament: The House of Commons, 1715–1754* (1970), i. 71.
[2] *The Commons, 1715–54*, i. 70.

Hanoverian opposition, such as William Pitt and Johnson's old acquaintance the Hon. George Lyttelton. A quite different group represents professional political writers and publishers: Nicholas Amhurst, the writer of *The Craftsman*, the bookseller Hitch who had commented that Johnson's Orgilio was a Roman rather than English character, Paul Whitehead the political poet, and Charles Molloy, writer of Chesterfield's opposition journal, *Common Sense*.[3] Molloy is worth a moment's attention. A writer for the Jacobite *Fog's Journal* earlier in the decade, he was recommended by James III in 1736 as a suitable person to conduct a journal in England supporting the Jacobite interest. In 1737 James was informed that the new paper was about to start, and that Pope (provided his contributions remained anonymous), Chesterfield, and Lord Grange, that is, the Hon. James Erskine, would all lend their support.[4] The journal in question was certainly *Common Sense*, and Molloy seems to have received a pension from James III for his efforts, though this was cut off when 'he ceased to give political satisfaction'.[5] Erskine was a Jacobite at heart (younger brother of the Earl of Mar of the 1715 Rising) but also a skilful trimmer devoted to restoring the fortunes of his family.[6] Two further names in this subscription list command attention. The first is that of John Murray of Broughton, Secretary of State to Prince Charles Edward during the Jacobite Rising of 1745, and subsequently an informer on so many other Jacobite supporters. The second is that of Samuel Johnson, probably, though not certainly, the Samuel Johnson who is the subject of this chapter.

The list is of course more extensive than these names suggest. Many names are unidentified—at least by me. But, not surprisingly, it contains no recognizable supporter of Walpole. It is an opposition list *par excellence*. In his later years Johnson would call it 'a very

[3] See B. A. Goldgar, *Walpole and the Wits: The Relation of Politics to Literature, 1722–1742* (1976), 157–8; Jeremy Black, 'An Underrated Journalist: Nathaniel Mist and the Opposition Press During the Whig Ascendency', *British Journal of Eighteenth-Century Studies*, 10 (1987), 36.

[4] G. H. Jones, 'The Jacobites, Charles Molloy and *Common Sense*', *RES* NS 4 (1953), 144–7; Goldgar, *Walpole and the Wits*, 157–8.

[5] Royal Archives, Stuart MSS 249/113 (Thomas Carte to James III, 4 May 1743); see also 196/14 (George Kelly to Daniel O'Brien, 3 May 1737), 199/108 (Charles Molloy to James III, 23 July 1737), 200/124 (George Kelly to James Edgar). Michael Harris, 'The London Newspaper Press, 1725–46', Ph.D. diss. (London University, 1973), 207–8.

[6] *The Commons, 1715–54*, ii. 14–17.

liberal subscription' and question the justice of prohibiting the play from performance.[7]

The mixed and ambiguous situation which these details reveal can hardly be too much stressed. How it looked to an intelligent man not in the confidence of some great aristocrat such as Chesterfield is another question again. All who know Johnson's earlier life will recognize the significance of some of the names in the *Gustavus Vasa* list—Lyttelton, Gower, Chesterfield, the bookseller Hitch, to name no more. Did their public conduct help Johnson assess the state of affairs? The extreme problems of interpretation for him and for us are well illustrated by two examples from the opposition culture, David Morgan and James Erskine. The two parts of Morgan's poem *The Country Bard* (1739, 1741) might well be called 'the merest commonplaces of opposition propaganda' though the implications of certain footnotes give us pause. So do the dedications to Sir John Morgan of Kinnersley, MP, and to Sir Watkin Williams Wynn, each of whom is in the *Gustavus Vasa* list. *London* seems more anti-Hanoverian than *The Country Bard*. Morgan, however, joined Prince Charles at Chester in 1745, urged him to march on London, deserted after the retreat from Derby, was captured, tried, and executed on Kennington Common. His dying speech is one of the best statements we have of undisguised and unrepentant Protestant Jacobitism.[8] Erskine, for his part, looked just like a member of the Whig opposition in the 1730s. Yet exiled Jacobites expected him to co-operate with Chesterfield in a Jacobite journal, in 1741 he handed a political invitation from James III to the Whig opposition leader, Pulteney, and he advised with the English Jacobites during the 1745 rebellion. He actually held a post under Frederick, Prince of Wales, until 1745, and became an ally of the Pelhams when the rebellion collapsed.[9]

Walpole, for his part, knew how to interpret a deceptive face of affairs. His opinion in 1738 was along the following lines:

No man of common prudence will profess himself openly a Jacobite; by so doing he not only may injure his private fortune, but he must render himself

---

[7] Life of Thomson, in *The Lives of the Poets* (1779–81), ed. G. Birlebeck Hill (Oxford, 1905), iii. 292.

[8] Robert Forbes, *The Lyon in Mourning*, ed. Henry Paton (Edinburgh, 1975), i. 43–7; Howard Erskine-Hill, 'Literature and the Jacobite Cause,' in Eveline Cruickshanks (ed.), *Ideology and Conspiracy* (Edinburgh, 1982), 56–7, 68.

[9] *The Commons, 1715–54*, ii. 14–17.

less able to do any effectual service to the cause he was embraced . . . Your right Jacobite, Sir, disguises his true sentiments, he roars out for revolution principles; he pretends to be a great friend to liberty, and a great admirer of our ancient constitution . . .[10]

Walpole had information which led him to distinguish between 'patriot Whigs' (such as Pulteney and Lyttelton) and 'Jacobites' who, if there were to be 'a revolution', 'the King's interest' being 'entirely lost', were determined that there should be 'a restoration'. Walpole also had a clear view of the policy of France, which, he believed, would never go to war with Britain during the life of Cardinal Fleury, but would do so after the Cardinal's death.[11] Walpole has been accused of exaggerating the Jacobite threat in order to prolong his own power, but it must be said that in the light of the most recent evidence and the public events of the time, his judgements have been vindicated. Another important witness is Lord Hervey (Pope's 'Sporus') whose then unpublished *Memoirs* never make light of the Jacobite threat, and are revealing on the extreme unpopularity of George II even though Hervey himself was committed to the Hanoverian cause.[12]

While the wishes of James III certainly contributed to the weakening of Walpole's position as first minister, there were some Tories and Jacobites who disliked this hunt to the kill. It seemed to them that, though Walpole might not have served the true king, he had served George I and George II as a loyal minister should serve a royal master, while the opposition Whigs only wanted to bring Walpole down to win office for themselves. William Shippen, 'head of the veteran staunch Jacobites', said that Walpole and he were 'two honest men; he is for King George and I for King James; but those men in long cravats only desire places . . .'. On the motion for Walpole's removal in February 1741 Shippen walked out of the House declaring that 'he would not pull down Robin on republican principles'.[13] On the same motion Edward Harley recalled Walpole's part in his uncle's imprisonment in the Tower despite a lack of evidence against him, and said: 'I am now, Sir, glad of this opportunity to return good for evil, and do that honorable gentle-

[10]   *The Commons, 1715–54*, i. 70.
[11]   Ibid.
[12]   Lord Hervey, *Memoirs*, ed. Romney Sedgwick (1952; rev. edn. 1963), 169–70.
[13]   *The Commons, 1715–54*, ii. 423.

man and his family that justice which he denied mine' and he then withdrew. Eight years later, the year when Johnson published *The Vanity of Human Wishes*, Harley was described to James III as 'one of the leading men of your Majesty's friends'.[14] On this vote, therefore, some notable Jacobites abstained, and many Tories evidently voted on Walpole's side.[15] While the long-term effort to bring Walpole down seemed to promise a new world, many Jacobite Tories began to have a rather different vision of what was to come. Evidently they did not all rejoice. Johnson's own reactions to Walpole's fall were complex.

Johnson's account of the debate on the motion to remove Walpole, in the *Gentleman's Magazine*'s 'Debates in the Senate of Lilliput', was eventually published in 1743, and has long been recognized as interesting and important. It is generally agreed that Johnson was as much composing speeches as reporting them in these debates,[16] and it has been noted that Walpole's speech in his own defence as given in William Coxe's *Memoirs of the Life of Sir Robert Walpole* (1798), replete with original documents, differs greatly from the speech given by Johnson.[17] Johnson gives Walpole an oration of exceptional power against his accusers and this is sometimes used to suggest that Johnson's heart had never been in the opposition, and that he had always approved of Walpole. This judgement requires some modification. Regarding the speech itself, it has been praised among other reasons for the way in which, at the start, Walpole asks that *all* the charges against him may be uttered before he speaks in his own defence, and for the way in which, in denying that he has personally profited from his great office, he makes an exception of 'a little house at a small distance from this city' that he could retire to 'without remitting my attendance on my office', and of the 'little ornament I wear on my shoulder' (his Garter ribbon) which he sees as an honour to the House of Commons.[18]

---

[14] *The Commons, 1715–54*, ii. 111; Donald Greene, *The Politics of Samuel Johnson* (New Haven, 1960), 129–30.

[15] *The Commons, 1715–54*, i. 45; Greene, *The Politics of Samuel Johnson*, 129.

[16] J. L. Clifford, *The Young Samuel Johnson* (1955), 247–8; Greene, *The Politics of Samuel Johnson*, 113.

[17] Greene, *The Politics of Samuel Johnson*, 128; Robert Giddings, 'The Fall of Orgilio: Samuel Johnson as Parliamentary Reporter', in Isobel Grundy (ed.), *Samuel Johnson: New Critical Essays* (1984), 98–100.

[18] Greene, *The Politics of Samuel Johnson*, 127–8; Giddings, 'The Fall of Orgilio', 99–100.

Only the ribbon is mentioned in Coxe.[19] These are indeed moving rhetorical moments but they were not Johnson's invention. Each is mentioned in Sir Dudley Ryder's shorthand account of the debate, deciphered and first published in 1970. Ryder was a close political colleague of Walpole and one of those who voted for him. Though he gives only a summary account he is a good witness.

It is worth stressing one point, Walpole's request that he may hear all the accusations, because this moment has both oratorical and political implications. Ryder's account shows that the question of whether Walpole be allowed to stay or required to leave had been raised early in the debate. Pulteney, Walpole's great Whig opponent, agreed he must be allowed to stay. After many speeches of patriot accusation, and some Tory speeches of reservation about the way the House was proceeding, there was a pause. Pulteney had still not spoken. Then Walpole asked if there were not more charges against him. Another long pause followed until Pulteney was obliged to stand up and make his speech of accusation, though he may not have been entirely ready. Walpole had effectively challenged him to do his worst, and made it seem that he was not playing fair. Walpole thus managed to cast a bad light on his most serious opponent among the Whig opposition, and one of the great orators of the time. According to Ryder, Pulteney talked for an hour 'in a very irregular and confused method' and raised several new charges.[20] All this shows Walpole's skill in the tactics of debate. It was evidently in the notes supplied to Johnson, who must have seen the political and dramatic significance of the moment. By contrast with the Tories who questioned the procedure against Walpole, Pulteney's tactics made him seem at once an unworthy opponent and yet one of the most probable beneficiaries of the minister's removal. This is one of those moments in Johnson when his capacity to create a drama, to think and feel with both sides of a case, creates a kind of equity. I do not think it means that Johnson was in his heart a supporter of Walpole all along. It is more probable, if we remember Johnson's works of 1738-9, that he shared the Tory and Jacobite sympathy with Walpole in the final crisis of his career, and recognized that he might be supplanted by politicians no better and

[19] William Coxe, *Memoirs of the Life and Administration of Sir Robert Walpole, Earl of Orford* (1798), i. 668.
[20] *The Commons, 1715-54*, i. 90-5; 94 for the quotation.

perhaps worse. This would be consistent with Johnson's later good opinion of Walpole as expressed in the *Lives of the Poets* and testified to by Hawkins and Boswell.

Walpole won the vote but could not last much longer. He had to resign the seals of office the next year. This great event revealed the different aims of the old opposition. Pulteney said: 'now, I thank God, we are out of the power of the Tories' and at once attempted to form a new, wholly Whig, administration. He was, however, opposed by the Duke of Argyle, a recent convert to the opposition, who had a far more radical aim. This was nothing less than to end the proscription of the Tories and to form a 'broad bottom' administration of Tories and Whigs, which, Jacobites believed, was likely to lead to a restoration. Argyle was indirectly in touch with James III, but was not formally committed to his service. Had his ambitions to be commander in chief of the armed forces been realized he might have attempted to emulate Monck and restore the exiled king. His opposition to Pulteney in 1742 seemed to promise all and more that the Tories had ever wanted since the reign of Anne: a broad, non-party, administration to serve the crown, and the crown to be worn by the *de jure* claimant. George II, when he heard of Argyle's moves, was in a 'great fright. He asked the Earl of Orford [Walpole] whether he was to be King any longer or not, and cried.'[21] George was right to see the danger. On 18 February 1742 Argyle agreed to accept the seals of office, but George held out against the admission to the new government of Sir John Hinde Cotton who (we remember) Walpole thought was James III's Secretary of State. With punctilious but fatal integrity, Argyle thereupon resigned, and all the Jacobite Tories with him. Britain had experienced for just three weeks the kind of government and expectation which Jacobite Tories had hoped and worked for, during a period of nearly thirty years.

Government now passed back to the Whigs, and not particularly now to Pulteney, but to Carteret and the Pelhams. The political change, which the author of *London* and *Marmor Norfolciense* probably desired, was checked in a thoroughly traditional way by the authority of the king on the throne. It was probably cold comfort that Pulteney did not lead the new administration.

[21] *The Commons, 1715-54*, i. 71, 51.

These disappointments pointed the more committed Jacobites back to the traditional mode of changing the dynasty: the landing of the rival claimant (or his representative) with a considerable body of foreign troops—William of Orange's successful method. Thus Watkin Williams Wynn declared in Parliament that 'England was made a mere province of Hanover' and Sir John Hinde Cotton 'averred it to be so in fact'.[22] Cardinal Fleury's death in 1743 removed the chief obstacle in France to supporting a Jacobite invasion, and thus the major invasion attempt of 1744 was planned, with 10,000 French troops under the formidable Marshal Saxe to be landed in Essex or in the Thames Estuary, a smaller body under the Earl Marischal in Scotland, and Wales to be raised by the Duke of Beaufort and Williams Wynn. The invasion was to be accompanied by Prince Charles Edward as regent, with a council composed of the Duke of Beaufort, Lord Barrymore, Wynn, Lord Orrery, John Hinde Cotton, Lord Cobham, and some others.[23] This was a serious, large-scale, military project, comparable in its conception with William's landing in 1688. The difference between the two was that, while William's invasion was an absolutely dedicated religious and political crusade against the power of France, Louis XV's plan was no more than a bold and intelligent attempt to open a new front in part of the enemy's territory. If storms had driven back William's ships, he would have tried again. When storms drove back the French transports, Charles Edward was promised that there would be another attempt, but the French were for the time being discouraged and diverted. As is well known, Prince Charles's own minor invasion attempt, although, starting from nothing it captured Scotland and in its march into England threw London into panic, was little more than a daring spin-off from the carefully planned and formidable Jacobite attempt of 1744.

The Jacobite rising of 1745, however, did have the advantage of complete surprise because it was virtually the Prince's own decision. Neither James III in Rome, nor the French authorities, nor the Jacobite leadership in England were informed. It was not what the Jacobites at home desired, and was nothing like the well-planned project they had encouraged the previous year. Unless they were assured of adequate military support from abroad, they could only

[22] *The Commons, 1715–54*, i. 72–3.
[23] Ibid.

see the Prince's expedition as promising disaster for his loyal subjects in England. This is the explanation for the sparse support the Prince received on his march to Derby, attracting only enthusiasts such as David Morgan, and the devoted Non-Jurors who formed the fated Manchester Regiment. There was substantial Jacobite support in England, but those who constituted it were not going to risk their lives and interests supporting what was, without foreign troops, a forlorn hope. There had been too many examples of such doomed loyalty already. They desired a peaceful restoration such as had taken place in 1660. At the same time, the apparent meteoric success of Prince Charles and his Highland army in possessing Scotland, capturing Edinburgh, and marching into the English midlands, after only one battle and that a Jacobite victory, was a real wonder. Those with sympathies for the Jacobite cause cannot but have been bedazzled by such an amazing achievement. In sheer historical drama it rivalled and contrasted with that other great political event of the 1740s: the fall of Walpole. Indeed these two events, the one civil and the other military, dominated the decade.

The poetic record alone shows with what horror the Jacobite rising was regarded by committed supporters of the House of Brunswick. In Ode XVIII of his First Book (1747), Mark Akenside, having reviewed the 'social good' and 'common welfare' established by William III, continued:

> Say, was it thus, when late we view'd
> Our fields in civil blood imbru'd?
> When fortune crown'd the barbarous host,
> And half the astonish'd isle was lost?
> Did one of all that vaunting train,
> Who dare affront a peaceful reign,
> Durst one in arms appear?[24]

It is interesting that Akenside mentions what is often overlooked in discussion of 1745: not that few Jacobites rose in arms for Prince Charles, but that few Hanoverians rose in arms for King George.

More interesting than Akenside is Young's poem to the Duke of Newcastle, 'Thoughts, Occasioned by the Present Juncture', published after Night the Eighth of the *Night Thoughts*, in the aftermath of the Battle of Preston Pans and the high tide of Prince

[24] *Poems* (1772), 304.

Charles's success. 'This political poem might be called a "Night Thought"', suggested the author of the Life of Young in the *Lives of the Poets*, iii. 385: it is a blank verse sermon which takes the Jacobite invasion seriously enough to see it as a divine judgement on the corruption of the times in Britain. Dramatizing itself as a moral vision in time of crisis, the poem seeks to recall politics and history to ethics and religion. 'Aid Divine the Crisis seem'd to call' and

> As, late, I walk'd the Night in troubled Thought,
> My Peace disturb'd by Rumours from the North;
> While Thunder, o'er my Head, portentous, roll'd;
> As giving Signal of some strange Event . . . .

Young has a vision over the white cliffs of Britain, a vision of 'The STATESMAN'S CREED'. It is a plain and indeed obvious moral, emphatically pronounced: 'Virtue, and Vice, are Empire's Life and Death.'[25] Though a Whig poem, it appropriates much opposition polemic against ambition and corruption in its diagnosis of the condition of Britain. Two features of the poem stand out. The first is its portrait of Cardinal Wolsey, fallen from power and royal favour. The second is the way Young presents Prince Charles and his Highland army. Each seems relevant to the poem Johnson was to write three years later, *The Vanity of Human Wishes*.

Young uses the example of Wolsey to recall political affairs to the spiritual. He also writes with an emphatically Protestant tone: thus it is Wolsey's 'Hart, un'Cardinal'd, | And sunk beneath the Level of a Man' which finally grasps true politics; and 'These, are Politics will answer, now, | (When common Men would fain to Statesman swell) | Beyond a *Machiavel's*, or a *Tencin's* Scheme.'[26] This is traditional anti-Catholicism brought up to date. While Machiavelli was probably invoked as often in the eighteenth century as in the sixteenth, the example of Wolsey is a reminder of the Protestant fears of the earlier time. Yet the old enemy is showing its face again: Pierre Guerin, Cardinal de Tencin, was the influential French churchman who had been a protégé of the exiled Stuarts and could now serve their cause. All this leads up to the contemptous vitupera-tion with which Young writes of Prince Charles and his Scottish Highlanders:

---

[25] *Lives of the Poets*, 385; Edward Young, *The Complaint . . . Night the Eighth* (1745), including 'Thoughts, Occasioned by the Present Juncture', 137–90.
[26] 'Thoughts', 123–4.

And shall a Pope-bred Princeling crawl ashore,
Replete with Venom, Guiltless of a Sting,
And whistle Cut-throats, with those Swords, that scrap'd
Their Barren Rocks, for wretched Sustenance,
To cut his Passage to the *British* Throne?[27]

These might be regarded as the merest commonplaces of anti-Jacobite propaganda, but Young is alarmed and outraged at the invasion. It is no surprise that he hates a papist prince brought up in the Papal States, but the facts that he had landed without foreign troops and arms, and was relying for support on hardy northern mountaineers, might have been given a very different construction: one need only recall *Gustavus Vasa*. Young resumes his onslaught on the Stuart Prince later in the poem, revealing:

A Foe, who (like a Wizard in his Cell)
In his dark Cabinet of crooked Schemes,
Resembling *Cuma's* gloomy Grot, the Forge
Of boasted Oracles, and real Lies,
(Aided, perhaps, by second-sighted *Scots*,
French Magi, Reliques riding Post from *Rome*,
A *Gothic* Hero* rising from the *Dead*,
And changing for spruce *Plad* his dirty Shroud . . .)

such a man, he says, with heavy irony, will lay the famous military, Protestant, Britain in the dust. 'How must *This* strike a Horror thro' the Breast . . .?' Young's own asterisk then leads his reader's eye to a footnote that is of great interest:

*The *Invader* affects the Character of *Charles* the Twelfth of *Sweden*.[28]

Young thus consciously reverses the Gothic and Swedish myth of liberty found in *Gustavus Vasa*. This '*Gothic* Hero' is in his eyes the mere pawn of Romish superstition and Scottish second sight: he is a nightmare from the past, dressed in the garb of the Scottish High-lander. The admission of the footnote, which turns on the word 'affects', does much to reveal what Young was so afraid of: a brave and resolute military leader who could face great odds and prevail, who could suffer defeat and yet survive and fight back. The real Charles XII had been a hero in Jacobite eyes. An uncompromising enemy of the House of Brunswick, he had been the great hope of the Gyllenborg Jacobite Plot in 1717, was a brilliant military leader,

---

[27] 'Thoughts', 127.   [28] 'Thoughts', 136.

3. Charles XII, 'the Valiant King of Sweden', engraving by Thomas Taylor, ?1719–29. By permission of the Ashmolean Museum, Oxford.

4. Prince Charles Edward Stuart, mezzotint, after Mercier, *c.* 1747.

inured to hardship and accustomed to share all the life of his common soldiers. He had been the subject of Voltaire's popular *Histoire de Charles XII* (1731), immediately translated into English. In 1742 Johnson had been preparing a drama on Charles XII. He must have seemed an attractive subject to the author of *London*, and *Gustavus Vasa* must have suggested how much better Johnson himself might dramatize the Swedish myth of liberty and military deliverence.[29] Be that as it may, it was not surprising that Jacobite propaganda sought to connect Prince Charles with Charles XII, and it is of great interest that Young, in what must have been a widely read poem in 1745–6, should have seized upon this claimed resemblance as a target for his derision.

II

The later stages of the Jacobite rising seemed only to extend the parallel already claimed. The second Jacobite victory, at Falkirk, was soon succeeded by the disastrous defeat at Culloden, when Prince Charles, like Charles XII after his defeat at Pultava, managed to make his escape to a friendly country only through protracted wandering through largely occupied or enemy territory with the aid of a few faithful followers. When Prince Charles eventually arrived in Paris the duc de Luynes wrote that his appearance irresistibly recalled that of Charles XII of Sweden, the warrior prince.[30] Frederick the Great wrote to him that: 'all Europe was astonished at the greatness of your enterprise; for though Alexander, and other heroes, have conquered kingdoms with inferior armies, you are the only one who ever engaged in such an attempt without any . . . My friend Voltaire . . . is . . . indebted to you for having at length furnished him with a worthy subject of his pen . . .'.[31] When the great European war, of which the Jacobite invasion and rising had been merely parts, came to be resolved in the summer of 1748 in the

---

[29] Samuel Johnson, *Letters*, ed. Bruce Redford (Oxford, 1992), i. 28 (Johnson to John Taylor, 10 Aug. 1742). Johnson may also have known the earlier (and obviously Jacobite) *A Short View of the Conduct of the King of Sweden* (1716). For the view of a modern historian on Charles XII's possible designs against George I, in 1718, see R. M. Hatton, *Charles XII of Sweden* (1968), 473–93.

[30] Frank McLynn, *Charles Edward Stuart: A Tragedy in Many Acts* (1988), 310.

[31] *Historical Manuscripts Commission*, 14th Report, Appendix, Part IV (1894), Kenyon Papers, 474 (1215).

Treaty of Aix-la-Chapelle, France which had at first given the Prince a hero's welcome was obliged to expel him from French territory. Prince Charles refused to agree to leave, and threatened to do as Charles XII had done when surrounded in his place of exile in Bender: defend himself by force of arms.[32] Reports of these comparisons had reached England by December 1748 at the latest: they were probably circulating during the course of the autumn.

In England the meteoric career of Prince Charles and his small army in 1745–6 must have been of compelling interest to the author of *London* and *Marmor Norfolciense*, and of the proposed drama on the subject of Charles XII. The experience was something he would take to the writing of *The Vanity of Human Wishes*. So was the experience of the fall of Walpole, which would have been brought back into his mind when in 1747 he looked at Warburton's *Shakespeare*, and especially that scene which he would describe as 'above any other part of Shakespeare's tragedies', Act IV, scene ii of *King Henry VIII*: the judgement of Wolsey. In his commentary on the character of Wolsey, Warburton appropriated much of the opposition rhetoric which had been directed against Walpole. He spoke of bribery, corruption, and the enslavement of the kingdom, and referred to Wolsey as a 'first minister'. These comments Johnson incorporated into his own deferred edition of Shakespeare, published in 1765.[33] It had been Pope, Warburton's patron and friend, who had teasingly applied the name to Walpole together with the parallel classical name of Sejanus: '*Sejanus, Wolsey*, hurt not honest FLEURY, | But well may put some Statesmen in a fury.'[34]

Thus it was that the two great political events in Britain in the 1740s, the fall of Walpole and the rising under Prince Charles, each lightly connected with a Johnsonian literary project, the drama on Charles XII and the edition of Shakespeare, commanded Johnson's attention in 1747–8. In each case something of what he may have thought and might have written could also find expression in a different literary form, one in which he had already excelled: the imitation of a classical formal satire. In particular Juvenal, Satire X, offered the opportunity of writing about both a fallen political

---

[32] McLynn, *Charles Edward Stuart*, 362; John Byrom, *Private Journal and Literary Remains*, ed. Richard Parkinson (Manchester, 1854–7), II. ii. 466–7.
[33] Samuel Johnson, *Works* (1810), v. 462, 455, 463, 383.
[34] 'Epilogue to the Satires, Dialogue' i. 51–2, ii. 136–7; *TE* iv. 301–2, 321.

favourite and a transient military hero who courted and found defeat. *In The Vanity of Human Wishes* it is not long before the commanding generality of the opening gives way to a poetic idiom more sensitive to human bewilderment:

> Where wav'ring Man, betray'd by vent'rous Pride,
> To tread the dreary Paths without a guide
> . . . .
> Shuns fancied Ills . . .
>
> (ll. 7–10)[35]

This in turn soon follows Juvenal in writing of public matters in a public style. Thus while Juvenal's 'Nocitura toga . . .' (ll. 8–9) is subsumed by Johnson, Juvenal's 'domos totas' (l. 7) is enlarged into something more public and historic; not whole households, or (Johnson's first thought in the MS) 'Families', but 'Nations sink, by darling Schemes oppress'd (l. 13). This brief prospect of national misfortune is, within the first 70 lines of the poem which Johnson appears to have written in one morning, soon altered and enlarged into a scene of civil war. Instead of following Juvenal in recalling some earlier tyranny, Johnson seems rather to have remembered lines from his own *Marmor Norfolciense*:

> Then o'er the World shall Discord stretch her Wings,
> Kings change their Laws, and Kingdoms change their Kings.
>
> (ll. 15–16)[36]

> Let Hist'ry tell where rival Kings command,
> And dubious Title shakes the madded Land,
> When Statutes glean the Refuse of the Sword,
> How much more safe the Vassal than the Lord,
> Low sculks the Hind beneath the Rage of Pow'r,
> And leaves the bonny Traytor in the *Tow'r*,
> Untouch'd his Cottage, and his Slumbers sound,
> Tho' Confiscation's Vultures hover round.
>
> (ll. 29–36)[37]

Civil war and rival kings are perennial, but Johnson's poem is at once general and contemporary. Only three years earlier Britain had

---

[35] Samuel Johnson, *The Poems*, ed. David Nichol Smith and Edward L. McAdam, rev. J. D. Fleeman (Oxford, 1974), 115–16.
[36] *Poems*, 87.
[37] *Poems*, 116–17.

suffered civil war stemming from 'dubious Title'. The word (in the first printing) which clinches contemporaneity as well as generality is the Scotticism, 'bonny', which certainly alludes to the four Scottish Jacobite Lords imprisoned in the Tower after the collapse of the rising (Balmerino, Cromarty, Kilmarnock, and Lovat), three of whom had been beheaded. Once the Scottish role in recent civil war is in our focus, the somewhat archaic 'Vassal' and 'Hind' fall into place in an implied allusion to Highland society; so does 'Confiscation', which was devastating in post-Culloden Scotland. The lines appear austerely impartial (most people thought one title was legal and the other not) but ll. 31, 33, and 36 seem to show compassion for the suffering side, and certainly no resentment against rebellion. The contrast with Akenside and Young is instructive.

The poem now turns away from imprisonment and deprivation to consider the pursuit of influence and wealth. Britain is named in this part of the poem (l. 61); British history resumes the centre of the poem's vision in a passage even more clearly contemporary than the one just considered:

> But will not *Britain* hear the last Appeal,
> Sign her Foes Doom, or guard her Fav'rites Zeal;
> Through Freedom's Sons no more Remonstrance rings,
> Degrading Nobles and controuling Kings;
> Our supple Tribes repress their Patriot Throats,
> And ask no Questions but the Price of Votes;
> With Weekly Libels and Septennial Ale,
> Their Wish is full to riot and to rail.
>
> (ll. 91–8)[38]

This satire on a declining parliamentary opposition alludes sarcastically to the Grand Remonstrance, the prelude to the seventeenth-century civil war. Then Parliament had been over-mighty and done what Walpole had later been accused of: degrading nobles and controlling kings. Now in the years after Walpole's fall the opposition has gone to the opposite extreme: dwindling into subservience and corruption. It has simply fallen into easy and ineffectual habits. Ale was as usual supplied to bribe the voters, but only every seven years. By the Septennial Act of 1716 parliaments had been extended to seven years from three. Johnson would later say of this that 'by the instigation of Whiggism, the commons, chosen by the people for three years, chose themselves for seven'.[39] This measure was crucial in helping the Whigs hold on to office during the reign of the first two Georges. This passage has taken us to the heart of the world of electoral politics in the 1730s and 1740s, very English, very familiar. Beyond the specific judgements it makes, its role in Johnson's poem is to alert the reader to the near contemporary relevance of what now follows: the narrative of the fall of Wolsey.

In *London* Johnson had replaced 'Sejano' (MS), a name suggestive of Walpole, with the abstract and general 'Orgilio'. The bookseller Hitch had then remarked that the character seemed more Roman than English. Now Johnson comes to imitate formally Juvenal's Sejanus (x. 54–113): he chooses an English proper name and an English historical figure as his parallel. This figure, as drawn by Shakespeare in *Henry VIII*, the most national and one of the most popular of his plays in the earlier eighteenth century, had been invoked by the opposition in their attack on Walpole. This is why, after a time, Shakespeare's character was so irresistible a reminder of Walpole, as Warburton's notes witness. Johnson certainly expected the Sejanus/Wolsey parallel to bring Walpole to mind as Pope's collocation: '*Sejanus, Wolsey*' had been meant to do.[40] Yet the Wolsey of this poem is not Walpole under another name. He remains the early Tudor Cardinal and is the example of a great minister within the recognizable structures of England's ancient Christian kingdom. He has so much in common with Walpole because, despite even the Reformation and the Revolution of 1688, England's ancient constitution had not greatly changed:

> In full-blown Dignity, see *Wolsey* stand,
> Law in his Voice, and Fortune in his Hand:
> To him the Church, the Realm, their Pow'rs consign,
> Thro' him the Rays of regal Bounty shine,
> Turn'd by his Nod the Stream of Honour flows,
> His Smile alone Security bestows:
>
> (ll. 99–104)[41]

[39] *Lives of the Poets*, ii. 114.
[40] Christopher Ricks, 'Wolsey in *The Vanity of Human Wishes*', MLN 73 (1958), 563–8; Howard Erskine-Hill, 'The Political Character of Samuel Johnson', in Isobel Grundy (ed.), *Samuel Johnson: New Critical Essays* (1984), 129.
[41] *Poems*, 119.

Unlike Juvenal and Young, Johnson does not open his narrative
with the fall of the favourite; rather the reader first sees him approaching the meridian of his power. The English 'full-blown' and
the latinate 'Dignity' bring together an idea of social advancement
and elevation with one of a flower in bloom. Unlike Shakespeare, in
the speech of Queen Katharine (IV. ii. 33–43), Johnson does not
accuse him of deceit, nor say he was 'ever double | Both in his words
and meaning'. Alone among these four writers Johnson gives us a
vision of the grandeur of power. This is consistent with his manner
of presenting the fall of Walpole in the parliamentary debates.
Nothing is allowed to interrupt Johnson's narrative of Wolsey's
power, ambition, and fall, not Juvenal's insistent questions about
whether the reader shares the desires of Sejanus, nor Young's insult-
ing style. Following out the implications of the term 'full-blown' the
fall comes inexorably:

> At length his Sov'reign frowns—the Train of State
> Mark the keen Glance, and watch the Sign to hate.
> Where-e'er he turns he meets a Stranger's Eye,
> His Suppliants scorn him, and his Followers fly;
> At once is lost the Pride of aweful State,
> The golden Canopy, the glitt'ring Plate,
> The regal Palace, the luxurious Board,
> The liv'ried Army, and the menial Lord.
> With Age, with Cares, with Maladies oppress'd,
> He seeks the Refuge of Monastic Rest.
> Grief aids Disease, remember'd Folly stings,
> And his last Sighs reproach the Faith of Kings.
>
> (ll. 109–20)[42]

As Johnson follows the traditional tragic pattern of the fall of
princes the reader's moral scrutiny moves from the ambition of the
Cardinal to the faithlessness of his followers. The result is a feeling
of real compassion towards Wolsey, different from what is felt
towards Sejanus in Juvenal. Young had shown hostility to Wolsey
as a prince of the Roman Catholic Church: it would lead on to his
polemic against modern cardinals such as Tencin, and thence to his
attack on the 'Pope-bred Princeling' Prince Charles. Johnson impar-
tially saw that Wolsey sought 'the Refuge of Monastick Rest'. Like

---

[42] Poems, 119–20.

Juvenal, Shakespeare, and Young, Johnson has his great minister fall by losing the favour of the monarch. This makes it clear that Johnson's Wolsey, while reminding his readers of Walpole, is no portrait of the fallen prime minister. Walpole had not lost his monarch's favour; on the contrary, George II wept at his minister's fall, and asked whether he himself would be king any longer. Johnson's art here is to see the present in the past and the past in the present. Sejanus, Wolsey, and Walpole, all different yet all with something in common, are seen as a series in the history of the world, marking its realm of politics with a recognizable pattern. And in keeping with his 'extensive View' Johnson's presentation of Wolsey has been Shakespearian in the fullest sense, not just in recalling a great scene from *Henry VIII*, or the whole presentation of Wolsey in that play, but in his combination of judgement with sympathy. Guided by Juvenal and Shakespeare, provoked probably by Young, Johnson responds as fully as any poet and humanist could to the first great political event of the 1740s, the downfall which so many had been hoping for and expecting so long.

Johnson did not follow Shakespeare in praising Wolsey as a patron of learning, perhaps because Walpole had not been one, perhaps because the vocation of learning was to be a major theme of his poem in its own right. Juvenal offered him two eminent examples of learning and eloquence, Cicero and Demosthenes, each of whom fell victim to his political enemies. Juvenal makes it easy for Johnson to teach that the profession of learning is not immune to the dangers of the historical and political world. Nevertheless the choice of William Laud as an English example to bring the account of the life of learning to its climax may seem surprising. Laud was remembered rather as a royalist martyr than a Greek scholar and supporter of oriental studies. Despite his fate, however, Laud was for Johnson a man whose learning led him to serve the British kingdoms as Demosthenes and Cicero had served the Athenian and Roman republics. A paragraph of energetic eloquence and incisive rationality on the subject of military glory (ll. 176–90) now mediates between the death of Laud and the next exemplary narrative of the poem, that of King Charles XII of Sweden.

Here Johnson's text remembers Juvenal's example of a great military commander, Hannibal, the Carthaginian general who, invading Italy from the north, seemed to have Rome at his mercy, before retreating by sea and seeking help from foreign courts. The name Sejanus had been connected with Walpole before Johnson came to write his poem. There was, as it happens, also an association of the name of Hannibal with Jacobite invasion. *Hannibal at the Gates: or, The Progress of Jacobitism. With the present danger of the Pretender* (1712) may have been the work of Defoe. It was answered by *Hannibal Not at Our Gates*, in the same year, to which a revised version of *Hannibal at Our Gates* replied in 1714. Around 1716 Richard Savage, later to be Johnson's friend, wrote explicit Jacobite poetry, perhaps circulated in manuscript. His poem *Britannia's Miseries* drew a parallel between Hannibal and the Jacobite exile Ormonde, a great military commander in his time, now 'Reduc'd to seek reliefe in Foreign Courts . . .': the comparison is entirely laudatory. The Jacobite association evidently survived, for as late as 1749 a poem protesting at Prince Charles's expulsion from France under the terms of Aix-la-Chapelle would praise him as 'A Hannibal, the Glory of Mankind | Fair Albion's Prince!'[43] This is a relatively slight tissue of comparison, but one which, if it came to Johnson's attention, would have helped guide the poet's choice of a modern Hannibal.

To produce a good parallel within the terms of his imitation Johnson needed a foreign commander of phenomenal success, catastrophic defeat, and subsequent exile as a persevering supplicant. The mark of his ambition had to be an invasion. Charles XII fitted his purpose admirably in these and other ways. Voltaire's *History* had extended Charles's fame while also providing a critical appraisal. As a hero to Tories and Jacobites Charles could be thought to continue the faint association of Hannibal with exiled Jacobite leaders. As a Protestant the Swedish king was an acceptable model for Jacobitism, a predominantly Protestant movement however paradoxical that may seem. Indeed it is possible that Johnson chose him, among other reasons, because he afforded so strong an answer to the invasion of the 'Pope-bred Princeling' as presented in Young's poem. Then, Charles, the valiant Swede, evoked those ideas of Gothic liberty and northern valour expressed in *Gustavus Vasa* and its Preface. Voltaire had praised Gustavus Vasa and shown him as

---

[43] 'Verses pasted on the Gates of M. Puissieux', *A Satyr: in French and English* . . . (Paris, 1749), 6–7. See David Foxon, Sect. 46. The anti-Jacobite marquis de Puysieux had become Foreign Minister of France in Jan. 1747.

an ancestor of Charles XII.[44] All this having been said, two differences between Juvenal and Johnson strike the reader. First, Hannibal
was only a general: Charles XII is a king. Secondly, Juvenal the
Roman saw Hannibal as an invader of Rome. Johnson the English-
man saw Charles XII as an invader of Russia. This interesting
divergence is resolved if the parallel claimed by Jacobites between
Charles XII and Prince Charles Edward (now clinched by Young's
'Thoughts Occasion'd by the Present Juncture') is borne in mind.
Charles Edward, heir of a royal house, had invaded Britain. 'Swedish Charles' is likely to have reminded the 1749 reader of Scottish
Charles, especially in view of the early sections of the poem. Like
Johnson's Wolsey, however, his Charles XII is an approximate
parallel with a contemporary figure, not a portrait corresponding in
every respect.

> A Frame of Adamant, a Soul of Fire,
> No Dangers fright him, and no Labours tire;
> O'er Love, o'er Fear, extends his wide Domain,
> Unconquer'd Lord of Pleasure and of Pain;
> No Joys to him pacific Sceptres yield;
> War sounds the Trump, he rushes to the Field;
> Behold surrounding Kings their Pow'rs combine,
> And One capitulate, and One resign;
> Peace courts his Hand, but spreads her Charms in vain;
> 'Think Nothing gain'd, he cries, till nought remain,
> 'On *Moscow's* Walls till *Gothic* Standards fly,
> 'And all be Mine beneath the Polar Sky.'
>
> (ll. 193–204)[45]

Johnson is working in a mode of extreme poetic compression. Much
here seems to draw on Voltaire (for instance Charles's repudiation
of pleasure and luxury) but much is excluded in order to achieve a
bold and simple example (for instance the origins of the hostility
between Charles and the Tsar). The word '*Gothic*' is striking:
conventionally applied to Sweden, it must carry the meaning of
primitive freedom and courage it had in the *Gustavus Vasa* Preface.
As such it somewhat modifies the hubristic egoism of the following
line. Charles is ambitious, but ambitious as a deliverer. When one
turns from the King's Herculean design to Prince Charles's small

---

[44] *History of Charles XII*, 5–9.
[45] *Poems*, 124–5.

anabasis, it is notable how much is applicable to him. Impatient with his father's 'pacific' sceptre, he had in the late 1730s and early 1740s schooled himself through physical hardship to become a warrior. On the abandonment of the 1744 invasion plan he raised arms and troops on his own initiative. Losing these in the sea fight on his voyage to Scotland, he still held to his purpose, and raised sufficient clansmen to capture the northern kingdom. Rejecting Scottish advice and French policy counselling consolidation and the detaching of Scotland from the Hanoverian crown, Charles's controversial march into England was so that 'all' should be his.[46] Line 200, however, can apply only to Charles XII:

> The March begins in Military State,
> And Nations on his Eye suspended wait;
> Stern Famine guards the solitary Coast,
> And Winter barricades the Realms of Frost;
> He comes, not Want and Cold his Course delay;—
> Hide, blushing Glory, hide *Pultowa's* Day:
> The vanquish'd Hero leaves his broken Bands,
> And shews his Miseries in distant Lands;
> Condemn'd a needy Supplicant to wait,
> While Ladies interpose, and Slaves debate.
>
> (ll. 205–14)[47]

The poetry's evocation of winter marches through inhospitable northern terrain may allude to both the greater and the lesser invasion, though 'the solitary Coast' and the exclamation 'He comes . . .' rather suggest the latter.[48] Each Charles meets his moment of defeat: Pultowa or Culloden; each, leaving a shattered army, becomes first a fugitive and then an exile: this is the moment in their two careers where, as we have seen, several contemporaries pointed out the resemblance.

---

[46] McLynn, *Charles Edward Stuart*, 168–74, 124–6.

[47] *Poems*, 125–6.

[48] Charles XII's route, in Voltaire's narrative, is from Dresden through Poland to Pultowa in the Ukraine, never anywhere near the sea. And why should the English poet say: 'He comes' when, historically, the hero marches away from western Europe into the Ukraine? Stuart propaganda reminded its sympathizers of Charles Edward in 1748 by striking a new medal, designed to recall the achievement of 1745, and to assert the Stuart claim during the period of the negotiations of Aix-la-Chapelle (see Noel Woolf, *The Medallic Record of the Jacobite Movement* (1988), 111–12. It bore the head of Charles, Prince of Wales, the date: '1745', and on the reverse Britannia on a seashore with ships in the distance, the legend: 'Amor et Spes'.)

Johnson's narrative of the career of Charles XII of Sweden now concludes with, perhaps, the most famous lines of poetry he ever wrote:

> But did not Chance at length her Error mend?
> Did no subverted Empire mark his End?
> Did rival Monarchs given the fatal Wound?
> Or hostile Millions press him to the Ground?
> His Fall was destin'd to a barren Strand,
> A petty Fortress, and a dubious Hand;
> He left the Name, at which the World grew pale,
> To point a Moral, or adorn a Tale.
>
> (ll. 215–22)[49]

As in his narrative of the career of Wolsey Johnson is unashamedly traditional. Great civil power is uncertain and dangerous; great military prowess brings nothing about, not even a sensational death. Yet within these well-accepted paradigms Johnson's effect is far from predictable. There is a measure of triumphal sarcasm in Juvenal as his narrative presses on through Hannibal's final years to his suicide:

> . . . sed ille
> Cannarum vindex et tanti sanguinis ultor
> anulus. i demens et saevas curre per Alpes,
> ut pueris placeas et declamatio fias!
>
> (ll. 164–7)

Johnson is dealing with a different life and a different death but, though he could have followed Juvenal in calling the great commander a madman, he does not. Brilliantly following Juvenal in the final couplet, Johnson plays down the circumstances of the death even beyond what was suggested by Juvenal's 'anulus': the little ring with poison in it. Voltaire had struck a very different note:

At the mouth of the river *Tistendall*, near the bay of *Denmark*, between *Bahus* and *Anslo*, stands *Fredericshall*, a place of great strength and importance, which is reckoned to be the key of that kingdom. *Charles* sat down before it in the month of *December*. The cold was so extreme that the soldiers could hardly break the ground.[50]

---

[49] *Poems*, 125–6.
[50] *History of Charles XII*, 166.

This 'place of great strength and importance' becomes Johnson's 'petty Fortress'. Voltaire's confident conclusion that Charles was killed by chain-shot from enemy canon gives way to the rumour Voltaire rejects, that Charles fell victim of friendly fire. Johnson's decisions are still more surprising when one looks at the manuscript. There the important Fredericshall was first 'A nameless Fortress' (l. 222) before the revision of the word to 'petty' yielded the line: 'A petty Fortress, and a nameless hand'. Johnson's poetic decision to work for a chastisement of hubris by playing down the death hardly explains his evident impulse to render everything about it remote and obscure. This impulse, I suggest, is to be explained by the likelihood that Johnson still bore in mind the claimed parallel between Charles XII and Charles Edward: at the same time as he contemplated the actual and well-publicized circumstances of 'Swedish Charles's' death he wished to propose a probable fate to which the lesser but nearer Charles was destined, a fate predictable only in its likely insignificance, unspecific otherwise, and nameless because in this case it lay still in the future. In revision, the manuscript version struck the right note of admonition in the word 'petty' and found the right balance between the two invaders. Fredericshall might be minimized into a place of less significance than it really was: it could never be 'nameless'.

One need not linger over Johnson's second example of transient conquest in the 1740s, Charles Albert of Bavaria who was elected Emperor, to see that *The Vanity of Human Wishes* is a highly political poem showing a deep concern with the processes of history. It explores two ways in which a state might suddenly change or be changed: the fall of a Favourite or a revolution brought about by military invasion. Johnson employs the literary mode of oblique allusion, practised by Dryden and Pope, to reflect on the British experience of the 1740s. '*Wolsey*' and '*Swedish Charles*' are not covert names for Walpole and Charles Edward, as I have tried to make clear: they are examples which cannot fail to remind of them when the poem is read in context, and they evoke much of the experience of the 1740s, when many hoped to see a national transformation in 1742, and then in 1744–6. *The Vanity of Human Wishes* is not a poem of generality in the sense that it excluded recent historical events, but is comprehensive in assimilating them to famous examples of the past. The long view thus constructed displays not least the vanity of human wishes as the tragedy of political hope.

It is a vision of the world from which one may turn either to Stoic or Christian doctrine to find a faith with which to live. Johnson's text turns to the Christian religion, though he has at least in common with Juvenal the rejection of chance and the advocacy of virtue.[51]

III

Such an analysis of *The Vanity of Human Wishes* may well be regarded with comprehensive disbelief. Yet it is supported by the anti-Hanoverian character of *London* and *Marmor Norfolciense*, by the obliquely allusive poetic modes established by Dryden and Pope which Johnson inherited, and by the biographical record of Sir John Hawkins and other evidence advanced above. It was no dishonour to Johnson to be drawn towards the Jacobite cause. Jacobitism was a major international movement of the early eighteenth century. If Johnson hoped for a second restoration he did so, perhaps, with a third of the nation. That Johnson's political views would change in the 1750s (or at least grow more complex) is already suggested by *The Vanity of Human Wishes*, which never incites to Jacobite action, but which, in the Tory and Jacobite spirit of many at that time, views with pity the fall of a great minister, and the defeat of a valiant invader and deliverer whose enterprise appeared in retrospect all the more a forlorn hope. Most significant of all is the emotional change from Juvenal's presentation of Hannibal to Johnson's presentation of Charles XII of Sweden, with all the implications which that seems likely to have conveyed to the contemporary reader of Johnson's poem. None of this depends on the testimony of Boswell; much of it, on the other hand, tends to support Boswell's portrait of the later Johnson as one who had been, and who in certain respects was still, a Jacobite sympathizer.

These, however, are biographical issues not strictly involved in a discussion of Johnson's poetry and affairs of state in the 1730s and 1740s.[52] More to the point is Johnson's conception of the poet's rôle

---

[51] Juvenal, x. 363–4; *Vanity of Human Wishes*, 349–68. See Greene, *The Politics of Samuel Johnson* (2nd edn. 1989), p. xxxvii.

[52] After 1749 anti-Jacobite or apparently anti-Jacobite statements begin to appear in Johnson's work, for example the Preface to the General Index to *The Gentleman's Magazine* (1753), partly written and wholly corrected by him, introd. Arthur Sherbo

as it is set forth in his *Prefaces Biographical and Critical* (1779–1781).[53] The *Lives* show the poet deeply involved in affairs of state. Not only those that discuss the seventeenth-century Civil War period, such as the Life of Milton and the Life of Waller, but a majority of the lives consider political principle and political situation. Together the *Lives* constitute an oblique history of England from before the Civil War to Johnson's own middle years.[54] The Life of Addison and the Life of Swift are of exceptional importance in the way they display the first great age of party. A close investigation of Johnson's language when he writes of some of the great revolutions of state during this period shows continuity as well as change. On 1688 his feelings are divided and his insight tragic; his language is tellingly reticent. He stresses necessity, but never claims that James II had abdicated or been legally deposed. Rather he was 'frighted away' and 'irremediably excluded'. On the Hanoverians, he writes of their taking possession of the throne, not of their right, and is explicit about the then persecuted and proscribed Tories. On Walpole, Johnson comes round in favour, bearing out the sense of sympathy conveyed in the Wolsey portrait in *The Vanity of Human Wishes*.[55] On the basis of evidence outside *The Lives of the Poets* it is of course clear that Johnson's political position changed from what it was in the late 1730s—indeed *The Vanity of Human Wishes* may be regarded as gaining some of its tragic power from its being a politically transitional work.

(Michigan State University, 1977); his Introduction to *The Political State of Great Britain* (1756) (*Works*, x. 142–3); and the anecdote of Thomas Cooper (*Works*, x, p. xxx). Once the Boswellian account opens there are, of course, statements to be found on both sides. I think it likely that after 1749 Johnson abandoned any Jacobite expectation, but that his conversation reflected an awareness of the claims of each side in a way which that of a man who had been a steady Hanoverian from the start would not have done.

53 *Lives of the Poets*.

54 This has been little recognized: See Greene, *The Politics of Samuel Johnson*, 221–2, but John A. Vance, *Samuel Johnson and the Sense of History* (Athens, Oh., 1984), rightly observes that Johnson 'on occasion offers information or analysis beyond what is required of a good literary critic or biographer' (104). See Howard Erskine-Hill, 'The Poet and Affairs of State in Johnson's *Lives of the Poets*', *Man and Nature* (1987), 93–113 (there are unfortunately minor uncorrected errors in this printing) and 'The Political Character of Samuel Johnson: *The Lives of the Poets* and a further report on *The Vanity of Human Wishes*', in Eveline Cruickshanks and Jeremy Black (eds.), *The Jacobite Challenge* (Edinburgh, 1988), 161–76.

55 Sir John Hawkins noted the change in Johnson's view of Walpole, *Life of Samuel Johnson*, 514.

The Lives of the Poets not only confirms and throws light on Johnson's political position in his major poetry; it also discloses, in the Life of Milton, the most potent political and poetic influence on the political poet who now seems to dominate the last decade of the eighteenth century and the first of the nineteenth: William Wordsworth. The example of a blank verse epic from a principled republican, something Johnson could never commend however much in that Life he sought to separate his critical from his political judgement, was a powerful incitement to the young Wordsworth. Not Lyttelton and Thomson, 'with clamours for liberty, of which no man felt the want', nor even Akenside with his 'unnecessary and outrageous zeal' for liberty (Johnson's later remarks)[56] meant so much to Wordsworth as Milton. Yet the political imagination of the later poet touched that of Johnson in two ways. Like Johnson he was moved by the myth of Gustavus Vasa arising from the northern mines to deliver his country; like Johnson he sensed in Juvenal a voice and a vision radically independent of the established order. Wordsworth's choice for imitation, however, was Satire VIII, the poem which praises worth above birth, and which argues that the noblest steed is the fastest, on whatever pasture it has been raised (ll. 60–1).

[56] Life of Thomson, Life of Akenside, *Lives of the Poets*, iii. 289, 411.

PART IV

The Politics of The Prelude

6

Wordsworth and the Conception of The Prelude

I

WHEN Vernon describes the 'noble horsemanship' of the young
Prince Henry, before the Battle of Shrewsbury in 1 Henry IV (IV. i.
98–111), his elaborate account not only signals that the apparently
scapegrace prince, frequenter of taverns and low company, has now
assumed his rightful place in his father's army, but offers also an
image of the inherent qualities of command, the command of the
will over the passions, and the command of a king over his people.
The lines are not without their invocations of natural and animal
energy ('As full of spirit as the month of May | . . . Wanton as
youthful goats, wild as young bulls', ll. 102–4) but the horse, though
like 'a fiery Pegasus', shows no sign of rebellion. Anyone who has
seen Sir Anthony Van Dyck's great painting of King Charles I on
horseback with M. de St Antoine, must feel that this is not only one
of the most majestic icons of monarchy ever painted for England,
but also an unforgettable image of the grace and harmony of rule,
explicable yet strange in view of the civil discord shortly to come.
The horse upon which the King rides is powerful but not constrained; the monarch's face is grave and assured; de St Antoine, an
important accompanying figure in the composition, leading the
horse and looking forward and upward, seems to express pleasure
and inspiration in his own subordinate rôle.[1] Van Dyck's equestrian
masterpiece comes of an ancient tradition concerning wisdom and
strength, will and energy, command and odedience, descending at
least from Plato's *Phaedrus*, and the battle of the Lapiths and the
Centaurs on the Parthenon freize. In the eighteenth century Swift,

---

[1] David Bevington (ed.), *Henry IV, Part I* (Oxford, 1987), 247, 108 n.; Van Dyck,
King Charles I on Horseback, in the Collection of HM the Queen.

with his usual analytically painful vision, not to mention his love of horses, recognized in *Gulliver's Travels*, Book IV, that horses were both sources of energy and subjects of obedience—and provocatively endowed them with secular wisdom too. For centuries human society had relied on the horse. The horse drew the plough in the country, and the carriage in the city. It carried the farmer to market, the gentleman on business or pleasure, the cavalryman or commander in the war. It was also a ubiquitous economic and functional presence like the motor car in the late twentieth-century West—except that the horse was alive. Swift, seeing horses as servants as well as masters, the Houyhnhnm master shocked to discover that horses were to Gulliver's countrymen as Yahoos were to Houyhnhnms, had his vision, half-comic, half-horrific, of a revolt of the horses in Gulliver's native land: we may wonder how many shared, in dream or waking, some vision like that, and whether, and in what ways, it seemed compelling.

One who seems to have had this vision, or nightmare, was the 17-year-old Wordsworth. It may have been peculiar to him; it may have expressed a widespread subconscious fear. In either case the image of the horse was to be of some significance in the poetry of political developments in the French Revolutionary period. Here is a prose fragment assigned to the year 1787:

Nay since the hours when in my infant bed with closed eyes I saw perpetually rising before me The face of [?] horses as wild as Lions have the form of [?Men] been [?dear] to me The half formed visions [?of] the long processions of solemn terror been dear [to] me[2]

What is striking here is 'horses as wild as Lions'; even more, the conjectural 'have the forms of [?Men]'. The link between the familiar and the fearful, the loved and the terrifying, is, at any rate, forged by the end of the fragment which, we may also note, opens with what sounds like a blank verse line. Some two years after setting down this fragment Wordsworth imitated the lines about the horse in Book III of Virgil's Georgics (75–94), attempting to convey the physical features of the beast, and his fiery spirit. Writing of the animal's eagerness for war Wordsworth uses an image more explicit than Virgil (or Dryden):

[2] William Wordsworth, *Prose Works*, ed. W. J. B. Owen and J. W. Smyser, 3 vols. (Oxford, 1974), i. 7; Jonathan Wordsworth, *William Wordsworth: The Borders of Vision* (Oxford, 1982), 1–2, opens his discussion with one of this poet's images of a horse, though without referring to the passage from *Prose Works*.

strained like a bow, his [? spine]
Doubles, and unbroken, springing back, he scorns
The Earth . . .

(ll. 14–16)[3]

The horse is envisioned as charged energy, a bow bent for destruction. This is of some interest since the editors of Wordsworth's *Prose
Works* plausibly connect the prose fragment with a verse draft for
The Prelude, *c.*1798–1800, where a vision of 'Processions,
multitudes in wake of fair', of 'Wild beasts, and standards waving'
is succeeded by another of horses, 'Hounds, and the uproar of the
ch[ase?] |, or steeds | That galloped like the wind through standing
corn'. This vision, which includes 'files of soldiery with dazzling
arms', is more fragmentary, horrific, and spectral. Each vision is a
vision of mounting succession ('mounting ever in a sloping line',
'Still mounting, mounting upward . . .') and the second concludes
(save for one word) with 'unimaginable change'.[4] Conjecturally
linked with *The Prelude* (1805), iv. 73, the draft may point forward
to the London or even the French revolutionary sequences of the
poem, though never incorporated in it.[5] Its vision of a terrifying
succession, of energy, armies, mutilation, and 'unimaginable
change' contrasts with the majestic succession of kings which confronted the horrified assassin Macbeth in Shakespeare.

Between the probable dates of the prose fragment and Virgil
imitation, on the one hand, and the verse draft on the other, fall
those experiences, and perhaps much of that reading, which led
Wordsworth to call himself 'a Republican'[6] in the title of his unpublished 'Letter to the Bishop of Llandaff' (1793) and 'a democrat' in
his letter to Matthews on 23 May 1794.[7] Though we should beware
of using *The Prelude* as a reliable autobiographical record[8] Wordsworth's visits to France during the early revolutionary years are not

---

[3] William Wordsworth, *Poetical Works*, ed. Ernest de Selincourt and Helen
Derbyshire, 5 vols. (Oxford, 1952), i. 285.

[4] *Prose Works*, i. 3.

[5] William Wordsworth, *The Prelude*, ed. Ernest de Selincourt and Helen Derbyshire (Oxford, 1959), 533. See W. J. B. Owen, ' "A Second-Sight Procession" in
Wordsworth's London', *Notes and Queries*, NS 16 (1969), 49–50.

[6] *Prose Works*, i. 29.

[7] William Wordsworth and Dorothy Wordsworth, *Early Letters . . . The Early
Years, 1787–1805*, ed. Ernest de Selincourt, 2nd edn. rev. Chester Shaver (Oxford,
1967), 116.

[8] Stephen Gill, *William Wordsworth: A Life* (Oxford, 1989), 56–9, 223.

in doubt, and history in the making must have greatly sharpened his sense of political direction. It is suggested that the young Englishman abroad could only have been confused at the turmoil of revolutionary politics in Paris in 1792.[9] No doubt there is some truth in this. But it should be noticed that two striking political developments occurred during Wordsworth's second residence in France: the Jacobin *coup* against the new constitution on 10 August, and the subsequent trial of Louis XVI as constitutional King of the French. No educated Englishman could miss the significance of such events. As Milton, as late as the very early 1640s seems not yet to have been a fully principled republican but became so, perhaps, after the time of *Areopagitica* in 1644, so public events are most likely to have drawn Wordsworth to a salient but minority tradition of English political radicalism by the early 1790s.[10] It should certainly not be thought that the republican Wordsworth was in the mainstream of eighteenth-century political thought, whatever apologia-like gestures he later made (e.g. *The Prelude* (1805), x. 229–41).[11] The tradition of *The Eighteenth-Century Commonwealthman*, and of *The Machiavellian Moment*, that flowed from the seventeenth-century Independents, and later freethinking and religious Dissent, articulate and provocative as it was in late eighteenth-century England, was not that national orthodoxy for Church and King which began to consolidate itself after 1760. With the ending of the proscription of the Tories and the waning of the Jacobite challenge, and after further challenge from Unitarianism and Dissent, this tradition, remarkably in view of the evils of the time, helped to carry the nation through the French Revolutionary and Napoleonic wars to eventual victory.[12]

[9] Ibid. 60, 63.

[10] Zera S. Fink, 'Wordsworth and the English Republican Tradition', *JEGP* 47 (1948), 107–26, is the starting-point for discussions on this matter; a continuation is found in Nicholas Roe, *Wordsworth and Coleridge: The Radical Years* (Oxford, 1988), and J. R. Watson (ed.), *The French Revolution in English Literature and Art, Yearbook of English Studies* (London, 1989).

[11] Quotations from *The Prelude*, except where indicated otherwise, are drawn from *The Prelude, 1799, 1805, 1850*, ed. Jonathan Wordsworth, M. H. Abrams, and Stephen Gill (1979): the 'Norton Prelude'.

[12] See Caroline Robbins, *The Eighteenth-Century Commonwealthman* (Cambridge, Mass., 1959); G. J. A. Pocock, *The Machiavellian Moment* (Princeton, 1975); E. P. Thompson, 'Disenchantment or Default? A Lay Sermon', in Conor Cruise O'Brien and W. D. Vanech (eds.), *Power and Consciousness* (1969) and Linda Colley, *Britons* (1992).

Wordsworth's own awareness of holding a possibly dangerous minority view is to be seen in what he published during this period, contrasted with what he wrote but did not publish. It can also be seen in the very terms of his discussion, in the 'Letter to the Bishop of Llandaff', originally intended for publication. Assuming, once again, that Wordsworth's first two visits to France made a deep impression on him of some kind, we find confirmation, not indeed in *An Evening Walk*, which goes back to an earlier period of his life, but in *Descriptive Sketches*, also published in January 1793, and largely composed during his second visit to France. Here he chooses to praise the traces of primitive freedom to be found among the republican Swiss, which he had apparently not noticed when he and Jones travelled among them in 1790;[13] and he concludes with a long peroration on liberty:

> —Tho' Liberty shall soon, indignant, raise
> Red on his hills his beacon's comet blaze;
> Bid from on high his lonely canon sound,
> And on ten thousand hearths his shout rebound;
> His 'larum-bell from village-tow'r to tow'r
> Swing on th' astounded ear it's dull undying roar:
> Yet, yet, rejoice, tho' Pride's perverted ire
> Rouze Hell's own aid, and wrap thy hills in fire.
> Lo! from th'innocuous flames, a lovely birth!
> With its own virtues springs another earth;
> Nature, as in her prime, her virgin reign
> Begins, and Love and Truth compose her train
> With pulseless hand, and fixed unwearied gaze,
> Unbreathing Justice her still beam surveys:
> No more, along thy vales and viny groves,
> Whole hamlets disappearing as he moves,
> With cheeks o'erspread by smiles of baleful glow,
> On his pale horse shall fell Consumption go.
>
> (ll. 774–91)[14]

Here, in fact, is revolutionary sentiment. Yet not only is it clear that this is a poet who has not yet found his voice; it is clear also that the use of personification and its widely generalizing idiom gives many

---

[13] *Poetical Works*, i. 325.
[14] *Poetical Works*, i. 88.

fewer hostages to fortune than is the case with other kinds of poetry, or, indeed, than practical political argument.

The 'Letter to the Bishop of Llandaff' helps us reach behind this rhetoric to positions and arguments of a more specific kind. Wordsworth's own judgement of the balance of political opinion in 1793—it would admittedly have been more equal three years earlier—can be found on the first page:

While, with a servility which has prejudiced many people against religion itself, the ministers of the church of England have appeared as writers upon public measures only to be advocates of slavery civil and religious, your Lordship stood almost alone as the defender of truth and political charity. The names of levelling prelate, bishop of the dissenters, which were intended as a dishonour to your character were looked upon by your friends, perhaps by yourself, as an acknowledgement of your possessing an enlarged and philosophical mind . . .[15]

Here is a strong awareness of us and them: the poet is the more offended at the Bishop because his change of opinion constitutes a desertion of the true-believing few (one might compare the Non-Jurors' assault on the deserting William Sherlock in the 1690s). Wordsworth soon comes to the event which occasioned the Bishop's defection from those of 'philosophical mind': the execution of King Louis XVI. Here he rejects pity save the fact that human weakness had forced 'an individual' into the 'unnatural situation' of being king, and declares that 'In France royalty is no more . . .'. He affirms his belief in representative republican principles as best able to secure common interest between rulers and ruled.[16] In response to the Bishop's consternation at what had recently been done in the name of liberty in France Wordsworth adopts an almost Tom Paine-like, Miltonic derision for his opponent:

What! have you so little knowledge of the nature of man as to be ignorant, that a time of revolution is not the season of true Liberty

At a later point he returns to the same argument, this time to deploy an image that would be significant in *The Prelude*:

I must also add that the coercive power is of necessity so strong in all the old governments that a people could not but at first make an abuse of the liberty which a legitimate republic supposes. The animal just released from its stall

---

[15] *Prose Works*, i. 31.
[16] *Prose Works*, i. 33, 36–7.

will exhaust the overflow of its spirits in a round of wanton vagaries, but it will soon return to itself and enjoy its freedom in moderate and regular delight.[17]

In *Descriptive Sketches* the 'pale horse' of death by consumption (cf. Revelation 6,8) was ranked with the forces of oppression; here the fiery horse of revolution has been wishfully rationalized into a horse of instruction. Here for the first time in Wordsworth the horse is used to express the events in France, specifically the Terror, and earlier September Massacres, which Wordsworth had himself witnessed from the provinces during 1791–2.[18] By comparison with the 1787 prose fragment, and even with the *Georgics* imitation, it is clear that the poet's republican commitment has led him, when confronted with events of contemporary history, deceptively to play down the capacity of popular revolution to be destructive as well as creative.

Explicit as Wordsworth was about his republicanism in the unpublished 'Letter', he was more explicit still in the unpublished version of Juvenal's 'democratic' Satire VIII 'Stemmata quid faciunt?' (1795–7). In this poem of Wordsworth, as might be expected, the idiom of both Pope and Johnson is plainly heard:

> A single word on Kings, and Sons of Kings
>
> (l. 100)

has Pope's manner of the later 1730s, while the couplet:

> But why for scoundrels rake a distant age
> Or spend upon the dead the muse's rage?
>
> (ll. 117–18)

has the slower, more comprehensive manner of Johnson. It also provides an interesting comment on Juvenal's Satire VIII which even at a moment of direct address ('His ego quem monui? tecum est mihi sermo, Rubelli/Blande', ll. 39–40) seems to name the dead rather than the living. Juvenal's most notorious target in this poem was of course the Emperor Nero, also long dead. Wordsworth follows Juvenal's lead in drawing examples from the past, and here some

---

[17] *Prose Works*, i. 33, 38.
[18] See George Watson, 'The Revolutionary Youth of Wordsworth and Coleridge', *Critical Quarterly*, 18: 3 (1976), 49–66; John Beer, 'The "Revolutionary Youth" of Wordsworth and Coleridge: Another View', *Critical Quarterly*, 19: 2 (1977), 79–87.

parliamentarian ideology from the seventeenth-century civil war
(and some Bolingbrokeian prejudice from the 1730s) find expression:

> Were Kings a freeborn work—a people's choice,
> Would More or Henry boast the general voice?
> What fool, besotted as we are by names,
> Could pause between a Raleigh and a James?
> How did Buchanan waste the Sage's lore!
> Not virtuous Seneca on Nero more.
> A leprous stain! ere half his prime was spun
> Ripe for the block that might have spared his son.
> (For never did th'uxurious martyr seek
> Food for sick passion in a minion's cheek.)
> To patient senates quibble by the hour
> And prove with endless puns a monarch's power,
> Or whet his kindly faculties to chase
> Legions of devils through a key-hole's space.
> What arts had better claim with wrath to warn
> A Pym's brave heart, or stir a Ham[p]den's arm?

(ll. 101–16)[19]

The republican Wordsworth's view of English history emerges clearly here, and we may note the propensity to attack the *institution* of
monarchy through the attribution to particular monarchs of odious
vices, traditionally so considered. In France Marie Antoinette had
been endlessly, and groundlessly, accused of incest and homosex-
uality; in Wordsworth's text, on the face of it, James VI and I
deserved execution for homosexual proclivities (and of course for
punning and pedantry) while Charles I, a more regularly sexual
man, did not. The poet's management of Juvenalian satire need not,
perhaps, be taken too literally, though given the dates of its composition it should not be dismissed as mere metaphor either.

The Johnsonian couplet quoted above also marks that logic by
which the eighteenth-century satiric imitation is carried inexorably
towards daring contemporary attack. 'Go, modern Prince,' declares
Wordsworth, 'at Henry's tomb proclaim | Thy rival triumphs—thy
Newmarket fame' and, as the draft draws to its close, he links, in

---

[19] *Poetical Works*, i. 304–5.

Commonwealthman's style, the age of Pym and Hampden with the founding of the American Republic.

> Let grandeur tell thee whither now is flown
> The brightest jewel of a George's throne.
> Blush Pride to see a farmer's wife produce
> The first of genuine kings, a king for use,
> Let Bourbon spawn her scoundrels, be my joy
> The embryo Franklin in the printer's boy.

(ll. 149–54)[20]

Probably completed two years before the 'Imitation of Juvenal', *Guilt and Sorrow* (?1791–4), partly published in 1798 as 'The Female Vagrant', introduced a new development in Wordsworth's political and wider human thought. It was one that would reach into *The Borderers* (1796–7), into *Lyrical Ballads* (1798) in 'Old Man Travelling', into *Lyrical Ballads* (1800) in 'The Old Cumberland Beggar' (Jan.–Mar. 1798), and into *The Prelude* (1805), Book IV, in 'The Discharged Soldier' (originally completed Jan.–Feb. 1798). This is the theme of vagrancy, part of a long-recognized evolution in the post-revolutionary Wordsworth towards attention to common life. In this body of poetry there is neither confident generalization about Liberty, as in *Descriptive Sketches*, nor lofty sarcasm about the killing of kings, as in the 'Imitation of Juvenal'. Instead we find a sometimes clumsy but ineradicably serious concern with the happiness and suffering of the poorest common folk, especially as affected by social oppression, national emergency, and war. *The Borderers* is exceptionally interesting in its folklore-like reduction of a baron to near vagrancy and to a vagrant's death, not exactly murdered, but left to die, aged, starving, and wounded, in the winter borderlands. While a sufficient contrast with Wordsworth's polemical revolutionary writings, *The Borderers* does not so much mark a conversion as the beginning of a phase of self-questioning concerning political morality. The drama focuses on the commissioning of the death of Baron Herbert, whether murder, or an act of exemplary justice. Rivers, who constantly urges this killing upon Mortimer, leader of the Borderers, is sometimes considered a Godwinian figure, but is more obviously one committed to the creed that it is

---

[20] *Poetical Works*, i. 305; see Peter Kitson, 'Sages and Patriots that being dead do yet speak to us . . .', in *Prose Studies*, 14 (1991), 205–30.

necessary to destroy in order to create. His favourite flower (an observation made early in the play) is that 'which, while it is Strong to destroy, is also strong to heal' (I. i. 18–19)[21]. His fuller view emerges in his exclamation to Mortimer:

> Happy are we,
> Who live in these disputed tracts that own
> No law but what each man makes for himself.
> Here justice has indeed a field of triumphs!
>
> (II. i. 51–4)[22]

In this situation, 'The wholesome ministry of pain and evil' (II. i. 73)[23] can have full sway. Uncomplicated personal justice for an exceptionally odious moral crime is what Rivers recommends. This crime, the betrayal by Herbert of a living adopted daughter into prostitution, is alleged but has never in fact been committed, as might have appeared through regular course of justice in undisputed tracts of the kingdom. The cold-hearted criminality of much of the aristocracy is not in dispute, but whether an innocent member of this class should be killed for its crimes is an issue implicitly raised by the action. Something of the political resonance of the situation for Wordsworth is probably revealed in the manuscript of I. i. where Mortimer, urged on to the execution by Rivers, says of the Baron Herbert: 'I tell thee he is a Tyrant | And most malignant in hypocrisy'.[24] Personal revenge might be wrong, but in several political creeds, not least that of Jacobin Paris in the early 1790s, tyrannicide was held justifiable.

Mortimer's frame of mind is not, however, straightforward. Confronted by a prospect of killing Herbert he talks of a '*transition* in my soul' (II. i. 92),[25] and is clearly a figure caught in second thought, and later feeling. Motivated to kill Herbert by his love of Herbert's daughter, Mortimer finds this very love an intuition which checks him at the instant of action. Yet when Rivers argues the case for abstract justice, and the perfection of their opportunity, Mortimer cannot answer him. The transition in his soul has to do with a memory of happiness and a growing recognition that reason, emo-

---

[21] William Wordsworth, *The Borderers*, ed. Robert Osborn (1983), 76.
[22] Osborn, 128.
[23] Ibid.
[24] Osborn, 319.
[25] Osborn, 130.

tion, and instinct should move together in any act of moral integrity. Still believing Herbert to be guilty, Mortimer can at most leave him to die. Or perhaps instinct subconsciously suggests the innocence of his victim.

When Wordsworth first published *The Borderers* in 1842, in revised form, he linked the drama explicitly with his experience of the French Revolution. He commented on the way 'sin and crime' could arise from their 'very opposite qualities' and how 'During my long residence in France, while the revolution was rapidly advancing to its extreme of wickedness, I had frequent opportunities of being an eye-witness to this process, and it was while that knowledge was fresh upon my memory, that the tragedy of "The Borderers" was composed.' In the record of comments kept by Isabella Fenwick (1843) he reverted to the question of 'transition in character', not now in relation to Mortimer but Rivers (Marmaduke and Oswald respectively in the 1842 text). It is said to be a phenomenon witnessed by Wordsworth in the 'changes through which the French Revolution passed'.[26] The change from 'Rivers' to 'Oswald' in the 1842 text recalled the bloodthirsty English Jacobin John Oswald, active in revolutionary France in the 1790s, as David Erdman has shown in his important discussion, 'Wordsworth as Heartsworth'.[27] While a corrupt transition of the mind can certainly be seen to have occurred in Rivers, in the 1797–9 text, as in the 1842, the term is explicitly attached to Mortimer/Marmaduke. The drama shows him in bewildered transition from the acceptance of revolutionary violence, an effect somewhat masked by the retrospective remarks of the poet. Far from having been simply a 'witness' of revolutionary 'wickedness', the author of *Descriptive Sketches*, 'Llandaff', and 'Juvenal' seems likely to have had a good deal invested in the character of Mortimer whose awakening compunction prevents him from actively killing his enemy, but not from leaving him to die.

[26] *Poetical Works*, i. 345–9.

[27] David Erdman, 'Wordsworth as Heartsworth: Was Regicide the Prophetic Ground of "Those Moral Questions"?', in Donald R. Reiman *et al.*,(eds.)*The Evidence of the Imagination* (New York, 1978), 12–41; see too Osborn, 18; Reeve Parker, 'Reading Wordsworth's Power: Narrative and Usurpation in *The Borderers, ELH* 54 (1987), 299–331; ' "In some sort seeing with my proper eyes": Wordsworth and the Spectacles of Paris', *SIR* 27: 3 (Fall 1988), 369–99, and Thomas McFarland, *William Wordsworth: Intensity and Achievement* (Oxford, 1992), ch. 7.

This gives us a clue to *The Borderers* as itself a work of transition from a creed of revolutionary violence. Within Mortimer are implanted those misgivings, as yet incapable of rationalization, concerning the Terror and regicide in France. Wordsworth has hitherto, in his unpublished writings, been an apologist for the Revolution including the September Massacres. He now uses drama to open up a wider range of opinion, and indeed something of the moral psychology of revolutionary violence. Nobody should be deceived by the Gothic plot and setting of *The Borderers*; like the late romantic dramas of Dryden it has a suggestive and equivocal relationship with recent political events. The land is oppressed by a cruel and predatory aristocracy which the Crown has latterly failed to control. Only in the ungoverned borderlands between two distracted countries can men of vision, unrestrained by the paralysed institutions of the law, help the needy, and execute pure justice. These geographical borderlands are like those temporal spaces created by fundamental revolution in the orders of history. For the moment neither the rejected authority of the past nor the desired authority of the future prevails. Caught in this exceptional situation is the Baron Herbert, deprived of his hereditary title and lands, reduced to near vagrancy and as vulnerable as a vagrant, allegedly but not actually as cruel and corrupt as the aristocratic order to which he belongs, and rumoured to be about to be restored to his old rank. In the aftermath of the execution of King Louis XVI Herbert's plight is, while not an allegorical allusion, suggestive in the extreme. As Erdman put it: 'the debate over the justice and necessity of the dethronement, trial and execution of Louis XVI is recapitulated in the central moral conflict in *The Borderers*'.[28] Robespierre and St Just, for example, favoured summary execution of the King. The view of St Just was that trial conceded the possible innocence of the King which in turn allowed the possible guilt of the 10 August *coup*, a conclusion unthinkable by him.[29] Herbert's vulnerability remembers the recent regicide and is the touchstone by which the differing moral psychologies of Mortimer and Rivers are judged.

With the exception of 'The Old Cumberland Beggar' the other poems of vagrancy allude to high politics in their concern with the impact of war on the lives of the poor.

---

[28] Erdman, 'Wordsworth as Heartsworth', 17.
[29] Simon Schama, *Citizens: A Chronicle of the French Revolution* (1989), 651.

                    My happy father died,
When threatened war reduced the children's meal:
Thrice happy! that for him the grave could hide
The empty loom, cold hearth, and silent wheel
                    'The Female Vagrant'

—I asked him whither he was bound, and what
The object of his journey; he replied
'Sir! I am going many miles to take
'A last leave of my son, a mariner,
'Who from a sea-fight has been brought to Falmouth,
'And there is dying in an hospital.'
        'Old Man Travelling: Animal Tranquility and Decay, a Sketch'

He told a simple fact: that he had been
A soldier, to the tropic isles had gone,
Whence he had landed now some ten days past;
That on his landing he had been dismiss'd,
And with the little strength he yet had left
Was travelling to regain his native home.[30]

Such allusions to war are unspecific ('the tropic isles' were a repeated theatre of conflict in the eighteenth century) but, Revolutionary France having declared war on Britain on 1 February 1793, and
Britain having then retaliated, these poems were composed and
published during time of war. Their reference to war certainly
suggested the current war in the first instance.

The pastoral and Virgilian relationship set up in 'The Female
Vagrant' (*Guilt and Sorrow*) shows the greater world breaking in
upon the idyllic but vulnerable smaller one of wife and husband.
Forces inexplicable to her abruptly cut off her family from their
living, eventually forcing them to emigration to 'the western world',
where all but her meet their death. This is related by the vagrant
herself, the narrative voice being suspended which, in the larger
structure of *Guilt and Sorrow*, has reached her story through that of
the fugitive soldier. Any implications that the economic process of
war which ended her domestic happiness was unnecessary, even
wrong, rests only on the fact of Wordsworthian authorship of the
poem. Wordsworth's art here is, as in old ballads, to present facts of
suffering without direct moral interpretation. Indeed the whole issue

[30] Beth Darlington, 'Two Early Texts', in Jonathan Wordsworth (ed.), *Bicentenary
Wordsworth Studies in Memory of John Alban Finch* (Ithaca, NY, 1970), 433–7.

of interpretation is raised in the next extract, from 'Old Man Travelling', as Heather Glen has rightly pointed out.[31] The narrative voice which seems to blend the old man with the landscape through which he moves, in an eloquent nature poem, is abruptly challenged by the old man's stark statement of his purpose in travelling. In his reply to his questioner the public world of the mariner, of naval engagements, and the hopeless refuge of the hospital, supplants the meditative voice of the poet. In a more challenging way than in 'The Female Vagrant' the wider world of public warfare breaks in upon the idyllic, in this case not a situation recalled but an interpretation checked in course. Nothing can better the drama with which the bald facts emerge to confront comments such as: '—He is insensibly subdued | To settled quiet'. (In later versions of the poem the old man's words were dropped, and 'Animal Tranquility and Decay' took over from the 'Old Man Travelling'.)

The lines from 'The Discharged Soldier' bear a very different relation with the rest of their poem. Bald and factual as they are, there is no tranquillizing discourse for them to contrast with; on the contrary, the earlier part of the poem conveys something of what the soldier is, creating a sense of desolation which his own words in no way disrupt.

> I could mark
> That he was clad in military garb,
> Though faded yet entire.

Such lines prepare and make subtle in advance the soldier's words and link with the later commentary which they prompt:

> Remembering the importance of his theme,
> But feeling it no longer.

Further, the soldier's statement is, as it happens, balanced. His home has not been destroyed, like the Female Vagrant's, nor is he going to lose a son, like 'The Old Man Travelling'. His dismissal might be construed as ingratitude on the part of the authorities, or as a release from peril. It was certainly a release into penury. But again no social or political moral is drawn, as it well might have been, from this human relic of war. Social and political awareness are implicit, but

---

[31] Heather Glen, *Vision and Disenchantment: Blake's Songs and Wordsworth's Lyrical Ballads* (Cambridge, 1983), 225–30.

give way to what is at the centre of the poem's focus: the mental state of the soldier, and the impact he has on the narrator. This poem will become one of the most telling and memorable episodes of the whole *Prelude*, the soldier, an early victim of the Revolutionary War, seeming with enigmatic resignation to dominate the earlier books of the poem. But it should be noted that nothing in the spiritual condition of this discharged soldier, nor in his reception by the narrator of the poem, relegates as of small concern the public circumstances of what Wordsworth's readers would, had he published in the decade prior to the Peace of Amiens in 1802, have presumed to be the French Revolutionary War: this 'just and necessary' war as Burke had called it in his *Letters on a Regicide Peace* in 1795.[32]

II

The 1798–9 *The Prelude* opens abruptly with a rhetorical question the antecedent of which is never formally identified: 'Was it for this | That one, the fairest of all rivers loved | To blend her murmurs with my nurse's song . . .' (i. 1–3).[33] This question, well known in eighteenth-century poetry and carrying with it a series of heroic and mock-heroic associations, goes back in its English form to Harington's version of Ariosto's *Orlando Furioso*.[34] (Wordsworth carried an Ariosto with him to read during his tour of France and Switzerland in 1790.)[35] The context from *Orlando Furioso*, and from the suggestive analogue in the opening of Milton's *Samson Agonistes* ('For this did the angel twice descend? For this 'Ordained thy nurture holy . . .?' (ll. 361–2), invokes a destined hero or heroic enterprise, apparently in utter defeat. In lines closely following this opening description of *The Prelude*, but dropped after 1799, Wordsworth, thinking of himself, alludes to those similarly marked out by higher powers:

[32] Edmund Burke, *Works* (1815), viii. 121–2; James K. Chandler, *Wordsworth's Second Nature: A Study of the Poetry and Politics* (1984).

[33] Norton, 1.

[34] Howard Erskine-Hill, '*The Prelude* and its Echoes', *TLS*, 3837 (Sept. 1975), 1094; Norton 1. Wordsworth's reading of *Orlando Furioso* is recorded in Duncan Wu, *Wordsworth's Reading, 1770–1799* (Cambridge, 1993), 7 (item 13).

[35] Gill, *Wordsworth*, 45, 431; Wordsworth to Sir George Beaumont 17 Oct. 1805, *EY* i. 529.

> I believe
> That there are spirits which, when they would form
> A favoured being, from his very dawn
> Of infancy do open out the clouds
> As at the touch of lightning . . .

(i. 69–72)[36]

After the addition of the preamble to *The Prelude* as completed in 1805, it seemed obvious that the disappointment in 'Was it for this . . . ?' stemmed only from Wordsworth's awareness of poetic talent so far unfulfilled,

> Like a false steward who hath much received
> And renders nothing back.

(1805 edn., i. 270–1)[37]

In view, however, of the poet's writing in the earlier 1790s, it seems possible that the rhetorical question out of Ariosto had become attached to the revolutionary hopes of 1790, and probable that 'Was it for this . . . ?' in the 1799 *Prelude* referred rather to political dismay than poetic unfulfilment, and thus accorded with the famous affirmation (answering the appeal of Coleridge[38]) with which Part II ended:

> —if, in this time
> Of dereliction and dismay, I yet
> Despair not of our nature, but retain
> A more than Roman confidence . . .

(ii. 486–9)[39]

This was a passage similar in its rhetorical patterning to the opening repetitions, 'for this' being now supplanted by 'If this . . .', 'If', 'If', 'If', 'if in this time . . .' (ii. 465–92)[40]. This concluding exordium

---

[36] Norton, 3; cf. *Samson Agonistes*, ll. 23–36.

[37] Norton, 42.

[38] Coleridge to Wordsworth, *c*.Sept. 1799, in S. T. Coleridge *Collected Letters*, ed. E. L. Griggs (Oxford, 1956), i. 527. It is much to be regretted that only so much of so important a letter of Coleridge should survive as Wordsworth chose to excerpt. On the political implications of this moment, see Nicholas Roe, 'Wordsworth, Milton, and the Politics of Poetic Influence', in J. R. Watson (ed.), *The French Revolution in English Literature and Art* (1989), 112–26.

[39] Norton, 26.

[40] Norton, 25–6.

makes it clear that the 1799 *Prelude* (whether Wordsworth originally envisaged its subsequent extension or not) had as its goal the
consolation available for those who have undergone political disappointment, and the reorientation of faith in—something radical
perhaps for the times—Human Nature.[41]

If the antecedent of 'this' is left undefined in 1799, what follows
the question is notable for its suggestive direction: the recollection
of an early childhood in rural Cumberland by Derwentside.

> Was it for this
> That one, the fairest of all rivers, loved
> To blend his murmurs with my nurse's song,
> And from his alder shades and rocky falls,
> And from his fords and shallows, sent a voice
> That flowed along my dreams?
>
> (i. 1–6)[42]

This recalls the image of 'a naked boy' among the river pools, and
concludes with the related but different image of 'A naked savage in
a thunder shower' (i. 26). [43] There was nothing subtle or recondite
in the choice of this image. From Montaigne to Dryden and Rousseau,[44] it conveyed a controversial sense of primal freedom, with
implications for the origin and nature of human government. If
primitive man had not been born into patriarchy then he enjoyed
pure, perilous freedom until contract established magistracy.[45] The
concept is so pervasive that it is probably instructive to cite an
example from a late eighteenth-century work of political controversy:

But hear, ye sons and daughters of liberty, the sounds which the winds are
wafting from the Western continent. The Americans are telling one another,

---

[41] Alan Bewell, *Wordsworth and the Enlightenment* (1989).

[42] Norton, 1.

[43] Ibid.

[44] Michel Eyquem de Montaigne, *Essaies* (1588), 24, 'Of Canibals'; John Dryden,
The Conquest of Granada (1670), Part I, i. i. 209; id., *Works*, xi. 30; Jean-Jeacques
Rousseau, 'Discours sur les sciences et des arts (1750), 'Discours sur l'origine et les
fondements de l'inégalité parmi les hommes' (1755).

[45] For this classic debate in European political theory see Quentin Skinner, *The
Foundations of Modern Political Thought* (Cambridge, 1978), ii chs. 7 and 9. For the
intervention into this debate of a great English poet, Alexander Pope, see Howard
Erskine-Hill, 'Pope on the Origin of Society', in Pat Rogers and George Rousseau
(eds.), *The Enduring Legacy: Tercentennial Essays on Alexander Pope* (Cambridge,
1988), 79–93.

what, if we may judge from their noisy triumph, they have but lately discovered, and what yet is a very important truth. "That they are entitled to life, liberty and that they have never ceded to any sovereign power whatever a right to dispose of either without their consent."

While this resolution stands alone, the Americans are free from singularity of opinion; their wit has not yet betrayed them to heresy. While they speak as naked sons of Nature, they claim but what is claimed by other men, and have withheld nothing but what all with-hold. They are here upon firm ground, behind entrenchments which never can be forced.[46]

Thus far Johnson will concede the claims of the American colonists. But if the colonists have ever enjoyed the protections of government, whether before leaving England or after arriving in the Western Continent, then the authority of the London government cannot be gainsaid. Johnson's argument sets history and common law above Nature; in his recollection of early childhood Wordsworth finds something of Nature's precontractual freedom in his own early life. The growth of this poet's mind will evoke some of the stages of the general progress of the human mind, as recently sketched, in unmistakably Lockeian manner, by Condorcet.[47] Condorcet opens his *Sketch* with the statement that 'Man is born with the faculty of receiving sensations' and later defines man as '*a being endowed with sensation*' (pp. 1, 231); combinations of pain and pleasure, recognized by reason, later lead him to morality. Wordsworth's whole passage is, of course, infused with the joy of sheer physical sensation. The episode appeals to the tactile imagination above all, in its sensations of warmth and cold, rest and action, 'Basked in the sun, or plunged into thy streams, | Alternate' (i. 20–1)[48] The description works towards the expression of a separate but not individualized life: in touch through perception with 'crag and hill, | The woods, and distant Skiddaw's lofty height' the boy 'stood alone, | A naked savage in a thunder-shower'.

That plunge back to the primal once past, the story of boyhood resumes, 'when upon the mountain slope | The frost and breath of frosty wind had snapped | The last autumnal crocus' (i. 28–30),[49]

[46] Samuel Johnson, *Taxation No Tyranny*, in *Works*, x. *Political Writings*, ed. Donald Greene (New Haven, 1977), 428.

[47] Marquis de Condorcet, *Esquisse d'un tableau historique de progrès de l'esprit humain* (Paris, 1794–5); *Outlines of an Historical View of the Progress of the Human Mind*, translated from the French (1795).

[48] Norton, 1.

[49] Norton, 2.

but the implications of the word 'savage' still reverberate, if with
some indulgent retrospective irony:

> That time, my shoulder all with springes hung,
> I was a fell destroyer.
>
> (i. 34–5)[50]
>
> Sometimes strong desire
> Resistless overpowered me, and the bird
> Which was the captive of another's toils
> Became my prey . . .
>
> (i. 42–5)[51]

Almost unnoticed, packed safely back into childhood memory,
these images of killing, predatory pursuit, and theft emanate from
the 'naked savage'. This picture is not one of innocent childhood.
Boyhood adventure is soon a matter of theft and death, albeit only
of birds, yet with analogies to a cruel adult world ('What! all my
pretty chickens and their dam | At one fell swoop?', *Macbeth*, IV. iii.
218–9). But, as before, the idyllic natural setting and form of
childhood memory control the theme of menace borne by the lines.
This was, after all, no more than the part sporting, part gainful
activity of a young country boy.

In subsequent famous episodes the themes of killing and theft are
picked up in the boy's bird-nesting and noctural rowing. 'In the high
places, on the lonesome peaks, | Among the mountains and the
winds' (i. 54–5) he was 'a rover' with 'inglorious' views (i. 53, 56)—
the episode is to be made more explicit in 1805. In its turn the
rowing boat episode takes up the theme of wrong to tell how
the mysterious forces of nature ('low breathings coming after me' in
the trapping, the 'strange utterance' of the wind in the bird-nesting)
are more powerful and more moral than before. Here the adventure
is cut short; the 'huge cliff Rose up between me and the stars'
and 'like a living thing | Strode after me', so that the boy turns back
in fear. As in all these episodes in Part I of the 1799 *Prelude*,
however, the moral aspect of the account, though developing, is
relatively subordinated, partly in the diminishing of retrospect, but
more through the repeatedly dramatic emphasis upon the alien,
mysterious, but not purposeless presences of Nature: its sublimity or
otherness.

---

[50] Ibid.   [51] Ibid.

The next episode, that of the skating, prompting or prompted by a letter from Coleridge, *c*.14 January 1799,[52] is remarkable in being the first communal episode of *The Prelude*, in 1799 as in the later versions. Opening with sunset and lighted cottage windows, the tolling of the village clock establishes human time and setting. The image of the horse, the first in *The Prelude*, beautifully strikes the mean between untrained and subordinate:

> I wheeled about
> Proud and exulting, like an untired horse
> That cares not for its home.
>
> (i. 155–7)[53]

The pride and freedom of the mettlesome horse, likely to have carried for Wordsworth the associations given it in the unpublished 'Llandaff', do not form the experience of a solitary creature, such as the bathing, trapping, or bird-nesting boy. This skating is a collective sport, and the horse leads on to images of the hunt and headlong gregarious exertion:

> All shod with steel
> We hissed along the polished ice in games
> Condederate, imitative of the chace
> And woodland pleasures, the resounding horn,
> The pack loud bellowing, and the hunted hare.
>
> (i. 156–60)[54]

This, for the moment, is the foreground, but in the distance other presences wait to make themselves felt:

> With the din,
> Meanwhile, the precipices rang aloud;
> The leafless trees and every icy crag
> Tinkled like iron; while the distant hills
> Into the tumult sent an alien sound
> Of melancholy, not unnoticed . . .
>
> (i. 163–7)[55]

---

[52] Griggs (ed.), *Collected Letters*, i. 462.
[53] Norton, 5.
[54] Ibid.
[55] Ibid.

The episode now wonderfully conveys the sensation of individual independence:

> I retired . . .
>
> . . .
>
> . . . . leaving the tumultuous throng,
> To cut across the shadow of a star
> That gleamed upon the ice.
>
> (i. 170, 172–4)[56]

And again, 'When we had given our bodies to the wind . . . then at once I Have I, reclining back upon my heels I Stopped short' (i. 175, 178–80):[57] the skater is not checked in full career, like the rower, but arrests his own course within the throng, and at that moment seems to see the movement of the earth itself in its slow revolution, as his senses slowly readjust to his individual stillness. The notable diminuendo, 'Till all was tranquil as a summer sea' (contrasting strangely with the winter scene and perhaps reinforcing the sense of heavenly motion) is a complete catharsis in the sense that all the energy of social and solitary movement is spent as this serene clemency supervenes. This is noticeably different from earlier conclusions, the 'naked savage' with its potential energy, the haunting 'almost as silent as the turf they trod', and more clearly psychological 'and were a trouble to my dreams'. Here the vigour of the boy has been spent without injury to others, constraint from society, or alienation from it. The vision of physical life in relation to society and nature which this yields, a moving spectacle of freedom, is the fullest human experience yet conveyed in this, Wordsworth's earliest *Prelude*.

At this point it may be asked what has become of affairs of state, those clear and conspicuous political events, the avowed focus of the present book? The early episodes of the 1799 *Prelude* are indeed not political (nor a-political), but prepolitical. They are physical experiences, sporting activities, but with spiritual and moral awareness growing out of sensation and energy. Yet they also have political implications. They concern the primal awareness of the untaught human being ('the naked savage'), the earliest predatory impulses, conscious guilt, enterprise, and rebuff, free enjoyment both social

---

[56] Ibid. [57] Ibid.

and solitary. They contain the germs of political ideas capable of being experienced later in practice, in specific historical situations, later still of being meditated upon and generalized. As a point of biography, the evidence available to us does not confirm whether these episodes are (as presented) close factual and emotional re-cords, or exemplary episodes, loosely based on childhood memory and fortified by more recent experience, designed to explore and respond to current political anxiety and error by offering the early ground for adult political attitudes and belief.

The notable advent in *The Prelude* of affairs of state proper, in the children's card-games of Part I, tends to confirm the latter interpre-tation, especially since the episode was added to Part I late, and it therefore seems deliberately, in the period of composition of the two-part *Prelude*.[58] The metaphor of politics as a game of cards remained fully current: as Burke had put it in his *Letters on a Regicide Peace* (1795): 'What signifies the cutting and shuffling of cards, while the Pack still remains the same?'[59] This is another social episode, and another sport, this time an indoor one:

> I would record with no reluctant voice
> Our home amusements by the warm peat fire
> At evening . . .
> We schemed and puzzled, head opposed to head,
>
>   . . . sate in close array,
> And to the combat—lu or whist—led on
> A thick-ribbed army, not as in the world
> Discarded and ungratefully thrown by
> Even for the very service they had wrought,
> But husbanded through many a long campaign.
>
>   (i. 206–19)[60]

Consistently with the view that *The Prelude* of 1799 is a poem seeking the fount of political engagement in early experience, the card-game embeds in childhood recollection a series of images for high affairs of state. Consistently, too, with the democratic nature of much of Wordsworth's earlier verse, the first reference here is popular, and invokes what we know to have been the subject of the recent, unpublished, poem on the Discharged Soldier (Jan.–Feb.

[58] Norton, 514.
[59] Burke, *Works*, iv. 65.
[60] Norton, 6.

1798). 'Discharged' or 'dismissed' now become 'Discarded' and Wordsworth's narrative reflects upon an ungrateful world that presses its manpower into military campaigns only to discharge it, later, into hospitals or penury. ('The Old Man Travelling' is as relevant here as 'The Discharged Soldier'.) This political allusion is now systematically extended:

> Oh, with what echoes on the board they fell—
> Ironic diamonds, hearts of sable hue,
> Queens gleaming through their splendour's last decay,
> Knaves wrapt in one assimilating gloom,
> And kings indignant at the shame incurred
> By royal visages.
>
> (i. 220–25)[61]

If the plebeian cards in Wordsworth's account carry the allusion suggested, so surely do the court cards. 'Queens gleaming through their splendour's last decay' is an ironic rejoinder to Burke's presentation of Queen Marie Antoinette in the celebrated passage of his *Reflections on the Revolution in France* (1790). Burke lamented the situation of the Queen, 'once glittering like the morning star, full of life, and splendour, and joy', now with 'disasters fallen upon her'.[62] Wordsworth's first response had been to describe the passage with some sarcasm as a 'philosophic lamentation over the extinction of chivalry' in the unpublished 'Letter to the Bishop of Llandaff' (1793). Now he gives the humble card-game of the lakeland children a pastoral rôle in prefiguring the downfall of regal splendour. The poet, one might suggest, had seen and felt the 'assimilating gloom' of Robespierre's ascendency, and witnessed the reaction among other crowned heads at the imprisonment and execution of Louis XVI. Quietly and with some humour, without revolutionary zeal, the card-game marks the two-part *Prelude's* awareness of itself

---

[61] Norton, 6–7.
[62] Burke, *Works*, v. 149. For recent essays on Wordsworth's card-game in the tradition of poems of political allusion, see Howard Erskine-Hill, 'The Satirical Game at Cards in Pope and Wordsworth', in Claude Rawson and Jenny Mezciems (eds), *English Satire and the Satiric Tradition* (1984), 183–95, and Nicholas Roe, 'Pope, Politics and Wordsworth's *Prelude*', in David Fairer (ed.), *Pope: New Contexts* (1990), 189–204. Roe presents further evidence for the currency of the card-game metaphor in the 1790s. Jerome McGann, *Don Juan in Context* (Chicago, 1976), 91–3, misses the point, perhaps, of so salient a late addition to the 1798–9 text.

as the poem of a revolutionary era. The episode has enough in common with other communal sports to belong in the narrative, but is sufficiently different to constitute some kind of pointer to the poet's concern. More, it is a wholly 'artificial' passage: its domestic intimacy contrasts not only with the tragedies of high politics, but with ferocious natural forces outside, where the 'splitting ice', no longer sustaining the delights of skating, sent forth 'its long | And frequent yellings, imitative some | Of wolves that howl along the Bothnic main' (i. 229–34).[63]

The concluding stretch of Part I of the 1799 *Prelude* is dominated by the two powerful and mysterious 'spots of time' episodes, the girl with the pitcher on the Beacon, and the news of the poet's father's death. These, and these two only, are designated 'spots of time' in the poem. Part of their power lies in paradox. Introduced always as possessing some fertile or restorative virtue, their immediate imaginative impact is rather daunting than cheering, and in the 1799 *Prelude* it is especially obvious that they belong with episodes of check and chastisement, such as that of the stealing of the rowing boat. They are located here, significantly, immediately after the recovery of the drowned man's body from Esthwaite Water (i. 263–88).[64] Here is another variation on beauty and fear, security and exposure, fulfilment and denial. And here too is a link between the drowned man, 'such tragic facts | Of rural history' (i. 282–3)[65] and the 'spots of time' in the resilience and resource of the assimilating mind: 'images to which in following years | Far other feelings were attached . . .' (i. 284–5)[66]

Part II of the 1799 *Prelude* turns from the Sublime to the Beautiful, and from Nature to, in greater measure, the works of man. In this way one is tempted to simplify the relationship, and there is some truth in saying so. Thus, in Part II, the 'smart assembly-room' supplants the 'stone | Of native rock' in the centre of Hawkeshead; thus ruins of an earlier age blend into the scenes of modern boys' activities. In each case a sense of specific historical change is introduced, complementary to the more primitive moments generally comprising Part I. This development is, in one way, taking the cue

---

[63] Norton, 7.
[64] Norton, 8.
[65] Ibid.
[66] Ibid.

offered by the card-game; the words and goals of men, some of them
heavenly, are now, in relics and icons, part of the theatre of youthful
life. Competitive impulse, whether in theft, race, or game, is, in this
part, transcended in scenes redolent of a more holy time. 'To beat
along the plain of Windermere I With rival oars . . .' was 'such a
race, I So ended', on a hermit's island, that 'We rested in the shade,
all pleased alike, I Conquered or conqueror' (ii. 55–67).[67] The salient
episode of Part II, the expedition to 'the antique walls I Of a large
abbey' (Furness Abbey), picks up both the energy and the reconciliation of these lines. The early part of this narrative is fresh with
energetic arrangement: food, time, horses. And what emerges from
all this is, first, the sheer physical pleasure and movement—'To feel
the motion of the galloping steed (ii. 102)—and then the presence all
around of the remains of a historic antiquity,

> . . . the antique walls
> Of a large abbey, with its fractured arch,
> Belfry, and images, and the living trees—
> A holy scene:
>
> (ii. 108–11)[68]

The fracture of historical wrong, the revolution that dissolved the
monasteries, is, without concealment, made good by the marks of
peace:

> Along the smooth green turf
> Our horses grazed. In more than inland peace,
> Left by the winds that overpass the vale,
> In that sequestered ruin trees and towers—
> Both silent and both motionless alike—
> Hear all day long the murmuring sea that beats
> Incessantly upon a craggy shore.
>
> (ii. 109–17)[69]

The feeling of the abbey in the late eighteenth century as a place of
respite, 'sequestered', is given in the treatment of the winds 'that
overpass the vale' and the 'murmuring sea' whose energy is heard
but at a distance, beating 'Incessantly upon a craggy shore': gales

---

[67] Norton, 15.   [68] Norton, 16.   [69] Ibid.

5. Furness Abbey, print by Townley, published in Lancaster, in the early nineteenth century.

and sea are here the agents of violent change, and the word 'murmur', while on the face of it having a gentle and lulling effect, is not quite without its earlier sense of a restless and resentful power.[70] Neither wind nor sea violate this holy scene, but the boys on horseback do:

> Our steeds remounted, and the summons given,
> With whip and spur we by the chantry flew
> In uncouth race, and left the cross-legged knight
> And the stone abbot, and that single wren
> Which one day sang so sweetly in the nave
> Of the old church that, though from recent showers
> The earth was comfortless, and, touched by faint
> Internal breezes, from the roofless walls
> The shuddering ivy dripped large drops, yet still
> So sweetly 'mid the gloom the invisible bird
> Sang to itself that there I could have made
> My dwelling-place, and lived for ever there,
> To hear such music. Through the walls we flew
> And down the valley, and, a circuit made
> In wantonness of heart . . .
>
> (ii. 118–32)[71]

This is much more than a picturesque backdrop for a further episode of rural sports. The 'smooth green turf' is, in a way, a field of energies in which old things and young life assume a dynamic relation one with another. The rough vigour of the boys on horseback is in dramatic counterpoint to the cold, still, and silent effigies of 'the stone abbot' and 'the cross-legged knight', icons of a feudal order, fallen supremacies. As Wordsworth was to put it in his 'Reply to Mathetes': 'Youth has its own wealth and independence; it is rich in health of Body and animal spirits . . . above all . . . in the possession of Time, and the accompanying consciousness of Freedom and Power.'[72] Knight and abbot, the life of action and the life of God, once had their power too, but, sketched in here with the most delicate sensibility, is a Protestant awareness, in which to disturb, if not desecrate, images and 'holy scene', by 'whip and spur' and the

---

[70] Cf. Milton, *Paradise Lost*, iv. 1015; and Dryden, *Absalom and Achitophel*, l. 45.
[71] Norton, 16–17.
[72] *Prose Works*, ii. 13.

impetuous pleasure of youth, is the purest freedom. Shakespeare, alluding to the more recently despoiled monasteries, wrote of 'Bare ruined choirs, where late the sweet birds sang';[73] here the voice sounding from amidst what we think of for the first time in the passage as the horrors of antiquity—'The shuddering ivy dripped large drops'—is not that of the monks of ancient devotion, but of 'the single wren', 'the invisible bird'. In a brilliant intervention of nature poetry, 'the invisible bird' is witness to the invisible world for which the church was originally built. A voice of Nature, in the song of the wren, seems to fulfil the vocation desecrated by history. It transcends the impetuous but harmless violation of the horseriders and leads to the 'still spirit of the evening air' which inspires them on the steeps of the hills or when, in a final assertion of physical power, '[they] beat with thundering hoofs the level sand' (ii. 39).[74]

The political implications of this episode are rather more than latent, though they will in any case be recalled at two more explicitly political moments, the visit to the Grande Chartreuse and the news of the death of Robespierre, in the later *Prelude* (1805: vi. 414–25; 1850: vi. 407–89; 1805: 559–67).[75] Taken as a whole it is an image of historical revolution, in which the young express their freedom from the past though they do it no wrong. Indeed they may keep some larger faith, within a natural spirit of overthrow and survival, licensing iconoclasm within a larger reverence.

Part II of the 1799 *Prelude* moves through further scenes of youthful life in a partly man-made and social environment to a summarizing personification skilfully stripped of the poetic dress which would have rendered it 'poetical' in much of the verse of the late eighteenth century: 'Blessed the infant babe . . . | Nursed in his mother's arms . . .'. The expressive unvatic idiom of this crescendo is partly achieved by the enhanced presence here of Coleridge as the addressee ('Thou my friend, art one | More deeply read in thy own thoughts . . . (ii. 249–67; cf. i. 447–9), partly by the well-judged prosaic parentheses and explanations: 'For with my best conjectures I would trace | The progress of our being—' (ii. 267–9).[76] There is a

---

[73] The probable recollection of Shakespeare's Sonnet 73, l. 4, is noted by Jonathan Wordsworth, *William Wordsworth*, 118–19. On this scene in *The Prelude*, see Geoffrey Hartman, *The Unremarkable Wordsworth* (1987), 10–11.

[74] Norton, 17.

[75] Norton, 208–11, 388.

[76] Norton, 20, corrected by the Cornell Edition.

convincing feeling of having arrived at a source of wisdom even as such explanation is sceptically disclaimed ('who shall parcel out | His intellect . . . Who that shall point as with a wand, and say | "This portion of the river of my mind | Came from yon fountain" ' (ii. 242–9).[77] What 'hath no beginning', Wordsworth writes to Coleridge, is here given a peculiarly Coleridgeian form, picking up the theme of infancy and parenthood from many of Coleridge's poems, notably 'Frost at Midnight' to which Wordsworth will shortly allude. This turning to Coleridge as in the mode of a conversation poem takes on further meaning as Wordsworth reaches the overtly political peroration of his work:

> If in my youth I have been pure in heart,
> If, mingling with the world, I am content
> With my own modest pleasures, and have lived
> With God and Nature communing, removed
> From little enmities and low desires,
> The gift is yours; if in these times of fear,
> This melancholy waste of hopes o'erthrown,
> If, 'mid indifference and apathy
> And wicked exultation, when good men
> On every side fall off we know not how
> To selfishness, disguised in gentle names
> Of peace and quiet and domestic love—
> Yet mingled, not unwillingly, with sneers
> On visionary minds—if, in this time
> Of dereliction and dismay, I yet
> Despair not of our nature, but retain
> A more than Roman confidence, a faith
> That fails not, in all sorrow my support,
> The blessing of my life, the gift is yours
> Ye mountains, thine O Nature.

(ii. 473–92)[78]

The argument of this passage, and even some of the keywords ('domestic', 'visionary') coincides with, if it does not necessarily derive from, Coleridge's letter to Wordsworth of c.10 September 1799, of which, unfortunately, the well-known fragment is all that has been preserved:

[77] Norton, 19–20.   [78] Norton, 26.

I wish you would write a poem, in blank verse, addressed to those, who, in consequence of the complete failure of the French Revolution, have thrown up all hopes of the amelioration of mankind, and are sinking into an almost epicurean selfishness, disguising the same under the soft titles of domestic attachment and contempt for visionary *philosophes*. It would do great good, and might form a part of 'The Recluse,' for in my present mood I am wholly against the publication of any small poems.[79]

If this request arrived soon after the date stated, and without anticipation in earlier correspondence or conversation, it came perfectly to cap Wordsworth's emerging design. His peroration seems to arise naturally from the body of the poem, the chief episodes of which powerfully militate against apathy and despondency. The rhetoric of the poem flows between 'Was it for this?' and 'Ah, not in vain . . .' (i. 1, 130).[80] To speak of 'the sudden entrance into the poem of a concern with "hopes o'erthrown" ', as the Norton editors do,[81] is to ignore the emotion of 'Was it for this . . . ?' at the outset, a lament not identified in the 1799 text with poetic unfulfilment.

We should beware of assuming that Coleridge had hitherto no idea of what Wordsworth was doing in the 1799 *Prelude*, or that the suggestion of the younger poet was totally novel to the recipient. Torn from its original context it may seem to have a rather contrived aptness, but however that may be the two poets had at this time minds well attuned to one another's concerns. Further, several passages of what came to be the 1799 *Prelude*, including the rowing boat and skating episodes, were sent to Coleridge by Dorothy Wordsworth when all three were in Germany. Thus when Coleridge requested a poem 'in blank verse' he will not only have had in mind the quasi-philosophic vein and mental preoccupation of 'Tintern Abbey' but the most recent—and finest—examples of blank verse from Wordsworth's hand. Is it too much to suppose that Coleridge saw, in the check to adventure in the rowing boat episode, and the alternation of communal and solitary in the skating, something that bore upon political engagement and disappointment? I think not, for in Coleridge's own *France: An Ode* (1798) the liberty betrayed when revolutionary France invades that fountain-source of free-

[79] Coleridge, *Collected Letters*, i. 527.
[80] Norton, 1, 4.
[81] Norton, 26.

dom, republican Switzerland, withdraws into the spaces and energies of Nature:

> Thou speedest on thy subtle pinions,
> The guide of homeless winds, and playmate of the waves!
> And there I felt thee!—on that sea-Cliff's verge,
>   Whose pines, scarce travelled by the breeze above,
> Had made one murmur with the distant surge!
> Yes, while I stood and gazed, my temples bare,
> And shot my being through earth, sea, and air,
>   Possessing all things with intensest love,
>   O Liberty! my spirit felt thee there.
>
> (ll. 97–105)[82]

By comparison with Coleridge's total turn in this ode, from the arena of history to the world of Nature, Wordsworth, in the early *Prelude* episodes, presents human and natural far more closely intertwined. In so doing he explores the blending of public, personal, and instinctive within experience more fully, and in a way more able to meet the challenge of Coleridge's request.

To return to the psychological and political image of the horse, considered at the opening of this chapter, how may we characterize the horses in the boys' expedition to Furness Abbey? The answer, it may be thought, discloses something of the relation of historical, personal, and natural in Wordsworth. Living creatures that gallop, graze, and pause for breath, they are more than merely mounts, borrowed from an innkeeper. They are extensions of the energies and exploring enterprise of their riders; their speed can be produced by whip and spur, they can be directed, but their momentum and power become, temporarily, those of youth, those of the poet, when

> We beat with thundering hoofs the level sand.

They will not always convey such harmonious energy.

---

[82] S. T. Coleridge, *Complete Poetical Works*, ed. E. H. Coleridge (Oxford, 1912), i. 247.

7
Experiencing Revolution

HOWEVER well attuned and prescient Coleridge's request of September 1799 may have been, it is obvious that it sketched the project to which Wordsworth finally addressed himself in the production of *The Prelude* of 1805. Perhaps urging Wordsworth towards Coleridge's own political judgement, the younger poet had roundly specified 'the complete failure of the French Revolution' as the occasion to be addressed, and recommended a long (at least not a small) poem: a poem presumably capacious and flexible enough to encompass striking historical change and the accompanying revolutions of thought and feeling within the mind. The thirteen-book *Prelude*, completed just after mid-May 1805, longer even than Coleridge is likely to have envisaged, includes three French revolutionary books, and fully explores the impact of revolution and ensuing war on the mind of the poet.[1]

Yet this extension of the poem, so clear in retrospect, must have appeared very different to Wordsworth himself in the earliest years of the new century. To him at least the post-revolutionary *occasion* of *The Prelude* did not necessarily, or at first, entail an account of his French revolutionary experience. His decision from early in 1804 to develop the work aimed first at a five-book model. This traced the poet's life to the summer of 1791, omitting his visit to France and the Alps in 1790, and concluding in Book V with his description of his ascent of Snowdon (recently composed) and the two 'spots of time' episodes, originally located in Part I of *The Prelude* of 1799. In this last disposition we can see Wordsworth's

---

[1] To engage in an extended discussion of *The Prelude* is not only to recognize the prolific body of recent criticism, but to acknowledge a general obligation to some salient earlier works, hardly remembered in the more recent studies: John Jones, *The Egotistical Sublime* (1954); Edmund Burke, *A Philosophical Enquiry into ... Our Ideas of the Sublime and Beautiful*, ed. J. T. Boulton (1958); Herbert Lindenberger, *On Wordsworth's Prelude* (Princeton, 1963); Carl Woodring, *Politics in English Romantic Poetry* (Cambridge, Mass., 1970).

recognition of the special importance of these episodes, and his first decisive break into a non-chronological design.[2]

It is hard to say when, and how, the design for the five-book *Prelude* was abandoned, but some probabilities may be proposed. On the same day, 6 March 1804, Wordsworth wrote to both Coleridge and De Quincy about the progress of the poem. To Coleridge, who was in ill-health, preparing to go abroad, perhaps expecting death, Wordsworth announced that he had 'positively arrived at the subject I spoke of in my last. When this next book is done, which I shall begin in two or three days time, I shall consider the work as finished'.[3] This communication seems premised on the five-book plan. Yet writing the same day to De Quincey, and again speaking unambiguously about the poem 'on my own life', Wordsworth only asserts that the poem 'is better [than] half complete, viz., 4 books . . .'.[4] It seems probable that Wordsworth, stricken with concern for the friend to whom he owed so much,[5] held back from him the news that the poem of which Coleridge might think himself almost the only begetter, was to be yet further postponed and extended. What we learn from this is that the notion of extending *The Prelude* to include the French Revolution was probably not conceived in March 1804 and must go back earlier.[6] Wordsworth now worked astonishingly fast. In the same month he began *The Prelude*, Book VI, he probably went on at once to the other French revolutionary books, Book IX and the first half of Book X. There thus emerged, in only fourteen further months, the 1805 *Prelude*, completed just after mid-May 1805, and now containing the long preamble in Book I to the question: 'Was it for this . . .?', the French revolutionary experience laid like a charge in the middle and later books, the 'spots of time' episodes placed as retrospects, in the

[2] *The Prelude*, 1799, 1805, 1850, ed. Jonathan Wordsworth, M. H. Abrams, and Stephen Gill (1979), 516–17; Stephen Gill, *William Wordsworth: A Life* (Oxford, 1989), 232. See too Alan Liu, *Wordsworth: The Sense of History* (Stanford, Calif., 1989), 398 (2nd para.).

[3] William Wordsworth and Dorothy Wordsworth, *Early Letters . . . The Early Years, 1787–1805*, ed. Ernest de Selincourt, 2nd rev. edn., Chester Shaver (Oxford, 1967), i. 386.

[4] *EY* i. 370.

[5] Cf. *EY* i. 379–80.

[6] That is to say, it must have been implicit in his taking seriously Coleridge's letter of *c.*10 Sept. 1799; S. T. Coleridge, *Collected Letters*, ed. E. L. Griggs (Oxford, 1956), 527.

post-revolutionary narrative, and the account of the ascent of Snowdon (also out of its chronological order) now the concluding episode.

Bald enough in summary, Wordsworth's decision to include his
French experience in *The Prelude* was one of the most momentous
of his literary career, comparable to Milton's decision in the year of
Oliver Cromwell's death to develop his projected drama 'Adam
Unparadised' into an epic with Satan in the pagan heroic rôle. In
each case an earlier literary project was opened up to historical
experience of a dramatically controversial interest. In each case an
involvement of idealism with political power afforded both a motive
for concealment and an exceptional opportunity for art. How did
Wordsworth come to take this decision? The answer must depend
on the poet's motive in presenting the French material. Was it in
order to convey a recantation of those earlier democratic and republican sentiments, known to his friends, and clear to those who
remembered *Descriptive Sketches* and 'Salisbury Plain?' Was it
autobiographical expression to challenge the whole generation of
recanters by affirming the validity of his original hopes in revolutionary France? Or was it, perhaps, to deny what Coleridge had
called 'the total failure of the French Revolution'? One thing at least
is clear, on biographical as on literary grounds: Wordsworth held no
brief for later revolutionary France. Indeed events after the collapse
of the Peace of Amiens, the protracted French invasion scare, and
the rise and conduct of Napoleon Bonaparte, First Consul after his
coup of November 1799, proclaimed Emperor of the French in May
1804, leave little doubt as to what Wordsworth thought about the
aftermath of the original revolution. On 3 October 1803, during the
invasion threat, Wordsworth enrolled with the military volunteers
of Grasmere and wore their uniform.[7] On Christmas Day 1804
Dorothy Wordsworth wrote to Lady Beaumont that: 'I grieve for
your anxiety and distress about your Sister, and for her sake I hate
if possible more intensely that cruel and foolish Emperor'.[8] In Book
X of the 1805 *Prelude* Wordsworth would compare the crowning of
Napoleon by Pope Pius VII to 'the dog | Returning to his vomit' (ll.
932–5): he was quoting from 2 Peter 2: 22 (as well perhaps as
Shakespeare's 2 Henry IV, 1. iii. 97–100) and thinking of the French

[7] Gill, *Wordsworth*, 233.   [8] *EY* 428.

people. Some words three verses earlier in the Epistle of Peter may
have seemed applicable: 'While they promise them liberty, they
themselves are the servants of corruption.'

It may be suggested that while Wordsworth recanted his political
and historical naïvety, his complicity, even, in historical evil, he did
not mean to repudiate all the principles behind his early revolutionary hopes. At this point in Wordsworth's life pamphlet evidence
(such as the 'Letter to the Bishop of Llandaff') is not to be had.
While Coleridge had recanted early and courageously, but would
later dissemble his Jacobin phase; while Southey changed his political views in a longer, more wavering, but equally public course;
Wordsworth, having refrained from publishing his own Jacobin
works,[9] now proposed to express what he had learned in a poetic
and semi-autobiographical *narrative*, thinking, perhaps, that only
thus might he do justice to the complexity of his political experience.
And this narrative he did not intend to publish until the distant
future. It was, however, read to Coleridge; on 4 January 1804, on a
remote Grasmere fell, Wordsworth read aloud to him Part II of the
1799 *Prelude*. In January 1807 Wordsworth completed his reading
of the thirteen-book *Prelude* to Coleridge and other friends. Coleridge's poem 'To William Wordsworth' (in its earliest version)
preserves something of the younger poet's immediate response. It is
interesting that, in the opening paragraph, he focuses on France:

> Now in thy hidden Life; and now abroad,
> Mid festive Crowds, *thy* brows too garlanded,
> A Brother of the Feast: of *Fancies* fair,
> Hyblaean Murmurs of poetic Thought,
> Industrious in its Joy, by lilied Streams
> Native or outland, Lakes and famous Hills!
> Of more than Fancy, of the Hope of Man
> Amid the tremor of a Realm aglow—
> Where France in all her Towns lay vibrating,
> Ev'n as a Bark becalm'd on sultry seas

---

[9] The term is admittedly general, but does not seem misapplied. Neither the
'Letter' nor the 'Juvenal' stress the need for constitutional process in the execution of
kings, the most crucial issue in the earlier 1790s over which Girondin had been at
odds with Jacobin. On the other hand the former work does recognize and seek to
excuse some wildness in the Revolution. For related senses of 'Jacobin' see Simon
Schama, *Citizens* (1989), 715–17, Nicholas Roe, *Wordsworth and Coleridge: The
Radical Years* (Oxford, 1988), 77–8, 138–9, and Gill, *Wordsworth*, 63–4 n.

> Beneath the voice from Heaven, the bursting Crash
> Of Heaven's immediate thunder! when no Cloud
> Is visible, or Shadow on the Main!
> Ah! soon night roll'd on night, and every Cloud
> Open'd its eye of Fire: and Hope aloft
> Now flutter'd, and now toss'd upon the Storm
> Floating! Of Hope afflicted, and struck down,
> Thence summon'd homeward—homeward to thy Heart[10]

In the frenzied and florid gestures of this passage we can see the importance for Coleridge of Wordsworth having been part of the early Revolution, 'A Brother of the Feast'. We can see too how cataclysmic events in affairs of state were, in response to Wordsworth's poem, expressed through images of Nature: sea, storm, and thunder—and the heart of man. These reactions, to Books VI and IX–X most obviously, suggest the way in which we should read *The Prelude*. The remaining sections of this chapter will therefore read the 1805 poem in its historic and political aspects, but always attending, as the nature of the work requires, to the subtle relationship it proposes between public, personal, and physical life, between history and nature.

I

Readers of the 1799 *Prelude* find much in common with Books I and II of the 1805 poem. To begin with, therefore, I shall consider 1805's changes to the 1799 *Prelude* in the light of the new, larger, structure. First, we encounter the long 'glad preamble' (1805: vii. 4) to the 1799 *Prelude* question, 'Was it for this? . . .'. It could not, I think, be argued that that abrupt and enigmatic original start is, in itself, a satisfactory opening to a well-thought-out poem. The hypothesis that 'this' in the opening question is what Wordsworth later in the same text called 'This melancholy waste of hopes o'erthrown', though biographically probable, cannot be fully demonstrated in terms of the coherence of the 1799 poem. A passage of 270 lines was therefore added as a preface to the question. It concludes, with a

---

[10] S. T. Coleridge, *Complete Poetical Works*, ed. E. H. Coleridge (Oxford, 1912), ii. 101–2.

New Testament invocation, in a confession in Miltonic and New Testament terms:[11]

> That I recoil and droop, and seek repose
> In indolence from vain perplexity,
> Unprofitably travelling towards the grave,
> Like a false steward who hath much received
> And renders nothing back.
>
> (1805: i. 267–71)[12]

One reaction to this might be to say that Wordsworth rejects the explicit political opening really required by 'Was it for this?'—and by Coleridge's 1799 letter—in favour of an opening that is merely literary. 'But who shall parcel out | His intellect by geometric rules . . .?' (1799: ii. 242–3). A more deliberate and spacious orchestration of the poet's major themes is now appropriate, and if we look at the nature of the literary ambitions expressed in the preamble we shall notice that its epic projects—and much of its personal expression—sound the note of liberty.

Personal freedom is the blessing of the breeze as the 1805 *Prelude* opens. A walled city, with London, Goslar, perhaps contributing to the metaphor, is set up as an emblem of servitude. Literary echoes are at the same time activated: of Coleridge's 'Frost at Midnight', where the poet confesses and affirms: 'For I was reared | In the great city, pent 'mid cloisters dim, | And saw nought lovely but the sky and stars. | But *thou*, my babe shalt wander like a breeze . . .' (ll. 51–4)[13] which in its turn recalls the poet and poem so often in the mind of Wordsworth in this part of *The Prelude*:

> As one who long in populous city pent,
> Where houses thick and sewers annoy the air,
> Forth issuing on a summer's morn to breathe
> Among the pleasant villages and farms
> Adjoined, from each thing met conceives delight . . .
> (*Paradise Lost*, ix. 445–9)[14]

---

[11] John Woolford, in observing a source in *Samson Agonistes* for 'Was it for this . . .?' ('*The Prelude* and its Echoes', *TLS* 3822 (6 June 1975), 627) has helped focus the numerous Miltonic echoes in the opening of the 1805 *Prelude*. See too Gill, *Wordsworth*, 231.

[12] Norton, 42.

[13] *Poems*, ed. Coleridge, i. 242.

[14] John Milton, *Poems*, ed. John Carey and Alastair Fowler (1968), 883.

If 'Frost at Midnight' is the primary reference here, the knowledge that Milton's lines present the experience of Satan in Eden is not prominently recalled: only some premonition of disaster to come—what freedom without check turns out to be—is intimated by the allusion. Meanwhile Wordsworth's diction is politically strong: 'captive', 'bondage', 'prison'; 'set free', 'enfranchised and at large'; 'Joyous, nor scared at its own liberty' (i. 5–9, 16).[15] Because the abstract principle of liberty is here, in spontaneous manner, presented in individual experience, the effect is far more telling than the introduction of Liberty in *Descriptive Sketches*. Further on in the preamble, the same note is sounded, though now in a new setting:

> So, like a peasant, I pursued my road
> Beneath the evening sun, nor had one wish
> Again to bend the sabbath of that time
> To a servile yoke.
>
> (i. 110–13)[16]

Even in this context, with the 'banded host' of the poet's inspirations and ambitions all 'dispersed', and the poet just a man, the choice of the *peasant* as an image of one who can follow his own pleasure and freedom on sabbath dispensation is notable. It must spring from Wordsworth's early revolutionary hopes and experience, yet to be recounted in *The Prelude*. This image of the peasant freed confirms something that has already been intimated, the great metaphor of the journey in *The Prelude*, whether a journey home or abroad. Movement in this poem is of many kinds: travel on horseback or on foot, the narrative that seems to flow down as naturally as a river, the pleasant vagrancy where, as here, there is nevertheless something in common with those who, like the Discharged Soldier, walk the roads from necessity. Such movements can in the long run seem providentially guided: we notice how the 1850 *Prelude* transforms the 'peasant' to the more Miltonic 'home-bound labourer' ('The world was all before them . . .' *Paradise Lost* xii. 631–2, 646–7). Whatever associations gather in these Miltonic echoes, doom to come, or fatal error behind, this passage brings to the preamble's earlier images of freedom an unmistakably democratic inflection.

---

[15] Norton, 28.   [16] Norton, 34.

If a Miltonic parallel has not been, in 1805, so far brought forward into the saliency of allusion, an explicit tribute is soon paid to the earlier poet. As Wordsworth reviews poetic projects of the most ambitious sort, he envisions:

> some old
> Romantic tale by Milton left unsung . . .
> (i. 179–80)[17]

The tribute is most adroitly managed. Milton had left romantic tales unsung on principle: he aimed at another sort of epic. By this time Wordsworth was aiming at a kind of epic more different still, with Milton's *démarche* as a precedent. Yet his present rehearsal of epic projects within an earlier tradition takes up the theme of liberty once more, not now in a personal or individual form, but as manifest in myth and history, peoples and nations. He speaks of 'the soul | Of liberty' as it animated Mithridates, Sertorius, Dominque de Gourges, and—a link here with the libertarian Jacobitism of the 1730s—Gustavus Vasa, a royal hero with plebeian support from the mines of Dalecarlia. The first of these examples is from the ancient world, the second bridges the gulf between antiquity and Renaissance, the two next are Renaissance examples. But the example with which Wordsworth's rehearsal reaches its climax is medieval: that of William Wallace in fourteenth-century Scotland. The life and death of Wallace, fresh in the poet's mind from his Scottish expedition of 1803, aptly fulfil that charge of stern self-liberation most associated with the republicanism of Milton. It is also notable that freedom here takes the form of armed national resistance against an alien oppressor. Wordsworth's preamble offers an overview of what is to come: this is not the revolutionary freedom of 1789 which is to be celebrated in *Prelude*, Book VI, but one which remembers revolutionary France's later invasion of free Switzerland and other European states. It points to the great political revolution which would ultimately be of most significance to Wordsworth and others of his generation and sympathy: the Spanish and Portuguese revolutions against the Napoleonic invader, which he was so powerfully to defend in his tract on the Convention of Cintra (1809).

[17] Norton, 39.

What is of greatest importance for the poem as a whole is the way in which a social and political rising against an occupying power flows over, through simile, into natural beauty, and into the geniuses of the place, the *patria*, the free native land:

> How Wallace fought for Scotland
> Of Wallace to be found like a wild flower
> All over his dear country, left the deeds
> Of Wallace like a family of ghosts
> To people the steep rocks and river-banks,
> Her natural sanctuaries, with a local soul
> Of independence and stern liberty.

(i. 213–19)[18]

In the light of this historical ideal the formal object of Wordsworth's discontent, as now restated in the remaining paragraph before the question, 'Was it for this . . . ?', takes on a political colouring. Of course the ostensible subject is the poet's personal dissatisfaction as he applies to himself the Parable of the False Steward (Matt. 25: 14–30). Yet the broad poetic projects concerning nationalism and liberty just invoked hardly allow the claim that the poet's desire to develop his talent was an a-political matter. In addition, certain phrases and overtones in this part of the poem help to join political and religious concerns. Earlier in the 'glad preamble' the poet had felt 'the sweet breath of heaven' blowing on his body (i. 41–2), recalling Samson, early in Milton's drama, feeling 'The breath of Heav'n fresh-blowing, pure and sweet' (i. 10); now, just prior to the application of the Parable of the False Steward, Wordsworth's declaration: 'I recoil and droop, and seeke repose' (i. 267) echoes Samson's 'So much I feel my genial spirits droop . . .' (i. 594), and all this prepares the ground for the question which originally began *The Prelude*, 'Was it for this . . . ?', itself an echo, of Manoa's words on Samson, 'For this did the angel twice descend? For this I Ordained thy nurture holy . . . ?' (ll. 361–2), among other salient texts.

Wordsworth's new expansion of this poem sets at a distance that political disappointment which, on largely biographical grounds, I have suggested was the antecedent of the opening question of the

[18] Norton, 40.

earliest *Prelude*. Nevertheless, in modes of expression less than overt but still perceptible, his rehearsal of epic projects and his delicate yet persistent echoing of *Samson Agonistes*, a drama presenting a revolution accomplished with God's grace by a single hero, Wordsworth impresses on his readers' minds the larger political expectations 'Of danger or desire' (i. 498).

The new opening of *The Prelude* must have been striking indeed to those few members of the poet's intimate circle who knew the two-part poem. Less noticeable perhaps but still significant, as we consider the poem in its political aspect, are several small revisions in the narration of particular episodes. Thus the very first childhood memory, the bathing episode, now had the simile (italics added):

> as if I had been born
> On Indian plains, and from my other's hut
> Had run abroad in wantonness to sport,
> A naked savage in a thunder-shower.
>
> (i. 301–3)[19]

The addition certainly renders more exotic a memory whose factual base was bathing in the Derwent as it flowed behind that classically styled gentleman's residence in Cockermouth, inhabited by the poet's father, the political agent of Lord Lowther. Wordsworth expands on the brilliant 'naked savage' of 1798–9, connecting the memory with an image of the primitive but heroically free Red Indian, who need own no political obligation. If, however, the simile adds a Rousseauistic touch to the passage, 'my mother's hut' somewhat mitigates our sense of a savage state of nature to yield a maternal picture taken up at the end of Book II in 'Blest the infant babe . . . Nursed in his mother's arms' (ll. 237–40).

When Wordsworth comes to the card-game, a series of changes extend the passage into a fuller system of political allusion. In a further echo of Pope he now writes of

> some, plebeian cards
> Which fate beyond the promise of their birth
> Had glorified and called to represent
> The persons of departed potentates.
>
> (i. 549–52)[20]

---

[19] Norton, 44.   [20] Norton, 56.

The knaves now become the 'sooty' playthings of a more mock-heroic humour, 'precipated down | With scoffs and taunts like Vulcan out of heaven' (i. 557–8). Kings now are 'surly' rather than 'indignant' and at 'wrongs' not 'shames' (i. 561), while, just before, a new feature appears:

> The paramount ace, a moon in her eclipse
>
> (i. 559)[21]

Wordsworth had added to the allusion to Marie Antoinette already in place another, the plebeian card, which in context of the time must point to Napoleon, First Consul since December 1799, crowned Emperor on 2 December 1804 (his monarchical status had long been clear, whenever Wordsworth redrafted the 1798–9 lines). Further particular reference ought not to be insisted on, though the aristocratic Talleyrand, so ostracized in London when on his republican mission there in 1792, now affords a good example of the 'knave'. 'The paramount ace', logically the Holy Roman Emperor, now seems another queen, already fallen: Maria Theresa, Empress *suo jure*, and mother of Marie Antoinette,[22] may be meant: the line expresses the decline of supreme power, and perhaps echoes Shakespeare's 'The mortal moon hath her eclipse endur'd' (Sonnet 108).[23] The general effect of the expanded passage is of a fuller picture of revolution in the old sense of the term: as the low born winds his way upward to the pinnacle of power, knaves are 'precipated down' 'like Vulcan out of heaven'; the supreme power wanes as the Queen of France, daughter of the Empress, gleams in her last decay. More even than before, the card-game prophesies fundamental change in the sources and patterns of political power.

The many further changes made by Wordsworth between 1799 and 1805 bear only slightly on the political character of the text, for example the alteration at the end of the skating episode from 'tranquil as a summer sea' (i. 185) to 'tranquil as a dreamless sleep' (i. 489). Further relevant inflections might, however, be noticed in the narrative of the visit to Furness Abbey, which Wordsworth now introduces 'within the Vale | Of Nightshade, to St. Mary's honour

---

[21] Ibid.
[22] Edmund Burke, *Works* (1815), ix. 53.
[23] Often glossed as an allusion to Queen Elizabeth I; see W. G. Ingram and Theodore Redpath (eds.), *Shakespeare's Sonnets* (1964; rev. edn., 1978), 246–7.

built . . . | a mouldering pile' (ii. 110–12). This very poetic name (which seems to have been local but may also have been influenced by the Vallombre of *Descriptive Sketches*) greatly increases our sense of the sequestered situation of the abbey, while throwing over it something of a Gothic pall. Another change concerns the distant presence of the sea. In the 1799 *Prelude* 'trees and towers' of 'that sequestered ruin'

> Hear all day long the murmuring sea that beats
> Incessantly upon a craggy shore.

> (ii. 113–177)[24]

The sea, throughout *The Prelude* an important image of peace, excitement, or, most often, danger, is somewhat diminished in power in the 1805 version. Now the abbey's 'more than inland peace' is challenged only by 'the sea-wind passing overhead' (ii. 115–16). It is interesting that the revisions for the 1850 *Prelude* restore the sea to its earlier force, as the poet writes of 'the west wind sweeping overhead | From a tumultuous ocean' (ii. 109–10). Finally, it is interesting that in both the 1799 and 1805 versions we read, at ii. 119 and ii. 123: 'with whip and spur we by the chantry flew . . .'. The surviving manuscripts of the one early draft read 'we through the gateway flew' (MS RV, l. 76),[25] with 'Through the walls we flew' a late addition to a later point in the passage (l. 88).[26] 'Through the gateway', while straightforward and perhaps autobiographically accurate, is tame. 'By the chantry flew' is an improvement, since it contrasts the flight of the boys on horseback with the ancient sanctity of the abbey, while the passage retains, later on, the important preposition 'through'. Yet 'by the chantry' is, in every sense, evasive, and only in the revisions for the 1850 version does Wordsworth achieve that climactic violation of antiquity by thoughtless and joyful youth which the whole episode requires:

> With whip and spur we thro' the Chauntry flew
> In uncouth race . . .

> (ii. 116–7; ii. 117–18)[27]

[24] Norton, 16.
[25] Williams Wordsworth, *The Prelude, 1798–99*, ed. Stephen Parrish (Ithaca, NY, 1977), 177.
[26] Ibid.
[27] William Wordsworth, *The Fourteen-Book Prelude*, ed. W. J. B. Owen (1985), 50, 429; Norton 16.

This is, in the modern political sense of the term, certainly the most revolutionary form of the episode.

II

Book VI, the first book of the third and final growth of *The Prelude*, is notable for its evolution from the boyhood books, and for its artistry of reprise in which *motifs* from earlier in the poem are repeated with altered and added significance. After a long, leisurely, reflective preamble, writing as present process, which among other things begins to associate Coleridge, as addressee of the poem, with the landscape of the 'spots of time' (vi. 239–49), the narrative of the two young mountaineers gets under way with their arrival in Calais, 'a mean city', on the eve of 'that great federal day' (vi. 357–8) which not only commemorated the fall of the Bastille but acclaimed the new constitution just established between King and people. The great ceremony of public oath-taking, the Fête de la Fédération on the Champs de Mars in Paris, was the culmination of many such ceremonies in the provinces 'of that great kingdom' (vi. 373). These nation-wide celebrations combined much from the symbolism of seventeenth-century metropolitan royal entries with, more ominously perhaps, the oath-taking of Hanoverian Britain. Yet what the world saw was a free popular commitment through public theatre to a new egalitarian monarchy: something without precedent. 'A series of new time' seemed indeed to have begun, in Dryden's earlier words, and Wordsworth's 1805 poem invokes both the language of seventeenth-century panegyric and of Tom Paine's praise of the new constitution, which had in fact something apocalyptic in common.[28]

> France standing on the top of golden hours,
> And human nature seeming born again.
>
> (iv. 353–4)[29]

The poem soon reaches beyond these more or less formulaic expressions. Political hope and confidence become one with the physical movement of the two travellers, first that of passage on foot,

---

[28] John Beer, *Wordsworth in Time* (1979), 40–1; Thomas Paine, *The Rights of Man*, ed. Henry Collins (Harmondsworth, 1969), 136; Schama, *Citizens*, 500–12.
[29] Norton, 204.

then travel by river, thirdly and finally that of dancing as invited and welcome guests of the newly enfrancised French people:

> Southward thence
> We took our way, direct through hamlets, towns,
> Gaudy with reliques of that festival,
> Flowers left to wither on triumphal arcs

—an obvious symbol but a proleptic moment—

> And window-garlands. On the public roads—
> And once three days successively through paths
> By which our toilsome journey was abridged—
> Among sequestered villages we walked
> And found benevolence and blessedness
> Spread like a fragrance everywhere, like spring
> That leaves no corner of the land untouched.
> Where elms for many and many a league in files,
> With their thin umbrage, on the stately roads
> Of that great kingdom rustled o'er our heads,
> For ever near us as we paced along . . .
>
> (vi. 360–74)[30]

Many will have felt something of this experience: brought up within one native national culture, to know the spontaneous hospitality of another people. It certainly extends political consciousness—and would prompt Wordsworth in future to be concerned with peoples before states. Here, in the 1805 *Prelude*, the common humanity of the experience is taken up into religious awareness; 'Benevolence' is not only the only word used, but 'blessedness':

> blessedness
> Spread like a fragrance everywhere, like spring

It is clear that the language of enlightenment, summed up here in 'benevolence', is inadequate to convey what the young travellers felt.

> Unhoused beneath the evening star we saw
> Dances of liberty, and, in late hours
> Of darkness, dances in the open air.
>
> (iv. 380–2)[31]

---

[30] Norton, 204–6.   [31] Norton, 206.

Here is something more effective than the panegyric language Wordsworth first used to express the events of the new France. 'Unhoused' is an important word here: liberty and Nature are subtly blended, and are the life of the travellers as well as the doings of the French people.

Wordsworth now seeks to develop the image of natural motion, more concerned with poetic effect than probable record.

> Among the vine-clad hills of Burgundy,
> Upon the bosom of the gentle Soane
> We glided forward with the flowing stream:
> Swift Rhone, thou wert the wings on which we cut
> Between thy lofty rocks. Enchanting show
> Those woods and farms and orchards did present,
> And single cottages and lurking towns—
> Reach after reach, procession without end,
> Of deep and stately vales. A lonely pair
> Of Englishmen we were, and sailed along
> Clustered together with a merry crowd
> Of those emancipated, with a host
> Of travellers, chiefly delegates returning
> From the great spousals newly solemnized
> At their chief city, in the sight of Heaven.
> Like bees they swarmed, gaudy and gay as bees;
> Some vapoured in the unruliness of joy,
> And flourished with their swords as if to fight
> The saucy air.
>
> (vi. 385–401)[32]

Through georgic scenes the two companions move with the natural movement of rivers. Their national identity remains ('a lonely pair of Englishmen') as they are carried forward in a communal movement of Frenchmen, 'clustered together'. This easy alignment of the two companions, the *fédérés* and the rivers, suggests a movement of mind as well as body. In a poem in which so much physical action and mental adventure is checked and reversed, this movement is unchecked. Huge peaks, black and huge, do not forbid further movement here; indeed the rôle of the Rhone is to penetrate formidable mountains, or seem to soar above them—'thou wert the wings

[32] Norton, 204.

on which we cut | Between thy lofty rocks . . .'. This is why Wordsworth's poetic narrative needs both the Soane *and* Rhone, and does not hesitate to transcend credible travel narrative.[33] Travel narrative is merely the idiom of the passage—its baseline—while interspersed, sparingly but tellingly, is the political language introduced with the landing of the two travellers at Calais. 'A merry crowd | Of those emancipated' catches both the momentous public character of the time, and, perhaps, the easy acceptance of all this by a couple of students on vacation. Yet the Fête de la Fédération remains in the back of the mind, garbed in Wordsworth's fittest Miltonic diction, and this Miltonic moment leads on to a Virgilian and even Dryden-like analogy between the returning *fédérés* and the commonwealth of the bees. This jaunty allusion, 'flourished with their swords as if to fight' (vi. 400; *Georgics*, iv. 58–87; Dryden, *Poems*, ii. 982–3) nevertheless intimates strife to come: ancestral voices prophesying war.[34]

As in the skating episode of *The Prelude*, Book I, Wordsworth is here ringing the changes on individuality and community. In the final phase of the passage, the entry of the two companions into the company of the *fédérés* is completed, not through total assimilation into the swarm of travellers, but through the welcome and recognition of their difference and distinct history:

> In this blithe company
> We landed, took with them our evening meal,
> Guests welcome almost as the angels were
> To Abraham of old. The supper done,
> With flowing cups elate and happy thoughts
> We rose at signal given, and formed a ring,
> And hand in hand danced round about the board;
> All hearts were open, every tongue was loud
> With amity and glee. We bore a name
> Honoured in France, the name of Englishmen,
> And hospitably did they give us hail

---

[33] Ibid.; Mark L. Reed, *Wordsworth: The Chronology of the Early Years, 1770–1799* (Cambridge, Mass., 1967), 101.

[34] This will not be the last time in *The Prelude* when 'vapouring' is the first reaction to a great public event: something similar is found in the poet's own first response to the news of Robespierre's death, four years further on in the poem's narrative (x. 539–53).

As their forerunners in a glorious course;
And round and round the board they danced
again.
(vi. 401–13)[35]

If in earlier books of *The Prelude* physical movement has seemed to bear implications of fresh political freedom, here physical movement is explicitly allied to political joy, the dance of liberty. The passage is something of a reprise on what has gone before (the skating episode, the horse-riding through the abbey) but now enacted in a specific historical world, the world only glimpsed in the childhood card-games of Book I. Detail here gives a more complex picture. There is something here of the *philosophes'* view of English history, naïve as it was, with an allusion to the 'Glorious' Revolution of 1688.[36] But the notion of succession which this reference acknowledges is not a secular one; what the narrative adds to the welcome by the *fédérés* is a notion of the succession of biblical patriarchs, and the significance for them of divine interposition. Deep within this comparison is that idea, noticed earlier in *The Prelude*, of those singled out for the accomplishment of some providential end. On the face of things, however, and at present, there is only the dance, the celebration of communal happiness, to which the poet returns again and again, as if he were repeating a spell. The 1805 version ends the sequence with the two companions just regaining their position as observers: 'they danced again'; the 1850 version's 'we danced' would show them at one with the revolutionaries.

The 1805 version gives us, in effect, a brief coda: the visit to the Carthusian monastery of the Grande Chartreuse. At the time of the companions' visit the monks were not yet expelled,[37] though this recurrence of what had been done in Reformation Britain would soon take place. The poet's mixed reaction to this event was first expressed in *Descriptive Sketches* (1793): 'I greet thee, Chartreuse, while I mourn thy doom' (l. 53). The considerable expansion of this episode in the 1850 version of *The Prelude* hardly seems to have been the result of a change in Wordsworth's attitude after 1805. Though the 1805 version considerably expands on *Descriptive*

---

[35] Norton, 206.
[36] F. M. A. de Voltaire, *Lettres sur les Anglais* (1733–4), Lettres VIII and IX.
[37] Norton, 208.

Sketches, and greatly improves on the early poem, there is expressed the same sorrow at the desecration of a shrine devoted to powers and mysteries that are above reason (1805: vi. 414–88; *Descriptive Sketches*, ll. 51–76). The episode in the 1850 version is, however, far more explicit, and much more suggestive as to the importance of its themes within the larger movement of *The Prelude*:

> Vallombre's groves
> Entering, we fed the soul with darkness; thence
> Issued, and with uplifted eye beheld,
> In different quarters of the bending sky,
> The cross of Jesus stand erect, as if
> Hands of angelic powers had fixed it there,
> Memorial reverenced by a thousand storms;
> Yet then, from the undiscriminating sweep
> And rage of one State-whirlwind, insecure.
>
> (1850: vi. 480–8)[38]

Two things should be said. First, as a matter of biography we know that Wordsworth and his companion did not see a 'riotous' revolutionary force approach the monastery, though a verb in the subjunctive mood ('though our eyes had seen', l. 423) binds his imagining of this event tightly into his narrative. The 1850 passage in the *Prelude* is here as an essential part of the poem's imagining of revolution, and experiencing it through imagination. Like much else in *The Prelude*, the account is exemplary, historical, and dramatic, rather than strictly autobiographical.[39] Secondly, the episode harks back to the horse-riding through Furness Abbey, though from a different standpoint. The boys were there the innocent heirs of the despoilers; here the two companions seem to witness the invasion of a sanctuary by forces acting in the name of that same 'merry crowd | Of those emancipated', that dance of liberty, in which they had themselves so recently joined. The 1850 *Prelude* further strengthens the link by a name: the 'Vale of Nightshade'. This had appeared in the 1805 version (ii. 104–5), perhaps linking with the Grande Chartreuse passage in *Descriptive Sketches* which specified Vallom-

---

[38] Norton, 211.

[39] This, doubtless, is the salient biographical and critical issue in the study of *The Prelude*; see Gill, *Wordsworth*, 59, though he is disposed to accept Bk. IX as autobiographically straightforward. See also Nicholas Roe, *The Politics of Nature* (1992), ch. 5.

bre as a neighbouring valley. In the 1850 *Prelude* 'Vallombre', dark vale, valley of the shadows, now interacts in the same text with 'Vale of Nightshade'. Something of the same relation between darkness and transcendent sanctity is found in the Grande Chartreuse episode, though travel in the lines quoted above has become a fully religious process. The great achievement in the 1850 version would be to link a later regret with an earlier, thoughtless, violation. In the 1805 *Prelude*, this is not yet achieved. Yet even here there is one significant touch, the word 'boisterous':

> And every spire we saw among the rocks
> Spake with a sense of peace, at intervals
> Touching the heart amid the boisterous crew
> With which we were environed.
>
> (vi. 418–21)[40]

This strongly recalls 'We ran a boisterous race . . .' (1805: ii. 48; 1850: ii. 47) which commences the introduction to the Furness Abbey episode in this version. The adjective carries us back from the deeds of the *fédérés* to the horse-riding of the lakeland boys. The different points of the narrative connect.

The richly meditative narrative of Book VI may, from my present approach, seem dominated by two episodes: the encounter with the *fédérés*, and the crossing of the Alps (the Grande Chartreuse not assuming its full importance until the 1850 text). The poet's account continues to be tellingly retrospective, for example the 'naked huts, wood-built, and sown like tents | Or Indian cabins' (vi. 450–1), seen in a remote Swiss valley, recall the new form of the earliest *Prelude* incident ('as if I had been born | On Indian plains, and from my other's hut | Had run abroad . . .' (i. 301–3), and it is significant that this is an impression of that land of pristine republican liberty, Switzerland. The crossing of the Alps, however, is bound to recall the mountain environment of the early books of *The Prelude* in a special way. The reader now becomes aware that despite boyhood poaching on the fells, and climbing above the raven's nest on perilous crags, no part of the early *Prelude* recounts the crossing of a mountain. The crossing of the Alps both fulfills and fails to fulfill the 'lofty speculations' fed by Nature, 'ye mountains, and ye lakes | And sounding cataracts . . .' (ii. 440–66) of which Wordsworth had

---

[40] Norton, 208–9.

previously written. Non-fulfilment is a *motif* introduced as the two
travellers first behold Mont Blanc:

> That day we first
> Beheld the summit of Mount Blanc, and grieved
> To have a soulless image on the eye
> Which had usurped upon a living thought
> That never more could be.
>
> (vi. 452–6)[41]

Fulfilment is offered in some measure by the Vale of Chamouny.
Following hard on this comes the long, circumstantial narrative, full
of practical detail, the mountain inn, the prompt departure of the
other travellers, the wrong choice of the track that led over 'a lofty
mountain' (vi. 506), the discovery of the mistake, and the anticlimactic news that they had already crossed the Alps. There is,
perhaps, no more courageous and effective artistic decision in
Wordsworth than his eventual resolve on an abrupt change from
that dry, disappointed narrative, to the quasi-philosophical but far
from wholly abstract paragraph on the 'Imagination' which follows.[42] There could be no more demanding or dramatic transition.
The anticlimax ('we had crossed the Alps') is as bad as an impene-
trable obstacle, or worse: 'I was lost as in a cloud, I Halted without
a struggle to break through' (vi. 529–30). We are reminded of the
earlier and unchecked progress of the two companions and the
fédérés ('Swift Rhone, thou were the wings on which we cut I
Between thy lofty rocks . . . '). The paragraph is avowedly retrospective and prophetic: it takes us far beyond youthful travel and
affairs of state to the human spirit and its metaphysical destiny. Yet
we should notice a stream of diction which palpably refuses to
abandon some of the earlier concerns of Book VI. Even the word
'progress' in 'progress of my song' (vi. 526) is worth pausing over in
a narrative which has spoken of 'human nature seeming born again'
(vi. 534). The term 'usurpation' in 'such strength I Of usurpation, in
such visitings I Of awful promise . . .' (vi. 532–4) brings something
from the theatre of the world to Wordsworth's spiritual subject.[43]

---

[41] Norton, 212.

[42] Norton 216–17; it supplants the passage with the simile of the cave which
came to rest in *The Prelude*, viii. 711–27.

[43] See David Bromwich, 'Between Two States', *TLS* 4,197 (6 Sept. 1983), 963–4,
who then urged a more political account of Wordsworth than that offered in

Had kings usurped the natural freedom of mankind? Did the revolutionary usurp the right of France's king and the vocation of the Grande Chartreuse? Was the spiritual power of man usurped by disappointments? May a higher end be revealed, or intimated, in a finite rebuff?

> when the light of sense
> Goes out in flashes that have shewn to us
> The invisible world, doth greatness make abode,
> There harbours whether we be young or old.
> Our destiny, our nature, and our home,
> Is with infinitude . . .
>
> (vi. 534–9)[44]

What is notable here is that to transcend affairs of state (the hopes of the *fédérés*) is not to abandon them but to raise them and strengthen them.

> With hope it is, hope that can never die,
> Effort, and expectation, and desire,
> And something ever more about to be.
> The mind beneath such banners militant
> Thinks not of spoils or trophies . . .
>
> (vi. 540–4)[45]

'Such banners militant' in context this phrase is almost avowedly inadequate: the words from the world of arms and epic are about to be split away from their customary ends, spoils, and trophies, and addressed to infinity. Even so, these words are the words of collective action and change, and therefore the words of politics. They are not dispensed with in Wordsworth's chastened higher vision.

Only after this, after the dry narrative and the philosophical discourse, does the poem give what the reader waits for: something of the scenic sublime. It is the sublime not of lofty mounting but of confounded descent, the more genuine sublime for the very reason that the downward physical motion of the travellers deepens the

Jonathan Wordsworth's *The Borders of Vision*. (Oxford, 1982). He has it and more, perhaps, in Alan Liu's *Wordsworth: The Sense of History*, 23–31, where it is argued that the usurper Napoleon is the significant absence in the narrative of crossing the Alps.

44 Norton, 216.
45 Ibid.

space between them and the articulate peaks which challenge and
overawe the understanding.

> The immeasurable height
> Of woods decaying, never to be decayed,
> The stationary blasts of waterfalls,
> And everywhere along the hollow rent
> Winds thwarting winds, bewildered and forlorn,
> The torrents shooting from the clear blue sky,
> The rocks that muttered close upon our ears—
> Black drizzling crags that spake by the wayside
> As if a voice were in them—
>
> (vi. 556–64)[46]

Those powers by which adventurousness is rebuffed and awed, in
several episodes of the early *Prelude* (the rowing boat, the snaring,
the kite-flying) are raised to a higher order here. The reader had not,
perhaps, expected *this* to be the fulfilment of the early books. After
'triumph, and delight, and hope, and fear' this is epiphany out of
disappointment:

> The unfettered clouds and region of the heavens,
> Tumult and peace, the darkness and the light,
> Were all like workings of one mind, the features
> Of the same face, blossoms upon one tree,
> Characters of the great apocalypse,
> The types and symbols of eternity,
> Of first, and last, and midst, and without end.
>
> (vi. 566–72)[47]

Nothing binds the centre of *The Prelude* together with the early
books so strongly as this episode. Even more, perhaps, than the
Discharged Soldier in Book IV, this scene assumes a dominance and
exerts a power backwards and forwards within the text. It holds
that central position of prophecy found in the sixth book in Miltonic and Virgilian epic: this is as it were Wordsworth's vision of the
future from the underworld, and his prophetic triumph of Christ in
the war in heaven. It might also be said (to allude to another form
and a more recent poem) that it is Wordsworth's *Vanity of Human
Wishes*. But that would not be quite right. This is not the Christian

---

[46] Norton, 218.   [47] Ibid.

devotion of Johnson. The very strength of Wordsworth's poetry raises action—'Effort, and expectation, and desire'—into his summation of life. But the goals of action are obscured in the power of the voice of the mountains.

III

Public events, those 'banners militant', still urged to action in the theatre of the world. Returning to England the two companions 'crossed the Brabant armies on the fret | For battle in the cause of Liberty' (vi. 691–2). Liberty is an easy word, and the viewpoint here is one of youth. The rebellion of a French landowning class against its distant sovereign the Emperor was not much fomented by revolutionary Paris, and was moderately supported by London. But it gave the impression of history on the move.[48]

Books VII and VIII of *The Prelude* (composed after Book IX and the first half of Book X) are complementary. Apart from their place in a broad chronological sequence, these books explore the idea of human community, its apparent absence in the poet's first experience of London, and its presence in such regular assembly as was exemplified in Helvelyn Fair in Book VIII: the metropolis versus lakeland life. These concerns are not overtly political; they are not 'affairs of state' but, like much else in the 1805 *Prelude*, they underlie and inform those parts of the text which engage explicitly with the great historical issues of the time. Examples of community, or the lack of it, run through the poem and relate to the realm of politics.

The narrator's return to France is recounted at the opening of Book IX. At the factual level it could hardly be put more baldly. He 'quitted' London and 'betook myself to France' in order to improve his French (ix. 31–7). With far more drama, though without more than hinting a motive, the 1850 version has: 'France lured me forth' (ix. 34). In each case, however, the return to France is poetically presented, with a long Miltonic classical simile which picks up the discursive procedure of the preceding books, their time shifts and retrospections, in the image of the river which flows meanderingly,

---

[48] J. M. Thompson, *The French Revolution* (Oxford, 1944), 248–9; John Ehrman, *The Younger Pitt: The Reluctant Transition* (1983), 49–50; Schama, *Citizens*, 684–5.

circuitously, towards the sea. The sea, earlier the symbol of excitement (i. 498–501), peace (1799: i. 185), or power held in check (ii. 115–19), is now 'devouring'. This is more ominous even that the 'ravenous' of the 1850 *Prelude* (ix. 4): it is France to which the river inexorably flows, where the narrator may be not merely in danger but utterly destroyed. This simile may have an appropriate Burkeian source. Denouncing the party of appeasement, Burke had written in his *Letters on a Regicide Peace* (1795) of

the fatal term of *local* patriotism . . . an end of that narrow scheme of relations called our country, with all its pride, its prejudices, and its partial affections. All the little quiet rivulets, that watered an humble, a contracted, but not an unfruitful field, are to be lost in the waste expanse, and boundless, barren ocean of the homicide philanthropy of France . . . it propagates by arms, and establishes by conquest, the comprehensive system of universal fraternity.[49]

In addition, the 1805 opening of Book IX, though sometimes maladroit and clumsy, has in common with the 1850 version the echo of a Miltonic warning, proper to Book IX of a shared epic model. Milton's own opening is not inapplicable to what has gone before in *The Prelude*:

> No more talk where God or angel guest
> With man, as with his friend, familiar used
> To sit indulgent, and with him partake

---

[49] Burke, *Works*, viii. 278–9. There are two interesting analogues to this important simile in Wordsworth's later prose. In the great tract *Concerning the Convention of Cintra* (1809) he was to write: 'I feel indeed with sorrow that events are hurrying us forward, as down the Rapid of an American river, and that there is too much danger *before*, to permit the mind easily to turn back upon the course which is past', ll. 240–3 (*Prose Works*, i. 230). More evocatively he was to write in his 'Reply to Mathetes' (Dec. 1809–Jan. 1810): '. . . let us allow and believe that there is a progress in the Species towards unattainable perfection, or whether this be so or not, that it is a necessity of a good and greatly gifted Nature to believe it—surely it does not follow, that this progress should be constant in those virtues, and intellectual qualities, and in those departments of knowledge, which in themselves absolutely considered are of most value—things independent and in their degree indispensable. The progress of the Species neither is nor can be like that of a Roman road in a right line. It may be more justly compared to that of a River, which both in its smaller reaches and larger turnings, is frequently forced back towards its fountains, by objects which cannot otherwise be eluded or overcome; yet with an accompanying impulse that will ensure its advancement hereafter, it is either gaining strength every hour, or conquering in secret some difficulty, by a labour that contributes as effectually to further it in its course, as when it moves forward uninterrupted in a line, direct as that of the Roman road with which we began the comparison' (*Prose Works*, ii. 142–58).

> Rural repast . . .
>   I now must change
>   Those notes to tragic . . .
>   (ix. 1–4, 5–6)[50]

In keeping with Milton's precedent, Wordsworth sounds his own
warning: 'oh, how much unlike the past' (ix. 14). The sea is hence-
forth an image to be particularly watched; so now is that other
image traced through various texts in the previous chapter: the
image of the horse. In the second paragraph of Book IX it is now
reintroduced: 'Free as a colt at pasture on the hills | I ranged at large
. . .' (ix. 18–19). But it is the sea that is present in the first standard
image of the France of 1792: 'I saw the revolutionary power | Toss
like a ship at anchor, rocked by storms' (ix. 49–50): it is the old
sense of the word 'revolution', indicating only upheaval and danger.

Book IX is an exceptional book though needed by the political
design within the poem. Here for the first time narrator and reader
encounter explicit political argument which thus develops much
foregoing experience of an implicitly political kind. It is now polarized between the figures of two army officers, one royalist, and
one, Michel Beaupuy, a republican. The narrator soon avows his
commitment:

>   I . . . thus did soon
>   Become a patriot—and my heart was all
>   Given to the people, and my love was theirs.
>   (ix. 122–5)[51]

The royalist officer shows himself a ruined archangel, sick of mind
(ix. 143–65).[52] In Miltonic dismissal Wordsworth sums up the
royalist position: '. . . in the regal sceptre, and the pomp | Of orders
and degrees, I nothing found . . .' (ix. 212–13). The narrator does
not speak at this point of the new constitution so triumphantly
celebrated by the *fédérés* on his first visit to France. Rather, the
word 'patriot' is allowed to link the narrator with the republican
officer, a man of noble birth, but a meek and gracious enthusiast for
a new form of government (ix. 294–335). 'Patriot' (redolent in

---

[50] Milton, *Poems*, 851–2.
[51] Norton, 318.
[52] Jonathan Wordsworth calls him Beaupuy's 'Satanic opposite' in *Borders of Vision*, 250.

England of Whig and Tory opposition) carried for Wordsworth and Coleridge in the early 1790s the additional sense of 'egalitarian', one who favoured the new France. The poet uses it in this sense in a letter to William Matthews, in the very year described in *The Prelude*, Book IX, while later letters to the same correspondent underline its connection with Wordsworth's own views as one of 'that odious class of men called democrats'.[53] Of the first relevance to Book IX of *The Prelude* is the denunciatory definition by Coleridge in his first Bristol Lecture (1795), drawing upon J. P. Brissot: 'No! you are not a Patriot. The most consummate pride returns in your heart, the pride of Birth, of Riches, and of Talents. With this triple pride, a man never sincerely believes the doctrine of Equality . . .'[54]

It would be a great mistake to underestimate the importance of Beaupuy to the poem. Apart from Coleridge and his sister Dorothy, addressed by Wordsworth throughout, there are few indeed with whom the narrator has any converse.

> Oft in solitude
> With him did I discourse about the end
> Of civil government, and its wisest forms,
> Of ancient prejudice and chartered rights,
> Allegiance, faith, and laws by time matured,
> Custom and habit, novelty and change,
> Of self-respect, and virtue in the few
> For patrimonial honour set apart,
> And ignorance in the labouring multitude.
>
> (ix. 329–36)[55]

These lines describe the traditional matter of high politics, whose relation with poetry is the subject of the present book. From them it

---

[53] Wordsworth to Matthews, 17 May 1792, 23 May 1794, June 1794 (*EY* 76, 115–16, 119–20). On the poetic presentation of the French Revolution, see Nicholas Roe, 'Imagining Robespierre', in Richard Gravil, Lucy Newlyn, and Nicholas Roe (eds.), *Coleridge's Imagination: Essays in Memory of Peter Laver* (Cambridge, 1985), 161–78, and id., 'Revising the Revolution . . . ', in Robert Brinkley and Keith Hanley (eds.), *Romantic Revisions* (Cambridge, 1992), 87–102, a volume of great interest for the themes of this chapter. As the war with France developed, 'patriotism' for the British took on a loyal and nationalistic sense. As Ehrman says 'Love of country remained a formidable binding force' (*The Younger Pitt: The Reluctant Transition*, 158). See also Linda Colley, *Britons* (1992), ch. 7.

[54] S. T. Coleridge, *Lectures 1795 On Politics and Religion*, in *Collected Coleridge*, ed. Lewis Patton and Peter Mann (1971), 47.

[55] Norton, 328.

is clear that, although Wordsworth's tribute to Burke would not appear in *The Prelude* until the revisions of 1850, his arguments concerning the revolution in France ('laws by time matured, | Custom and habit'), are now present if not explicitly endorsed in the poet's account of his own political conversion. 'Virtue in the few' is, in all this discourse, the phrase that strikes the most ominous note, reminding as it does of *A Readie and Easie Way* and Milton's final, desperate stand against the choice of the English people for the return of their kings. (It links with the theme of the divinely chosen in the 'glad preamble' in Book I, and with those later moments when the poet seems to have mentally revolved some way in which he might, singly, serve the revolution, x. 117–57.) This discourse between the narrator and Beaupuy is later given a dramatic human focus:

> And when we chanced
> One day to meet a hunger-bitten girl
> Who crept along fitting her languid self
> Unto a heifer's motion—by a cord
> Tied to her arm, and picking thus from the lane
> Its sustenance, while the girl with her two hands
> Was busy knitting in a heartless mood
> Of solitude—and at the sight my friend
> In agitation said, ''Tis against that
> Which we are fighting', I with him believed
> Devoutly that a spirit was abroad
> Which could not be withstood, that poverty,
> At least like this, would in a little time
> Be found no more, that we should see the earth
> Unthwarted in her wish to recompense
> The industrious, the lowly child of toil,
> All institutes for ever blotted out
> That legalised exclusion, empty pomp
> Abolished, sensual state and cruel power,
> Whether by edict of the one or few—
> And finally, as sum and crown of all,
> Should see the people having a strong hand
> In making their own laws, whence better days
> To all mankind.
>
> (ix. 511–34)[56]

---

[56] Norton, 338.

With the girl and the bold argument holding our attention, we could not hope to find a moment of more striking and unequivocal egalitarian idealism in any English poet of this time. In the Aristotelian terms which the narrator invokes, government by the many— democracy—can alone redeem the misery of the oppressed and exploited. There is no physical excitement in these lines, yet behind their universal hope is felt an energy and reach which, checked or unchecked, found expression in physical action in the earlier *Prelude*. Yet the great social change here welcomed is seen as both something to be striven for, and as an irresistible natural force, 'Which could not be withstood'. In the dual structure of this shared hope there lurked disaster. For the moment, however, Wordsworth added to the 'hunger-bitten girl', as a mark of the oppression of the old order, 'Vaudracour and Julia', a verse tale of love which bears an oblique relation to his own love affair at that time with Annette Vallon.

Considering that it contains so momentous a political avowal, Book IX has a surprisingly muted tone. That is perhaps its strategy: for the narrator to announce his own commitment humbly and briefly, thereafter to use Beaupuy as a means of urging and expanding on his political theme. This is in accord with the narrator's extreme marginality to historical events in the opening, his picking up a stone from the fallen Bastille as a 'relick', affecting more emotion than he felt (ix. 65–71), and his disguise within Vaudracour and Julia at the end.

Book X brings the poet's centre of consciousness to the centre of historical consequence, making at the same time much fuller demand on Wordsworth's poetic resources than was the case with Book IX. It has a strikingly calm and serene opening:

> through scenes
> Of vineyard, orchard, meadow-ground and tilth,
> Calm waters, gleams of sun, and breathless trees,
> Towards the fierce metropolis turned my steps
> Their homeward way ...
>
> (x. 4–8)[57]

invoking again the georgic landscapes, through which the two companions had passed with the *fédérés* in more peaceful times.

[57] Norton, 358.

Such beauty expressed here has something of the tragic irony of Malory's conventional Spring opening to his 'Piteous Tale' of betrayal, civil discord, and disaster. The land reminds us of hope and happiness as the narrator turns to confront Paris after the September Massacres. His diction reminds us of the *fédérés* as also of the commonwealth of bees:

> Say more, the swarm
> That came elate and jocund, like a band
> Of eastern hunters, to enfold in ring
> Narrowing itself by moments, and reduce
> To the last punctual spot of their despair,
> A race of victims—so they seemed—themselves
> Had shrunk from sight of their own task, and fled
> In terror . . .
>
> (x. 13–21)[58]

This quasi-mathematical demonstration of the self-defeat of the violent strikes a rather defensive note. Wordsworth was among the first, and far from the last, to try to play down the terrors of the Revolution and absolve himself by detecting in them something inevitable. The events themselves had been fairly remarkable. Marat's *coup* of 10 August had been well prepared and completely unconstitutional. Louis XVI, now a limited monarch, may have tried to avert bloodshed among his Swiss Guards by ordering their retreat, but they (and by mistake the similarly garbed Brest *fédérés*) were indiscriminately slaughtered. 'Mutilators hacked off limbs and scissored out genitals and stuffed them in gaping mouths or fed them to dogs.'[59] Nine days later the impending Continental powers invaded French soil. As a consequence mass arrests of those suspected to be traitors within became the order of the day or, as the weeks went by, the night. Hundreds fell victim to summary execution: 'A race of victims—so they seemed' as Wordsworth put it, or, in the words of another poet, Danton's friend Fabre d'Eglantine, 'the first holocaust to Liberty'.[60] These phrases could hardly seem more ominous, though even with d'Eglantine we have not yet arrived at the modern meaning of 'holocaust'. The September Massacres were at all events the precursor of the Terror. Those who

---

[58] Ibid.
[59] Schama, *Citizens*, 615.
[60] Schama, *Citizens*, 630.

Those who are excited by the image of the French Revolution, and find admirable Wordsworth's unpublished extenuations of it in the earlier 1790s, must dispose of the judgement of at least one notable historian: 'Bloodshed was not the unfortunate by-product of revolution, it was the source of its energy . . . the September massacres . . . exposed a central truth of the French Revolution: its dependence on organised killing to accomplish political ends.'[61]

Biographically speaking it is impossible to consider Wordsworth a simple country youth in a foreign land, unaware of what went forward in Paris. His one surviving letter to Matthews from France indeed observes that London might be better informed about events in Paris than Blois, but this is probably the shrewd remark of a vigilant observer and prudent correspondent. This letter and a letter to his brother show how eagerly he followed the fortunes of the Revolution while he was in France.[62] Taken together, his letters from France and his subsequent affirmations and extenuations suggest that revolutionary violence could not deflect him from his political principles. Violence was either weighed and found an acceptable price to pay or, more likely, the poet did not let himself think about it too much. One purpose of Book X is to set that wrong to rights. As Book IX had avowed his revolutionary patriotism, Book X would confront the September Massacres in an episode which may be closer to retrospective fiction than autobiography.

> This was the time in which, enflamed with hope,
> To Paris I returned. Again I ranged,
> More eagerly than I had done before,
> Through the wide city, and in progress passed
> The prison where the unhappy monarch lay,
> Associate with his children and his wife
> In bondage, and the palace lately stormed
> With roar of cannon and a numerous host.
> I crossed—a black and empty area then—

---

[61] Schama, *Citizens*, 615, 637.

[62] Wordsworth to William Matthews, 17 May 1792, Wordsworth to Richard Wordsworth, 19 Dec. 1791 (*EY* 76, 67). Mary Moorman, *William Wordsworth: A Biography: The Early Years, 1770–1803* (Oxford, 1957), 171–7, and, to a lesser extent, Gill, *Wordsworth*, 56–64, are inclined to stress Wordsworth's probable innocence and bewilderment as he lived in the revolutionary France of 1792, though Gill's important political footnote at pp. 63–4 draws a sharper picture. Naïve Wordsworth may certainly have been, but the direct early evidence shows him capable of making a decisive assessment.

> The square of the Carousel, few weeks back
> Heaped up with dead and dying . . .

(x. 38–48)[63]

This achieves one of *The Prelude*'s most effective flashbacks—to the
card-games of 'monarchs surly at the wrongs sustained | By royal
visages' (i. 534–5): one notices here the effectiveness of the 1805
Prelude's change from '*kings* indignant at the *shame*' (my italics
from the version 1799). The game has now become historical reality
with a vengeance. And here the physical description 'a black and
empty area' is an image remarkably appropriate, one may think, for
precarious mental and moral omissions. At all events a factual
record is now filled out with acknowledgement of the dead on both
sides. The following image, of all this being to the poet as a volume
'whose contents he knows | Are memorable but from him locked up'
(x. 50–1), has all the air of an apology, but may be a true and severe
judgement on his response to events at that time. He saw, not felt,
how terrible they were.

> But that night
> When on my bed I lay, I was most moved
> And felt most deeply in what world I was;
> My room was high and lonely, near the roof
> Of a large mansion or hotel, a spot
> That would have pleased me in more quiet times
>
> . . . .
>
> The fear gone by
> Pressed on me almost like a fear to come.
> I though of those September massacres,
> Divided from me by a little month,
> And felt and touched them, a substantial dread
> (The rest was conjured up from tragic fictions,
> And mournful calendars of true history,
> Rembrances and dim admonishments):
> 'The horse is taught his manage, and the wind
> Of heaven wheels round and treads in his own steps;
> Year follows year, the tide returns again,
> Day follows day, all things have second birth;
> The earthquake is not satisfied at once'—

[63] Norton, 360.

And in such way I wrought upon myself,
Until I seemed to hear a voice that cried
To the whole city, 'Sleep no more!' To this
Add comments of a calmer mind—from which
I could not gather full security—
But at the best it seemed a place of fear,
Unfit for the repose of night,
Defenceless as a wood where tigers roam.

(x. 54–82)[64]

As often in Wordsworth, the episode turns effectively from an external, descriptive account to an inner drama. As hope has always hitherto been associated with a path, progress, a way through, so the cycle, hinted at in 'France standing on top of golden hours' (ix. 353),[65] carries a peculiar terror. Between the fear gone by and the fear to come there is only the black and empty area. These two fears, after a dream-like parenthesis concerning fact and report, precipitate the terrible vision of the following lines which disclose an energy beyond control. Yet the energy does display a pattern and a character, that of the circle. The training of a horse involves its moving in circles at the end of a long rein; this image of discipline is then aligned with the notion of a cycle, that of the wind of heaven which treads its own path like a man, and that of the tide whose ebb opens a way, only to endanger and destroy on its return. Natural recurrence is at this historical moment menacing rather than harmonious. These lines are full of significance in relation to Wordsworth's earlier writing. The wind is like a supernatural being (cf. i. 328–32), and the horse has the terror of some of the poet's earliest fears, not now an image of how revolutionary excesses will 'from their round of wanton vagaries' return to 'moderate and regular delight', as the poet had argued in *Llandaff*, nor like the steeds on which the boys 'a circuit made | In wantonness of heart' (ii. 135–8) after the visit to the ruined abbey in *The Prelude*, Book II. The recall of those lines measures a terrible distance from the wanton freedom of boyhood experience, for here the trained horse is more dangerous than the wild one. Warhorses were taught to charge. The image

---

[64] Norton, 360–2.
[65] Beer, *Wordsworth in Time*, 41–2. See also John A. Hodgson, 'Tidings: Revolutions in *The Prelude*', *Studies in Romanticism*, 31: 1 (Spring 1992), 45–70. Hodgson is concerned with exactly the ideas and moments in the poem that I am here, but our conclusions differ.

picks up what Schama tells us about these months. The Revolution was now *skilling* itself in death.

The invocation of *Macbeth*, 'I seemed to hear a voice that cried | To the whole city, "Sleep no more!" ' constitutes the most dramatic possible climax to the passage, and, in effect, an implicit recantation, from the viewpoint of the 1805 *Prelude*, of those positions which had led Wordsworth to excuse or play down revolutionary violence. Shakespeare's words recalled the murder of a king, perhaps also the cycles of his royal posterity; only a few lines before has Wordsworth reminded us of the doomed Louis XVI. The connection is there to be made.[66] The imagery of the end of the passage returns the narrator into a savage situation, not that of primal freedom as early in *The Prelude*, Book I, but of ferocious, predatory life, or of something worse.

Book X is a prolonged, retrospective, soliloquy on affairs of state in the early 1790s, punctuated by two public events, one early and one late in the book, each concerning Robespierre. If Book IX had a revolutionary figure of love in Beaupuy, Book X has a figure of revolutionary destruction in Robespierre. The black and empty area of the poet's mind is next filled by the 1805 poet with that occasion when the editor of *La Sentinelle*, Jean-Baptiste Louvet de Courvray, denounced Robespierre as a new Catiline.[67] The obvious admiration with which the 1805 narrative responds to Louvet's act of lonely defiance, together with a horror at the violence into which the Revolution now sank, has suggested to some that Wordsworth was a principled Girondin, detesting Robespierre and Jacobin excess. This is probably the impression that the 1805 *Prelude* seeks to give; it is not evidence of where Wordsworth stood in 1792. In addition, Stephen Gill rightly remarks that the Girondin faction was hardly moderate in any ordinary sense, though accused of being so by the Jacobins.[68] Perhaps the Girondins can only be said to have been somewhat closer to constitutional republicanism than the Jacobins, and the fact that the poet of the 1805 *Prelude* sought to give his poem a Girondin slant does show his acute understanding of the situation and his skill in combining a confessional resolve with a strategy to set his record in the best light.

[66] See the debate of George Watson and John Beer in *The Critical Quarterly*, 18: 3 and 19: 2 (1976–7).

[67] Schama, *Citizens*, 649.

[68] Gill, *Wordsworth*, 63–4.

Like the poet's avowal of his patriotism in Book IX, his decision to return to England is recorded in the humblest and most
candid way (x. 189–91). His refusal to make much of this moment
is impressive. Back in England worse awaited him on his inner
pilgrimage. Such was his faith in France that even the abolition of
the slave trade seemed to him a secondary matter; the success of
France was the key to the liberty of the whole world. At this point
France and Britain declared war upon one another, France making
the first move, after some confused and unsuccessful last-minute
diplomacy. Pitt's government was essentially traditional and reac-
tive; it did not take initiatives so much as respond to those of others.
Alarmed at the spread of egalitarian ideas at home it had taken
measures to repress them. Much more alarmed, now, at the prospect
of a newly and unpredictably aggressive France, Pitt's government
went to war not to put down the Revolution but to preserve the
balance of power. Pitt's chief demand of the French was:

The withdrawing of their Arms within the limits of The French territory; the
abandoning of their conquests; the rescinding of any Acts injurious of the
sovereignty or rights of any other Nations, and the giving, in some public,
and unequivocal manner a pledge of their intention no longer to foment
troubles, or to excite disturbances against other Governments.[69]

If France agreed to this, there would on the part of Britain be no
attempt to interfere with the revolutionary regime. On this basis the
hitherto neutral Britain went to war with the new republic. And this
was the occasion of Wordsworth's first using the word 'revolution'
in *The Prelude*. Revealingly enough, his sense of the word is traditional, meaning a violent upheaval, or reversal, not a great leap
forward. Yet in one respect he uses the word in a new way: 'revolution' is here for him an upheaval of the mind rather than in the
state.[70] Further, the notion of progress is a premise for the inner
upheaval he felt. In keeping, perhaps, with the thinking of the
philosophe and revolutionary Condorcet, Wordsworth argues that
all to this moment had been a steady advance to Liberty 'on the
self-same path | On which . . . | I had been travelling'. Britain's

---

[69] Ehrman, *The Younger Pitt: The Reluctant Transition*, 240.
[70] So it had been for Burke in his *Reflections*: 'Oh! what a revolution! and what
an heart must I have, to contemplate without emotion, that elevation and that fall!',
he had written of Marie Antoinette (*Works*, v. 149).

declaration of war, by contrast, caused 'change and subversion' in
the heart of his being:

> No shock
> Given to my moral nature had I known
> Down to that very moment—neither lapse
> Nor turn of sentiment—that might be named
> A revolution, save at this one time.
>
>   (x. 202–38)[71]

Back in May 1792 Wordsworth had written of the public events in
France as 'a Revolution';[72] the internalization of the word here is
appropriate to the concern and idiom of the book. But it is also clear
that 'revolution' was not, for Wordsworth, synonymous with 'progress'.

A profound and paradoxical deracination now occurred in the
poet's mind. His sense of belonging to his own country had been
proved to mean more to him than he had reckoned: he had been 'a
green leaf on the blessed tree | Of my beloved country' or—in the
inspired Burkeian revision of the 1850 *Prelude*—a 'pliant harebell,
swinging in the breeze | On some grey rock—its birth-place . . . the
ancient tower | Of my beloved country' (x. 253–5; cf. 1850: x.
274–80). Even the revisions of Henry James could hardly improve
on that. In the retrospective narrative now set forth, the agonies of
political conflict, feeling as well as thought, derive from what
Wordsworth admits to having then judged a wholly mistaken decision by 'the unhappy counsel of a few weak men' (x. 292): Britain's
declaration of war. They derive too from a deracination even more
dire, by 'the men who for desperate ends | Had plucked up mercy by
the roots' (x. 306–7) in the new France. The 1805 *Prelude* conveys
the terrible Kafka-like experience more abruptly, less fully, than the
1850, *Prelude* but well enough:

> Such ghastly visions had I of despair,
> And tyranny, and implements of death,
> And long orations which in dreams I pleaded
> Before unjust tribunals, with a voice
> Labouring, a brain confounded, and a sense

---

[71] Norton, 368–70.
[72] Wordsworth to Matthews, May 1792 (*EY* 76).

Of treachery and desertion in the place
The holiest that I knew of—my own soul.

(x. 374–80)[73]

Not only in its change of the hubristically secular final line for: 'In
the last place of refuge—my own soul', but also in its attention to
innocent prisoners, whether in cells or crowds, is the 1850 *Prelude*
a superior achievement. But even in 1805 it is clear that Book X of
The Prelude has here achieved a new kind of poetry, not now the
exhilarating physical and scenic poetry of the boyhood books, with
all its political implications for the life to come, but a poetry of
current confusion and guilt, introspective, confessional, psychological. *The Prelude* is a great poem because it can command both these
modes, and relate them together.

In the central position of Book X of *The Prelude* is recounted the
public event which, for a time at least in the poem, serves as a
moment of political catharsis, inward as well as outward, to clear up
the nightmare-like entanglements just exposed. Back in the lake
country, after a visit to the grave of his old headmaster, William
Taylor, 'in Cartmell's rural town' (x. 491), a place also likely to
have reminded the poet what a great medieval monastic church
would have seemed like if not despoiled at the Reformation, or in
the French Revolution, the narrator entered on the often dangerous
crossing 'over the smooth sands | Of Leven's ample estuary' (x.
474–5) to Ulverston on the further shore. This is a sheer triumph of
social and scenic description:

> All that I saw, or felt, or communed with,
> Was gentleness and peace. Upon a small
> And rocky island near, a fragment stood—
> Itself like a sea rock—of what had been
> A Romish chapel, where in ancient times
> Masses were said at the hour which suited those
> Who crossed the sands with ebb of morning tide.
> Not far from this still ruin all the plain
> Was spotted with a variegated crowd
> Of coaches, wains, and travellers, horse and foot,
> Wading, beneath the conduct of their guide,
> In loose procession through the shallow stream
> Of inland water; the great sea meanwhile

---

[73] Norton, 378.

6. J.M.W. Turner, watercolour of crossing the Lancaster Sands. British Museum.

7. Alfred Mouillard, 'Robespierre and St. Just leave for the Guillotine' (nineteenth century). By permission of the Galerie Dijol, Paris.

> Was at a safe distance, far retired. I paused,
> Unwilling to proceed, the scene appeared
> So gay and chearful—when a traveller
> Chancing to pass, I carelessly inquired
> If any news were stirring, he replied
> In the familiar language of the day
> That, *Robespierre was dead.*
>
> (x. 514–35)[74]

The 'devouring sea' (1850: ix. 4), the tide which turns again (x. 72), is 'at a safe distance': though, in this and other estuaries on this coast, the tide comes in with terrifying speed, passage is for the moment possible, even easy. The France of the Terror is far away, and the remains of a 'Romish chapel' stand as a good omen for the crossing. The 'variegated crowd'[75] display a natural communal occasion, a movement under guides but not commanders. It recalls Helvellyn Fair, another regular, easy assembly. Into this calm provincial scene is dropped the momentous news from the world of high politics. The episode of the accusation of Robespierre by Louvet is of course recalled, as also the mention of Robespierre and his 'atheist crew' (x. 456–7); further, the narrator's outburst of joy and triumph has all the effect of a pent-up force suddenly released. At first sight, what follows seems to answer the agonies, the complexities, the 'unintelligible chastisement', explored in the first half of Book X:

> 'Come now, ye golden times',
> Said I, forth-breathing on those open sands
> A hymn of triumph, 'as the morning comes
> Out of the bosom of the night, come ye.
> Thus far our trust is verified: behold,
> They who with clumsy desperation brought
> Rivers of blood, and preached that nothing else
> Could cleanse the Augean stable, by the might

---

[74] Norton 386. This stress on community, on people, is the answer to Alan Liu, who in his *Wordsworth: The Sense of History*, 383–4, notes an absence of reference to the revolutionary people, which he reads as an evasion, or an unacknowledged fear. Taken as a whole the Leven Sands episode redeems the image of popular life, accuses Robespierre and his supporters of revolutionary destruction, and reminds us of their popular support by the phrase 'madding factions' (l. 554). On this episode see also Alan Bewell, *Wordsworth and the Enlightenment* (1989), 254–7, and Hodgson, 'Tidings: Revolution in *The Prelude*'.

[75] Cf. J. W. M. Turner's *Lancaster Sands* of c.1826.

> Of their own helper have been swept away.
> Their madness is declared and visible;
> Elsewhere will safety now be sought, and earth
> March firmly towards righteousness and peace.'

(x. 541–52)[76]

These are crucial lines for any interpretation of Wordsworth's French Revolutionary faith. To the extent that the poet of the 1805 *Prelude* may read back later attitudes into the earlier record, as I have sometimes suggested, this passage might imply the lasting nature of his early radicalism. The forced march to Liberty had been terribly betrayed, but was now back on course. The narrator's inward oration surely does reaffirm, for example, the creed of Beaupuy. There can, I think, be no doubt that this moment is in itself a sort of liberation from bondage. Yet one cannot forget the placing of this internal oration within the poem. Golden times had been hailed once before (vi. 352–5). Further, the frenzied delight of the oration (note the rapid succession of 'vengeance and eternal justice') contrasts notably with the gentleness and peace of the surrounding scene. The concluding lines of the episode, it seems to me, effect a distancing without a repudiation:

> Then schemes I framed more calmly, when and how
> The madding factions might be tranquillized,
> And—though through hardships manifold and long—
> The mighty renovation would proceed.
> Thus, interrupted by uneasy bursts
> Of exultation, I pursued my way
> Along that very shore which I had skimmed
> In former times, when, spurring from the Vale
> Of Nightshade, and St. Mary's mouldering fane,
> And the stone abbot, after circuit made
> In wantonness of heart, a joyous crew
> Of schoolboys, hastening to their distant home,
> Along the margin of the moonlight sea,
> We beat with thundering hoofs the level sand.

(x. 553–67)[77]

Phrases such as 'more calmly' and 'uneasy bursts' do qualify what went before; and the general subsiding of emotion suggests a

---

[76] Norton, 388.   [77] Norton, 388.

measure of 'vapouring' (cf. vi. 399) in the narrator's first response
to the news from France. Yet as the narrator's political passions
subside, the landscape and its memories enter unawares into his
mind, giving access to an earlier joy and strength. The mountains
around Hawkshead and Windermere are visible to the north in
crossing the Leven Sands; arriving on the further shore the narrator
found himself on the route of the 'wanton circuit' made by the boys
on horseback returning from Furness Abbey home to Hawkshead.
If *indeed* Wordsworth heard the news of Robespierre's death as the
narrator tells the tale (which there seems small reason to doubt) it
was the most wonderful piece of creative opportunism to conclude
the episode in this way. Not only are boyhood and manhood,
personal and political, lakeland and France, brought together, but
this a genuine moment of time regained. The familiar landscape
draws us nearer and nearer to the earlier experience until the Book
X narrative coincides with Book II in the repetition of the final line
(ii. 144, x. 567). At this point a primal joy and energy is released
into later experience. Not the wanton circuit nor the cycle of terror
described earlier in Book X: a wider circle is completed here, more
comprehensive, more creative. The horse gallops onward, neither
constrained nor destructive. The reader is very near that fresh
setting forth of the 'fructifying' or 'vivifying' or 'renovating' virtue
mysteriously possessed by certain moments of the past.

In December 1804 Book X was supposed to end with this episode.
So it would do in the revisions/for the 1850 *Prelude*. Wordsworth's
interim decision, however, was that the long ensuing discourse,
lacking any great imaginative moment, should be appended to the
Leven Sands episode rather than stand on its own. It goes over some
of the history already recounted, for example Britain's declaration
of war on France, while also reaching forward to the enthrone-
ment of Napoleon as Emperor. It is a yet more retrospective discussion, by turn confessional, self-justifying, defiant. It certainly is
poetry on affairs of state. And it is no less severe on the efforts of
Pitt's government to repress sedition than on the French, as a dog
returning to its vomit, for allowing Napoleon to be crowned.

The passage on Pitt's administration:

> Our shepherds (say this merely) at that time
> Thirsted to make the guardian crook of law
> A tool of murder. They who ruled the state,

Though with such awful proof before their eyes
That he who would sow death, reaps death, or worse,
And can reap nothing better, childlike longed
To imitate . . .

$$(x. 645-56)^{78}$$

said by the Norton editors to be not an 'excessive' judgement, shows
some loss of sense of proportion on Wordsworth's part. Would Pitt
really have proved a Robespierre if he had had the courage? As Fox
conceded, *habeas corpus* had been suspended before, during threat
of invasion, under William in the 1690s, under George I in 1715,
and under George II in 1745. An intelligence network was indeed
newly active, as the disaffected and supposedly disaffected, including Coleridge and Wordsworth, found to their cost. Several egalitarian ideologues, Hardy, Tooke, Thelwall, were tried and, thanks to
the skilled defence by Thomas Erskine, acquitted. It was satirically
effective to link Pitt's 'Terror' with Robespierre's Terror, but a
rising attitude of British patriotism increasingly rejected such an
equation, as the career of William Frend demonstrates.[79] It might
also be thought that if, after so extraordinary a decade of change,
the French people had acquiesced again in a monarchy, there were
reasons for thinking monarchy a desirable political state. But
against each of these views the latter half of Book X is powerfully,
sarcastically, unyielding. The voice of the Juvenal translation is
heard again.

IV

The brief preamble to the two original 'spots of time' (1799: i.
288–94), suggesting their potential for the future, always meant that

[78] Norton, 394, n. 4.
[79] For Fox's speeches on the suspension of *habeas corpus* in May 1794, see I. C.
Willis (ed.), *Speeches During the French Revolution by Charles James Fox* (1924),
180–202, p. 187 for the suspension during the Jacobite crises, which Fox presents as
greater threats to security than any in 1794. For a sober and detailed account of Pitt's
repressive measures from his government's point of view, see Ehrman, *the Younger
Pitt: The Reluctant Transition*, ch. 4, '1792: The Dimensions of Unrest', especially
pp. 156–7. On the trial and acquittal of Hardy, Thelwall, and Tooke, see Roe,
Wordsworth and Coleridge, ch. 5, and Gill, *Wordsworth*, 88–9; it is Gill (pp. 234–5)
who notes the significance of the radical William Frend's publishing, in 1804, of
Patriotism: or, The Love of our Country.

this part of that early narrative was appropriate for removal. As it happens Wordsworth proposed a new place for the sequence at two different stages in the growth of *The Prelude*. During the short period when a five-book *Prelude* was in prospect, these two episodes were to have held the final place, in the last book, after the account of the ascent of Snowdon.[80] That is strong evidence of the poet's faith in their power and importance. Later Wordsworth removed them still further from their original chronological position. They became, 'with no particular appropriateness' Jonathan Wordsworth has suggested,[81] the dominating poetic sequence of Book XI. It may be that a political approach to the whole text of *The Prelude* can suggest the appropriateness of what Wordsworth did, albeit only through consideration of delicacies and details of the poem. First, in the 1805 poem it is actually in Book VI that the narrator first alludes to 'the Border Beacon' and its waste and naked surroundings, upon which 'was later scattered love— I A spirit of pleasure, and youth's golden gleam' (vi. 239–45). Book VI is a book peculiarly taken up with hope, and the 'golden gleam' of this personal recollection of the transforming power of happiness links with 'France standing on the top of golden hours I And human nature seeming born again' (vi. 352–3). This in turn involves Wordsworth's new use of the old idea of the renewal of the age of gold for a historical period of revolutionary hope. Secondly, we have just seen how another early episode, the horse-riding through Furness Abbey, though not formally a 'spot of time', could release its power into later experience. In the preceding 'hymn of triumph' breathed by the narrator at the news of the death of Robespierre, that keyword from the tradition of panegyric, 'renovation', was invoked to express the continuing hopes of the narrator for what Tom Paine had expressed as 'a Regeneration of man'.[82] Now, in Book XI, after several earlier tries, Wordsworth settles on a word to convey the long-lasting and germinating 'virtue' of early experience. The word chosen is the political and religious word: 'renovating':

---

[80] Norton, 516.

[81] Norton, 568–9.

[82] Paine, *The Rights of Man*, 136: '. . . the name of a Revolution is diminitive of its character, and it rises into a Regeneration of man.' See Duncan Wu, *Wordsworth's Reading 1770–1799* (Cambridge, 1993), 109–10 (item 194).

> spots of time,
> Which with distinct preeminence retain
> A renovating virtue . . .
>
> (xi. 257–9)[83]

It links the Beacon episode, which immediately follows, with the previous episode, the news of the death of Robespierre. The Beacon episode shows features which recall earlier episodes having political implication. Here is another horseback ride, but one where 'proud hopes' (ix. 280) end in dismounting and a stumbling descent on foot. Here is another narrative that aims high, 'towards the hills' (ix. 281) but where the travellers lose their way. This and the bleak and daunting mountain scene partly remind us of the crossing of the Alps in Book VI. But here also are two new features: the memorial to violent crime, cut in the turf, and, most mysterious and powerful of all, the girl bearing the pitcher on her head, who

> seemed with difficult steps to force her way
> Against the blowing wind. It was, in truth,
> An ordinary sight, but I should need
> Colours and words that are unknown to man
> To paint the visionary dreariness
> Which, while I looked all round for my lost guide,
> Did at that time invest the naked pool,
> The beacon on the lonely eminence,
> The woman with her garments vexed and tossed
> By the strong wind.
>
> (xi. 306–15)[84]

In the new position, and prefaced by the word 'renovating', the memorial to the murder now picks up the poem's horror at French revolutionary violence, 'the Carousel . . . heaped up with dead and dying' (x. 47–8). What renovates, in the post- revolutionary situation, must be a figure of hope living in the face of, not prior to or innocent of, man's inhumanity to man. So here; but there is more to it, because the girl is not only a part of her surroundings but combats with their dreariness. Comparison seems invited with the pauper girl with the heifer in Book X. By contrast with her 'languid' movement this figure is able to 'force her way | Against the blowing

---

[83] Norton, 428.   [84] Norton, 432.

wind'. She expresses both vigour and determination. For her there is no check and rebuff, as there has so often been for the narrator. As the poet brings together the various components of this episode—dispersed as they have been throughout the earlier poem—the memorial to crime, the naked pool and common crags, the Border Beacon, the idea of renovation, the age of gold, the spirit of pleasure, and youth's golden gleam, we can see that what in the end gives a renovating virtue to this episode, making it a beacon in the poem to the world, is the resolution and independence of the girl, and the fortitude with which she pursues her life amidst what might have otherwise been felt a landscape of 'unintelligible chastisement' (x. 414).

The twinned 'spot of time', the expectation of Christmas, and the poet's father's death, notable for its similarity in diction and scene, lacks only this central figure of hope. In her place there is a father who dies; well might the boy have sat, upon 'the highest summit', '*half* sheltered by a naked wall' (italics added; xi. 355–67). In his orchestration of this sequence of episodes, Wordsworth so manages common motifs that a shared vision and melody dies austerely away into providentialism and morality. The old order has gone; the reader is left with the picture of the narrator facing two roads, in a landscape 'Stormy, and rough, and wild' (xi. 356). From whichever way they come, the longed-for horses bear the narrator only towards loss.

V

Wordsworth writes as openly and directly about affairs of state, and as allusively and obliquely, as any poet in the tradition explored in this book. At the same time *The Prelude* does something quite new. It combines an explicit concern about contemporary political history with a myth of physical action. The motif of physical movement is variously extended, repeated, orchestrated. Action, sometimes individual and solitary (the snaring), sometimes communal and gregarious (the horse-riding), is sometimes movement to a destination (the hills in the Beacon episode), sometimes enjoyed for its own sake (dancing for liberty with the *fédérés*). It is sometimes a completed action (the skating), but sometimes checked, interrupted, redirected (crossing the Alps). This intense physical experience is present to put to the proof within the poem certain pervasive and dominating ideas, among which progress, revolution, and providence are perhaps the most salient. A high proportion of the poem's episodes of physical action are versions of progress, attempted, achieved, or chastised. Revolution, first a destination or at least a stretch on the 'public road' (xii. 145–84) of progress, later its tragedy, assumes in the end the contours of an intervening and chastising providence, a cliff or huge peak, black and huge (i. 406; 1850: i. 378–80), barring onward movement, a road hid in the stony channel of the stream (vi. 515–16), leading inexorably down. In this way powerful ideas of the era are received into individual consciousness, personal and public, there to be explored and put to the test, assessed against the other resources of the poem. (Such another resource is the Discharged Soldier of Book IV: an incitement to change, or an example of the courage of resignation?) All this not only takes place within the poem; it is in fact the form of the poem. Adventure and progress, rebuff, recovery, repeated within *The Prelude*, form a sequence which constitutes the structure of *The Prelude* itself. The deeply satisfying inwardness of the poem comes from its very artistic openness: as we learn from the preamble to Book I and its conclusion the path of the poem is its narrative task as well as what is narrated. As in *Tristram Shandy* and *Don Juan* (otherwise so different) the form of the work is its own creative process; and the creative process here means taking the weight of, and seeking to reconcile, potentially incompatible political principle and experience. *The Prelude*, in the way it undergoes revolutionary experience, holds a unique and central position in Wordsworth's writings, connecting the egalitarian idealism of 'Llandaff', 'Salisbury Plain', and 'Juvenal' with the later and more detached treatment of the French Revolution in *The Excursion*. It takes an individual consciousness into the heart of revolutionary events, a consciousness with a sense of being religiously elect (recall the echoes of Milton's Samson in the preamble to Book I) and is significant in that later eighteenth-century notions of progress were more commonly notions of spiritual progress to some millennial goal or vision of infinity, than secular concepts of indefinite social advance.[85]

---

[85] The proposal that *The Prelude* puts the notion of progress to the test of experience may be explored with the help of J. B. Bury, *The Idea of Progress: An Inquiry into Its Origin and Growth* (1920), and David Spadafora, *The Idea of*

It was with all this in mind, perhaps, that Wordsworth resolved to make the ascent of Snowdon the final episode of *The Prelude* in 1805 and 1850, rather than the 'spots of time' as in the earlier five-book scheme. This decision almost certainly gives the poem a stronger and more positive conclusion. Yet at the same time the episode powerfully and subtly recalls the crossing of the Alps, the other notable mountain-climbing experience of the poem. That account, it will be remembered, revealed no extended mountain view; the 'black, drizzling crags' as the travellers descended are what stay in the mind. The ascent of Snowdon, for the first time in *The Prelude*, reveals a prospect from a lofty mountain. Here, however, there is no effect of anticlimax: there is rather difference, surprise, and awe. To descend, in Book VI, was an anticlimax, until the experience of descent itself provided the longed-for sublime. The aim of the expedition in Book XIII is 'to see the sun | Rise from the top of Snowdon' (ll. 4–5). *That* possible climax is never mentioned again. Yet without any anticlimax the hurried and breathless climb, interrupted only by the shepherd's dog putting up a hedgehog (ll. 23–5) moves imperceptibly into a brightness shed on the ground. A brightness, not of the dawn, but of the moon:

> I looked about, and lo,
> The moon stood naked in the heavens at height
> Immense above my head, and on the shore
> I found myself of a huge sea of mist,
> Which meek and silent rested at my feet.
> A hundred hills their dusky backs upheaved
> All over this still ocean, and beyond,
> Far, far beyond, the vapours shot themselves
> In headlands, tongues, and promontory shapes,

Progress in Eighteenth-Century Britain (1990). The aspect suggested by Spadafora, following M. H. Abrams in *Natural Supernaturalism* (1971), as bearing on the Romantics, namely advance towards a millennial goal, is by no means the only version of progress to be exemplified within *The Prelude* (see n. 53 above). The concept was undoubtedly important within Wordsworth's early radical milieu. My own hypothesis, however, is that that milieu was not representative of later 18th-cent. English culture: progress was not a central idea of that era—not, by comparison with the concept of resignation to a special providence. Wordsworth's questioning of the idea of progress in his poem, I suspect, marks a move on his part from a marginal to a more comprehensive culture. The probability or improbability of this supposition, however, is unlikely to be demonstrated before the issue has been addressed by a quantitative form of the history of ideas. See also Deirdre Coleman, *Coleridge and The Friend* (Oxford, 1980).

Into the sea, the real sea, that seemed
To dwindle and give up its majesty,
Usurped upon as far as sight could reach.

(xiii. 40–51)[86]

We are first struck by the displacement of the word 'naked'. The
narrator, not 'naked in external things' (i. 165), has taken us from
the 'naked boy', the 'naked savage' (i. 292, 304), over the naked
crags and pools of vi. 243 and xi. 303, to the 'naked' moon which,
now personified, stands in the heavens. The word has moved from
an expression of inherent vitality, through a terrain of danger and
destitution, to this unexpected epiphany of light. Next, the sea, an
image partly political since the 'devouring sea' (ix. 4) and 'the great
sea' which heaved 'at a safe distance' at the news of the death of
Robespierre (x. 568–9), is now 'meek and silent' at the very feet of
the narrator. This 'huge sea of mist' shapes a total vision, lands and
promontories seeming to rise out of the encompassing oceans of the
world, while far below 'the real sea' (l. 49), once a devouring power,
now diminished by distance, yields its majesty, usurped (note these
political words, one already used in the account of the crossing of
the Alps) by this vision of a new heaven and earth, the first heaven
and first earth seeming to have passed away, when there shall be no
more sea (Revelations 21: 1). In the light of this vision the devouring
majesty of worldly power is set at a distance, apparently transcended.[87]
But transcendence is only temporarily the effect, not finally the
word.

Meanwhile, the moon looked down upon this shew
In single glory, and we stood, the mist
Touching our very feet; and from the shore
At distance not the third part of a mile
Was a blue chasm, a fracture in the vapour,
A deep and gloomy breathing-place, through which
Mounted the roar of water, torrents, streams
Innumerable, roaring with one voice.
The universal spectacle throughout

[86] Norton, 460.
[87] My debt to M. H. Abrams in *Natural Supernaturalism*, 78–9, 286–7, and
371–2, will be obvious. At the same time I think I see the Snowdon vision as less fully
and finally a triumph of mind, a lasting transcendence, than Abrams seems to do.

Was shaped for admiration and delight,
Grand in itself alone, but in that breach
Through which the homeless voice of waters rose,
That dark deep thoroughfare, had Nature lodged
The soul, the imagination of the whole.

(xiii. 52–65)[88]

While peace and glory are above the mist, the 'chasm' is a 'deep and gloomy breathing-place': through this the energies of the world find utterance, the choice of 'roar' and 'roaring' conveying a menacing power. These 'waters, torrents, streams'

Roll darkling down the Torrent of [their] fate[89]

as the narrative of *The Prelude* and the life it recounted have often seemed to do. This sense, less of blind than of a bewildered energy, 'Effort, and expectation, and desire' (vi. 541), is finally expressed— in one of Wordsworth's supreme moments—in the words: 'the homeless voice of waters', and shows how little the ascent of Snowdon is an easy transcendence. The energy, the lostness, and the grief cannot be forgotten. This mountain vision is poised between heaven and earth. Torrents and rivers reach the devouring sea; their voices like the voices of poets seek another home: 'with infinitude— and only there . . . And something ever more about to be' (vi. 539, 542).

The ascent of Snowdon is the furthest reach of *The Prelude* from affairs of state, yet the poem has been so framed that we cannot read of the 'homeless voice of waters' without thinking of revolution. This episode dominates the final book, not to make us forget or reject state affairs, but to set them in perspective, seeking to reveal something of what 'mid all revolutions in the hopes | And fears of men, doth still remain unchanged . . .' (xiii. 449–50)—something 'of fabric more divine' (xiii. 449–52).[90] It is on this note that Wordsworth choses to leave his poem and the reader. Its concluding statements (hedged about with quasi-philosophical qualification) are clearly religious and hardly pantheist—so much we learn from the treatment of the moon at the end of the Snowdon episode. But does the poem show Wordsworth—the poet of 1798–1805—a con-

---

88 Norton, 460.
89 *The Vanity of Human Wishes*, 1. 346; *Poems*, 132.
90 Norton, 482.

servative or a radical? If to have repudiated the French Revolution from Robespierre on is to have been conservative, then certainly he was conservative—conservative in the sense that George Orwell and Pasternak's Zhivago became conservative. He had the slow retrospective integrity to stand back from the world's distortion of his early hopes and the consequences of some of his early principles. If to trace a youthful political radicalism back, through complicity in the holocaust of revolutionary violence, to early experience, to put it to the proof and still, despite guilt, sorrow, and rebuff, not to repudiate its essential idealism, is to have been a radical, then he was a radical in 1805. When, in 1850, the poem was first published, in a version which a chorus of commentators has declared orthodox and conservative, the Whig Macaulay set it down as 'to the last degree Jacobinical, indeed Socialist'.[91] But, more important even than the answers to these questions, is the achievement of the poem which has led the reader, ultimately defenceless, into the heart of political and historical process, and set it in a larger physical and metaphysical landscape of the life of man. The pale horse, taught its manage in revolution, is now known; other steeds remain to ride towards the hills.

[91] Norton 560.

Epilogue

WHAT vision of 'present, past, and future' does poetry alluding to the realm of politics reveal? As previously explained in this book, and in its predecessor, *Poetry and the Realm of Politics*, I have not aimed at exploring the pure state poem, but those more complex works in which political moments, aspects, and structures are nevertheless integral to their aesthetic achievement. The question, therefore, does not come down to an enquiry about particular political complaints or desires, though we are usually aware of these, but turns rather on how poetry sees past and future in relation to each other.

Perhaps the most breathtaking poetic *coup* of *The Prelude* is its repetition of the line: 'We beat with thundering hoofs the level sand', after the news of the death of Robespierre (x. 567), which was first used eight books earlier as the last line of the narrative of the visit to the ruined abbey in the Vale of Nightshade (ii. 139). This is a masterstroke in the art of memory, connecting the potential politics of personal recollection with a song of political experience. Nothing could better dramatize the creative memory of the chastened but still resolved protagonist of *The Prelude* than this poetic juxtaposition of an earlier episode asserting young life against antiquity with the later, more uneasy and more qualified, sense of release from the trap into which latent political energy had ridden. This repetition is itself an allusion to an epic structure and corresponding vision, for the line certainly echoes the 'quadrupedante putrem sonitu quatit ungula campum' of *Aeneid*, viii. 596, which Virgil repeated in xi. 875 of his poem. (Dryden had translated: '. . . And shake with horny Hoofs the solid ground'—viii. 790—but did not observe the repetition).[1] In Virgil the line first occurs not after but just before Aeneas reaches a sacred and sequestered place, where the goddess Venus presents him with arms, including the famous shield, fashioned by Vulcan, which depicts the future history of Rome.

---

[1] See John A. Hodgson, 'Tidings: Revolution in *The Prelude*', *Studies in Romanticism*, 31: 1 (Spring 1992), 45–70 (acknowledging forthcoming work by Richard Graver).

Aeneas's sally on horseback leads to a divine vision, and through a divine gift to a historical prophecy. No goddess appears to the hero of *The Prelude*; here it is the song of the wren which animates the scene, but the inaugurative part played by this visit to an ancient and sacred site is clear in Wordsworth's as in Virgil's narrative. When the Latin line reappears in the *Aeneid*, at xi. 875, Aeneas is advancing in his conquest of Latium and thus into the history of the politics of Rome. Here the line, altered in one word, is associated not with setting out but with retreat, the flying horsemen enemies of the Trojans. The situation is much changed: not a bright vision, but a death-dealing rout; nevertheless the Trojans have gained the advantage. It is with this at least in mind that Wordsworth repeats his Virgilian line on the news of the death of Robespierre. The brave outset is recalled in the awareness of grief and death, but the old impetus is felt, and the quest is on course again. This course is in the largest sense political, for Virgil all that the Rome of Augustus meant to him, for Wordsworth 'The mighty renovation' of 'righteousness and peace' (x. 556, 552). Not just foes and erstwhile friends are here overcome; time too is conquered, especially in Wordsworth, as memory of the earlier experience runs through the same terrain into the repeated line. Wordsworth has widened greatly the narrative span between the two lines. In each case the poet has invoked the future of his epic, not only in the places just mentioned, but in a central (or nearly central) Book VI. There in the *Aeneid* is an earlier vision of the Rome of Augustus (the source of so much poetic and political programme in later panegyric); and in the crossing of the Alps in *The Prelude* (in terms characteristically more general)

> Effort, and expectation, and desire,
> And something evermore about to be.
>
> (vi. 541–2)[2]

Virgilian structure which so poignantly relates present, past, and future links Wordsworth back, through Pope, Dryden, and Milton, to Virgil himself. Yet Pope's later mock-epic, in its most famous moment, might seem to see only the past and present, its no-future being the burden of its extraordinary rhetorical *coup*:

---

[2] William Wordsworth, *The Prelude, 1799, 1805, 1850*, ed. Jonathan Wordsworth, M. H. Abrams, and Stephen Gill (1979), 216.

> As one by one, at dread Medea's strain,
> The sick'ning stars fade off th'ethereal plain
>
> .   .   .   .
>
> Lo! thy dread Empire, CHAOS! is restor'd;
> Light dies before thy uncreating word:
> Thy hand, great Anarch! lets the curtain fall;
> And Universal Darkness buries All.
>
>   (*The Dunciad* (1743), iv. 635–6, 653–6)

Much turns here on Pope's use of the present tense. Visions of the
end are conventionally in the future tense. Thus Dryden's 'So when
the last and dreadful hour | This crumbling Pageant shall devour . . .'
and Shakespeare, in a passage we know Pope admired:

>   . . . the great globe itself,
> Yea, all which it inherit, shall dissolve
> And, like this insubstantial pageant faded,
> Leave not a rack behind.[3]

In keeping with the metaphor of the great theatre of the world, the
fall of Pope's curtain marks the end of Nature, but here not only
'*Physic*' but '*Metaphysic*' dies. The present tense intensifies the tones
of religious prophecy, and also mediates, in a high-risk strategy on
Pope's part, the two sides of the paradox that poet and reader see
the curtain fall which is the end of everything (the end of the line
precluding questions concerning from which side of the curtain the
End is seen). Political and metaphysical are here made to meet (the
previous passage has been conspicuously political), but, at the point
of meeting, the metaphysical collapses into nothingness. If affairs of
state can ever revive after such a vision it must be because some
metaphysical resource remains unextinguished by the apparently
absolute darkness of the poem's concluding vision. The passage
constitutes a challenge to the reader to find the wherewithal to
respond to its 'Great Negative'.[4] Obviously its reversed terms help
in this, so that, for example, 'thy uncreating word' makes us wonder
about any continuing virtue, despite the vision of the text, in the
Word, the light which shineth in darkness, and the darkness com-

---

[3] John Dryden, 'A Song for St. CECILIA's Day, 1687', ll. 59–60 (*Poems*, ii. 539);
William Shakespeare, *The Tempest*, IV. i. 153–6, and Pope, *Corr.* l. 186.

[4] Rochester's phrase in 'On Nothing', l. 28. Pope imitated the poem in his 'On
Silence', *TE* vi. 17–19.

prehended it not.[5] Commentaries have detailed the earlier lines on which Pope's famous last line was modelled, and which it surpassed, from Shakespeare to Dryden.[6] Less attention has been paid to a line perhaps more remarkable, in its visual power:

> The sick'ning stars fade off th'ethereal plain . . .

The reader here is still looking at a sky, not quite yet confronted by Pope's final negative. Yet this entranced and entrancing line also seems to have an analogue, deep in the early Christian poetic tradition:

> tristia squalentis aethrae palluerunt sidera,

strengthened, three lines later in the same hymn of Prudentius, by a parallel less rare and more obvious:

> fertur horruisse mundus noctis aeternae chaos

This has reverberations within Book IV of *The Dunciad*, here and elsewhere. Prudentius (b. AD 348)—not so remarkable a source to propose for an early eighteenth-century Roman Catholic poet—is describing the darkness which covered the earth (Luke 24: 44), or the land (Matthew 27: 45; Mark 15: 33) on the crucifixion of Christ. It will be remembered that in *The Dunciad* of 1729 Pope's vision of a final darkness was alleviated by a concluding couplet which intimated that it was but a false dream. In 1743 that couplet was removed, with powerful effect. But if, as the Prudentian analogue suggests, Pope is here alluding to a unique moment of darkness in Holy Scripture, that challenged reader has a particular resource, ironically concealed but latent in the reversed religious terms of the passage: Christ's resurrection. This Prudentius, for his part, did at the end of his own text express in the terms of nature poetry:

> Flumen lapsus et undae, littorum crepidines,
> imber, aestus, nix, pruina, silva, et aura, nox, dies . . .[7]

---

[5] John 1: 5.

[6] See *TE* v. 409; Emrys Jones, *Pope and Dulness*, British Academy Chatterton Lecture (1968), 260–3.

[7] Aurelius Preudentius Clemens, *Cathemerinon*, ix. 78, 81, 112–13; *The Hymns of Prudentius*, ed. and trans. R. Martin Pope and R. F. Davis (1905), 104, 108. Good editions of Prudentius were produced from that of Aldus Manutius (1501–4) to those of Chamilard (1687) and Cellarius (1703). Further, as Bernard M. Peebles points out (*The Poet Prudentius* (New York, 1951), 63), 'All [the poems of *Cathemerinon*] have yielded hymn-texts to the Catholic liturgy.'

Poetry of the realm of politics is essentially an art of memory. Allusive detail of the kind touched on above suggests pasts and futures within the text and beyond it. Present poetry of political allusion is in no way constrained, embarrassed, or burdened, but wholly enriched and empowered by poetry of the past. Earlier vision lends direction and point to that of the present:

> For all the world,
> As thou art to this hour was Richard then
> When I from France set foot at Ravenspurgh;
> And even as I was then is Percy now.
>
> (1 Henry IV, III.ii.93–6)

If we search the poetic record for more specific programmes of a desired future we are in more difficulty. The earlier literature, much concerned with title to rule and forms of government, has a desired political future, in view chiefly in the neo-Virgilian programme of the golden age. Its particular form is then the positive side of the example of Augustus: rule which is strong, pacific, clement, a dominant position within the wider world, and a flourishing of the arts of peace. Poetic phrases associated with this ideal we have already seen in Wordsworth—'golden hours', 'golden times'—but here they are connected with a more radical and social political desire. Pope's concern with the alleviation of poverty in his Epistles on the use of riches is supplanted by a wider political ambition in the discussion with Beaupuy of the 'hunger-bitten girl' in *The Prelude*, when

> it is hoped: that poverty,
> At least like this, would in a little time
> Be found no more, that we should see the earth
> Unthwarted in her wish to recompense
> The industrious, the lowly child of toil . . .
>
> (ix. 522–6)[8]

The presentation of poverty in Wordsworth and Pope prompts a further question concerning past, present, and future. How far does the poetic record as here exemplified display an advance of the idea of progress? It would seem that it offers no evidence of steady,

---

[8] Norton, 338.

evolutionary change. As previously suggested, continuity and disruption, rather than what Wordsworth called in 1804, 'one steady progress . . .' is the pattern which emerges most strongly. The progress of the concept of progress, as argued for in David Spadafora's notable recent book,[9] seems unclear in the poetic record, though the concept (if to a religious rather than secular goal) is certainly present in the mind and art of Wordsworth. Perhaps there may have been a visible and slow transformation of progress as a recurrent stage in a cyclical concept of history, such as is found in Dryden and Pope, into progress as a comprehensive and indefinite idea.

The purpose of these two books, however, has not been to use poetic evidence to demonstrate some major movements of ideas, but, in a series of detailed readings, to show the political awareness which belongs to poetry of the most complex and subtle kind. A tradition of the moral scrutiny of rulers and governments becomes very clear, but one mingled with hopes and fears more specifically political or religious. Such scrutiny is generally mediated through an artistry which allows a many-sided and many-sighted understanding of bewildering historical situations. Dramatic structure and epic structure go far beyond prose argument in registering the difficulties of political experience. The same is true (though to a lesser extent and with distinguished exceptions) if we compare epic and tragedy with the state poems, or with works of one-to-one political allegory.

At the end of *Poetry and the Realm of Politics* I suggested that there may be a mental alliance between poetry and high politics, itself history with a human face, and I saw them as twin pillars of the great theatre of the world. The theatre of the world, however, if figured in this way, is not only a drama of rulers whose deeds sway the life of society but also a resonant arena of what poets say and have said. As in the earlier part of this conclusion, so in *Poetry and the Realm of Politics* and *Poetry of Opposition and Revolution*, I hope to have shown how a specific and detailed verbal art in the resonant theatre of the world may call up the words of the past to judge the present and strive to envision the future.

---

[9] David Spadafora, *The Idea of Progress in Eighteenth-Century Britain* (1990).

SELECT BIBLIOGRAPHY

Place of publication is London unless stated otherwise

PRIMARY

ADDISON, JOSEPH, *Miscellaneous Works*, ed. A. C. Guthkelch (1914).
Poems Relating to State Affairs (1705), BL Pressmark, c. 28.e.15, Pope's copy.
AKENSIDE, MARK, *Poems* (1772).
BAKER, DANIEL, 'Arabella, 1689', BL Add. MSS 11723, 299–302.
Belson Family Papers, Berkshire Record Office, D/EBT Q71/2.
BLAKE, WILLIAM, *Complete Poems*, ed. W. H. Stevenson and D. V. Erdman (1971).
BL Lansdowne MSS 927, fo. 86.
BOSWELL, JAMES, *Life of Johnson*, ed. George Birkbeck Hill, rev. L. F. Powell (Oxford, 1934).
BROOKE, HENRY, *Gustavus Vasa, The Deliverer of his Country* (1739).
BURKE, EDMUND, *Works*, 14 vols. (1815).
—— *A Philosophical Enquiry into . . . Our Ideas of The Sublime and Beautiful*, ed. J. T. Boulton (1958; rev. edn. 1970).
BYROM, JOHN, *Private Journal and Literary Remains of John Byrom*, ed. Richard Parkinson (Manchester, 1854–7).
CARYLL, JOHN, *The Duumvirate*, Bodleian Library, Oxford, Carte MSS 208, Item 62, fo. 397.
CHURCHILL, CHARLES, *Poetical Works*, ed. Douglas Grant (1956).
COLERIDGE, S. T., *Complete Poetical Works*, ed. E. H. Coleridge, 2 vols. (Oxford, 1912).
—— *Collected Letters*, ed. E. L. Griggs, 6 vols. (Oxford, 1956–71).
—— *Collected Works*, 16 vols. (Princeton, 1969–).
A Collection of all Her Majesty's Speeches . . . from Her Happy Accession to the Throne, to the Twenty First of June 1712 (1712).
CONDORCET, J. A. N. C., Marquis de, *Esquisse d'un tableau historique de progrès de l'esprit humain* (Paris, 1794–5); *Outlines of an Historical View of the Progress of the Human Mind*, translated from the French (1795).
DEFOE, DANIEL [?], *Hannibal at the Gates: or, The Progress of Jacobitism. With the Present Danger of the Pretender* (1712).

DENHAM, Sir JOHN, *Poetical Works*, ed. T. H. Bankes, Jr. (New Haven, 1928).

FORBES, ROBERT, *The Lyon in Mourning*, ed. Henry Paton, 3 vols. (Edinburgh, 1975).

FOX, CHARLES, JAMES, *Speeches During the French Revolution*, ed. I. C. Willis (1924).

FREND, WILLIAM, *Patriotism: Or, The Love of Our Country* (1804).

GUERINOT, J. V., *Pamphlet Attacks on Alexander Pope, 1711–44* (1969).

Hannibal Not at our Gates (1712).

Hannibal at our Gates (1714).

HAWKINS, Sir JOHN, *Life of Samuel Johnson, LLD* (1787).

HERVEY, JOHN, Lord Hervey of Ickworth, *Memoirs*, ed. Romney Sedgwick (1952; rev. edn. 1963).

HIGGONS, BEVILL, *The Mourners, POAS*, vi. 362.

Historical Manuscripts Commission, 14th Report, Appendix, Part IV (1894), Kenyon Papers.

HOGG, JAMES, *The Jacobite Relics of Scotland . . .* (Edinburgh, 1819–21).

JOHNSON, SAMUEL, Preface to the General Index to *The Gentleman's Magasine* (1753), introd. Arthur Sherbo for the Johnson society of the central regions (Michigan state University, 1977).

—— *Prefaces Biographical and Critical (Lives of the Poets)* (1779–81), ed. G. Birkbeck Hill, 3 vols. (Oxford, 1905).

—— *Works*, 12 vols. (1810).

—— *Poems*, ed. E. L. McAdam, Jr., with George Milne (New Haven, 1964).

—— *Complete English Poems*, ed. David Fleeman (Harmondsworth, 1971).

—— *The Poems*, ed. David Nichol Smith and Edward McAdam, rev. McAdam and David Fleeman (Oxford, 1974).

—— *Letters*, ed. Bruce Redford, 5 vols. (Oxford 1992–3).

KENNETT, BASIL, 'Le Nouveau Jeu de l'ombre, 1707', BL Lansdowne, MSS 927, F. 86.

MACK, MAYNARD, *The Last and Greatest Art: Some Unpublished Poetical Manuscript of Alexander Pope* (1984).

MANLEY, MARY, DE LA RIVIÈRE, *The New Atalantis* (1709).

MORGAN, DAVID, *The Country Bard* (1739, 1741).

NAIRNE, DAVID, Diary, National Library of Scotland, MS 689. 'On March 1703', *POAS*, vi. 614.

PAINE, THOMAS, *The Rights of Man*, ed. Henry Collins (Harmondworth, 1969).

Poems on Affairs of State. Augustan Satirical Verse, 1660–1714, George de Forest Ford *et al.* (New Haven, 1963–75).

POPE, ALEXANDER, *Works*, (1717).

—— *Correspondence*, ed. George Sherburn, 5 vols (Oxford, 1956).

—— *Poems*, ed. John Butt *et al*, 11 vols. (1939–69).

—— *Prose Works*, i. 1711–20, ed. Norman Ault (Oxford, 1936), ii. 1725–44, ed. Rosemary Cowler, (Oxford, 1986).

'Verses pasted on the Gates of M. Puissieux', *A Satyr: in French and English* . . . (Paris, 1749).

READE, A. L. (ed.), *Johnsonian Gleanings* (1909–52).

ROUSSEAU, JEAN-JACQUES, 'Discours sur l'origine et les fondements de l'inegalité (1755).

—— 'Discours sur les sciences et des arts (1750). *The Royal Gamesters or, The Old Cards new Shuffled for a Conquering Game, The Harleian Miscellany*, 8 vols. (1744–6). SACHEVERELL, HENRY, *The Tryal of Dr. Henry Sacheverell* . . . (1710).

ST JOHN, HENRY, Viscount Bolingbroke, *Remarks on the History of England* (1730–1).

—— *Works*, 5 vols. (1754).

SAVAGE, RICHARD, *Works*, ed. Clarence Tracy (Cambridge, 1962).

SEDGWICK, ROMNEY (ed.), *The History of Parliament: The House of Commons, 1715–1754*, 2 vols. (1970).

SEWARD, ANNA, *Poetical Works*, ed. Walter Scott (Edinburgh, 1810).

SMITH, MARGARET M., and LINDSAY, ALEXANDER (eds.), *English Literary MSS*, iii. *1700–1800* (1992).

SPENCE, JOSEPH, *Observations, Anecdotes and Characters of Books and Men*, ed. J. M. Osborn, 2 vols. (Oxford, 1966).

A Short View of the Conduct of the King of Sweden (1716).

SWIFT, JONATHAN, *Prose Writings*, ed. Herbert Davis, 14 vols. (Oxford, 1939–68).

—— *Gulliver's Travels*, ed. Paul Turner (Oxford, 1971).

—— *Poems*, ed. Pat Rogers (Harmondsworth, 1983).

VOLTAIRE, FRANCOIS-MARIE AROUET DE, *The History of Charles XII. King of Sweden* . . . *Translated from the French* (1732).

WAINGROW, MARSHALL (ed.), *The Correspondence and other Papers of James Boswell Relating to the Making of the Life of Johnson* (New York, 1969).

WOOLF, NOEL, *The Medallic History of the Jacobite Movement* (1988).

WORDSWORTH, WILLIAM, *The Prelude*, 1799, 1805, 1850, ed. Jonathan Wordsworth, M. H. Abrams, and Stephen Gill (1979): the 'Norton Prelude'.

—— *Poetical Works*, ed. Ernest De Selincourt and Helen Darbishire, 5 vols. (Oxford, 1940–9).

—— *The Prelude*, ed. Ernest de Selincourt and Helen Darbishire (Oxford, 1959).

—— *Prose Works*, ed. W. J. B. Owen and J. W. Smyser, 3 vols. (Oxford, 1974).
—— *The Borderers*, ed. Robert Osborn (Ithaca, N.Y. 1983).
—— *The Fourteen-Book Prelude*, ed. W. J. B. Owen (Ithaca, N.Y. 1985).
—— *The Thirteen-Book Prelude*, ed. Mark L. Reed (Ithaca, N.Y. 1991).
—— and WORDSWORTH, DOROTHY, *Letters . . . The Early Years, 1787–1805*, ed. Ernest de Selincourt, 2nd edn. rev. Chester Shaver (Oxford, 1967).
YOUNG, EDWARD, *The Complaint . . . Night the Eighth*, with 'Thoughts Occasioned by the Present Juncture' (1745).
—— *Works of the Author of the Night Thoughts* (1762).

SECONDARY

ABRAMS, M. H., *Natural Supernaturalism* (1971).
ADEN, JOHN M., *Pope's Once and Future Kings* (Knoxville, Tenn. 1978).
BEER, JOHN, 'The "Revolutionary Youth" of Wordsworth and Coleridge: Another View', *Critical Quarterly*, 19: 2 (1977), 79–87.
—— *Wordsworth in Time* (1979).
BEWELL, ALAN, *Wordsworth and the Enlightenment* (1989).
BLACK, JEREMY, 'An Underrated Journalist: Nathaniel Mist and the Opposition Press During the Whig Ascendency,' *British Journal of Eighteenth-Century Studies*, 10 (1987), 27–41.
BRINKLEY, Robert, and HANLEY, KEITH (eds.), *Romantic Revisions* (Cambridge, 1992).
BROOKS-DAVIES, DOUGLAS, *Pope's Dunciad and the Queen of the Night: A Study of Emotional Jacobitism* (Manchester, 1985).
BROWER, R. A., *Pope: The Poetry of Allusion* (Oxford, 1959).
BURY, J. B., *The Idea of Progress: An Inquiry into its Origin and Growth* (1920).
BUTTERFIELD, HERBERT, *The Whig Interpretation of History* (1931).
CHANDLER, JAMES K., *Wordsworth's Second Nature: A Study of the Poetry and Politics* (1984).
CLARK, J. C. D., *English Society, 1688–1832: Ideology, Social Structure and Political Practice during the Ancient Regime* (Cambridge, 1985).
—— *The Language of Liberty, 1660–1832* (Cambridge, 1993).
Samuel Johnson: Literature, Religions and English Cultural Politics from the Restoration to Romanticism (Cambridge, 1994).
CLIFFORD, J. L., *The Young Samuel Johnson* (1955).
—— *Dictionary Johnson* (1979).
COLLEY, LINDA, *Britons: Forging the Nation, 1707–1837* (1992).

CORP, EDWARD T., and SANSON, JACQUELINE (eds.), *La Cour des Stuarts à Saint-Germain-en-Laye au temps de Louis XIV* (Saint-Germain-en-Laye, 1992).

COXE, WILLIAM, *Memoirs of the Life and Administration of Sir Robert Walpole, Earl of Orford*, 2 vols. (1798).

CRUICKSHANKS, EVELINE, *Political Untouchables: The Tories and the '45* (1979).

—— (ed.), *Ideology and Conspiracy: Aspects of Jacobitism, 1689–1759* (Edinburgh, 1982).

—— and BLACK, JEREMY, (eds.), *The Jacobite Challenge* (Edinburgh, 1988).

DAVID, ALUN, ' "A Tragic Scene of Endless Woe": Daniel Baker's *History of Job*', *Critical Survey* (1991), 208–14.

DAVIES, BERTRAM H., 'The Anonymous Letter Proposing Johnson's Pension', *Transactions of the Johnson Society of Lichfield* (Lichfield, 1981), 35–9.

EHRMAN, JOHN, *The Younger Pitt: The Years of Acclaim* (1969).

—— *The Younger Pitt: The Reluctant Transition* (1983).

ERDMAN, DAVID, 'Wordsworth as Heartsworth: Was Regicide the Prophetic Ground of "Those Moral Questions" ', in Donald R. Reiman *et al. The Evidence of the Imagination* (New York, 1978).

ERSKINE-HILL, HOWARD, *Alexander Pope: The Dunciad* (1972).

—— 'Dryden the Poet and Critic', in Roger Lonsdale (ed.), *Dryden to Johnson* (1972; rev. edn., 1987).

—— '*The Prelude* and its Echoes', *TLS*, 3887 (Sept. 1975), 1094.

—— *The Social Milieu of Alexander Pope* (1975).

—— 'Scholarship as Humanism', in *Essays in Criticism*, 39: 1 (Jan. 1979).

—— 'Alexander Pope: The Political Poet in his Time', *Eighteenth-Century Studies*, 15 (Winter 1981–2), 123–48.

—— 'Literature and the Jacobite Cause', in Eveline Cruickshanks (ed.), *Ideology and Conspiracy: Aspects of Jacobitism, 1689–1759* (Edinburgh, 1982).

—— '*The Augustan Idea in English Literature* (1983).

—— 'The Political Character of Samuel Johnson', in Isabel Grundy (ed.), *Samuel Johnson: New Critical Essays* (1984).

—— 'The Satirical Game at Cards in Pope and Wordsworth', in Claude Rawson and Jenny Mezciems (eds.), *English Satire and the Satiric Tradition* (1984), 183–92.

—— 'Life into Letters, Death into Art: Pope's Epitaph on Francis Atterbury', *The Yearbook of English Studies*, 18 (1988), 200–20.

—— 'Pope: The Political Poet in his Time', in Leopold Damrosch (ed.), *Pope: New Critical Essays* (Oxford, 1988).

—— 'Pope on the Origin of Society', in Pat Rogers and George Rousseau *The Enduring Legacy* (Cambridge, 1988),79–93.

—— 'The Political Character of Samuel Johnson: *The Lives of the Poets* and a further report on *The Vanity of Human Wishes*', in Eveline Cruickshanks and Jeremy Black (eds.), *The Jacobite Challenge* (Edinburgh, 1988).

—— 'On Historical Commentary: The Case of Milton and Dryden', in Howard Erskine-Hill and Richard A. McCabe *Presenting Poetry: Essays in Honour of Ian Jack*,(Cambridge, 1995), 52–74.

FAIRER, DAVID (ed.), *Pope: New Contexts* (1990).

FERRARO, JULIAN, 'Political Discourse in Alexander Pope's *Episode* of Sarpendon: Variations on the Theme of Kingship, *MLR* 88: 1 (Jan. 1993), 15–20.

FINK, ZERA S., *The Classical Republicans . . .* (Evanstan, Iu., 1945).

—— 'Wordsworth and the English Republican Tradition', JEGP 47 (1948), 107–26.

GERRARD, CHRISTINE, 'Pope and the Patriots', in David Fairer, (ed.) *Pope: New Contexts* (1900), pp. 25–43.

GIDDINGS, ROBERT, 'The Fall of Orgilio: Samuel Johnson as Parliamentary Reporter', in Isabel Grundy (ed.), *Samuel Johnson: New Critical Essays* (1984).

GILL, STEPHEN, *William Wordsworth: A Life* (Oxford, 1989).

GLEN, HEATHER, *Vision and Disenchantment: Blake's Songs and Wordsworth's Lyrical Ballads* (Cambridge, 1983).

GOLDGAR, BERTRAND, A., *Walpole and the Wits: The Relation of Politics to Literature, 1722–1742* (1976).

GRAVIL, RICHARD, NEWLYN, LUCY, and ROE NICHOLAS, (eds.), *Coleridge's Imagination: Essays in Memory of Peter Laver* (Cambridge, 1985).

GREENE, DONALD, *The Politics of Samuel Johnson* (New Haven, 1960; Athens and London, 1989).

GREGG, EDWARD, *Queen Anne* (1980).

—— *The Protestant Succession in International Politics, 1710–16* (New York, 1987).

GRUNDY, ISABEL (ed.), *Samuel Johnson: New Critical Essays* (1984).

HARRIS, MICHAEL, 'The London Newspaper Press, 1725–46', Ph.D. diss. (London University, 1973).

HARTMAN, GEOFFREY, *The Unremarkable Wordsworth* (1987).

HATTON, R. M., *Charles XII of Sweden* (1968).

HODGSON, JOHN A., 'Tidings: Revolution in *The Prelude*', *Studies in Romanticism*, 31: 1 (Spring 1992), 45–70.

HOLMES, GEOFFREY, *The Trial of Dr Sacheverell* (1973).

JONES, G. H., 'The Jacobites, Charles Molloy and *Common Sense*', *RES* NS 4 (1953), 144–7.

JONES, JOHN, *The Egotistical Sublime* (1954).

KAMINSKY, THOMAS, *The Early Career of Samuel Johnson* (Oxford, 1985).

KITSON, PETER, 'Sages and Patriots that Being Dead Do Yet Speak To Us . . .', *Prose Studies*, 14 (1991), 205–30.

KRAMNICK, ISAAC, *Bolingbroke: The Politics of Nostalgia* (1968).

LANGFORD, PAUL, 'Convocation and The Tory Clergy, 1717–61', in Jeremy Black and Eveline Cruickshanks (eds.), *The Jacobite Challenge* (Edinburgh, 1988).

LENMAN, BRUCE, *The Jacobite Risings in Britain, 1689–1746* (1980).

LEVINSON, MARJORIE, *Wordsworth's Great Period Poems* (Cambridge, 1986).

LINDENBERGER, HERBERT, *On Wordsworth's Prelude* (Princeton, 1963).

LIU, ALAN, *Wordsworth: The Sense of History* (Stanford, Calif., 1989).

MACCUBIN, R. P., 'The Ironies of Dryden's *Alexander's Feast*', *Mosaic*, 18 (1985), 33–47.

—— 'Pope's Pastorals', *Scriblerian*, 12: 2 (Spring 1980).

MCFARLAND, THOMAS, *William Wordsworth: Intensity and Achievement* (Oxford, 1992).

MCGANN, JEROME J., *The Romantic Ideology: A Critical Investigation* (1983).

—— *Don Juan in Context* (Chicago, 1976).

MACGREGOR C. P., unpublished Paper on *Alexander's Feast*, communicated by the author.

MACK, MAYNARD, *The Garden and the City: Retirement and Politics in the Later Poetry of Pope, 1731–43* (1969).

—— and WINN, J. A. (eds.), *Pope: Recent Essays by Several Hands* (Brighton, 1980).

MACLYNN, FRANK, *Charles Edward Stuart: A Tragedy in Many Acts* (1988).

MONOD, PAUL KLEBER, *Jacobitism and the English People, 1688–1788* (Cambridge, 1989).

MOORE, J. R., '*Windsor Forest* and William III', *MLN* 66 (1951), 451–4.

MOORMAN, MARY, *William Wordsworth: A Biography: The Early Years, 1770–1803* (Oxford, 1957).

NOKES, DAVID, 'Lisping in Political Numbers', *Notes and Queries*, NS 24 (June, 1977), 228–9.

O'BRIEN, CONOR CRUISE, *The Great Melody: A Thematic Biography and Commented Anthology of Edmund Burke* (1992).

OWEN, W. J. B., ' "A Second-Sight Procession" in Wordsworth's London', *Notes and Queries*, NS 16 (1969), 49–50.

PALEY, MORTON, *The Apocalyptic Sublime* (New Haven, 1986).

PARKER, REEVE, *Coleridge's Meditative Art* (Cornell, 1975).

—— 'Reading Wordsworth's Power: Narrative and Usurpation in *The Borders*', *ELH* 54 (1987), 299–331.

—— ' "In some sort seeing with my proper eyes": Wordsworth and the Spectacles of Paris', *SIR* 27: 3 (Fall 1988), 369–90.

REED, MARK L., *Wordsworth: The Chronology of the Early Years, 1770–1799* (Cambridge, Mass., 1967).

RICKS, CHRISTOPHER, 'Wolsey in *The Vanity of Human Wishes*', *MLN* 73 (1958), 563–8.

ROBBINS, CAROLINE, *The Eighteenth-Century Commonwealthman* (Cambridge, Mass., 1959).

ROE, NICHOLAS, *Wordworth and Coleridge: The Radical Years* (Oxford, 1988).

—— 'Wordsworth, Milton, and the Politics of Poetic Influence', in J. R. Watson (ed.), *The French Revolution in English Literature and Art*, (1989).

—— 'Pope, Politics and Wordsworth's *Prelude*', in David Fairer (ed.), *Pope: New Contexts* (1990), 189–204.

—— *The Politics of Nature: Wordsworth and Some Contemporaries* (1992).

ROGERS, PAT and ROUSSEAU, GEORGE (eds.), *The Enduring Legacy: Tercentennial Essays on Alexander Pope* (Cambridge, 1988).

SCHAMA, SIMON, *Citizens: A Chronicle of the French Revolution* (1989).

SCHLESS, HOWARD H. (ed.), *Poems on Affairs of State*, iii (1968), 225–36.

SEDGWICK, ROMNEY (ed.), *The History of Parliament: The House of Commons, 1715–1754*, 2 vols. (1970).

SHERBURN, GEORGE, *The Early Career of Alexander Pope* (Oxford, 1934).

SMITH, RUTH, 'The Arguments and Contexts of Dryden's *Alexander's Feast*', *Studies in English*, 18 (1978), 465–90.

SOWERBY, R. E., 'Dryden and Homer', Ph.D. diss., University of Cambridge, 1975.

SPADAFORA, DAVID, *The Idea of Progress in Eighteenth-Century Britain* (1990).

THOMPSON, E. P., 'Disenchantment or Default? A Lay Sermon', in Conor Cruise O'Brien and W. D. Vanech (eds.), *Power and Consciousness* (1969).

THOMPSON, J. M., *The French Revolution* (Oxford, 1944).

VANCE, JOHN, *Samuel Johnson and the Sense of History* (Athens, Oh., 1984).

WATSON, GEORGE, 'The Revolutionary Youth of Wordsworth and Coleridge', *Critical Quarterly* 18: 3 (1976), 49–66.

WATSON, J. R., (ed.), *The French Revolution in English Literature and Art*, Yearbook of English Studies (1989).

WEINBROT, HOWARD D., *Alexander Pope and the Tradition of Formal Verse Satire* (Princeton, 1982).

—— *Augustus Caesar in 'Augustan' England: The Decline of a Classical Norm* (Princeton, 1978).

—— *Britannia's Issue, The Rise of British Literature from Dryden to Ossian* (Cambridge, 1993)

WIMSATT, W. K., 'Belinda Ludens: Strife and Play in *The Rape of The Lock*, in Maynard Mack and J. A. Winn (eds.), *Pope: Recent Essays by Several Hands* (Brighton, 1980).

WOODRING, CARL, *Politics in English Romantic Poetry* (Cambridge, Mass., 1970).

WOOLFORD, JOHN, '*The Prelude* and its Echoes', *TLS* 3822 (6 June 1975), 627.

WORDSWORTH, JONATHAN, *William Wordsworth: The Borders of Vision* (Oxford, 1982).

WU, DUNCAN, *Wordsworth's Reading 1770–1799* (Cambridge, 1993).

Index